CATHOLIC SOCIAL TEACHING ON LIBERATION THEMES

Christine E. Gudorf

University Press
of America™

Copyright © 1980 by

University Press of America, Inc.

4720 Boston Way, Lanham MD 20801

All rights reserved
Printed in the United States of America
ISBN: 0-8191-1080-9 (case)
         0-8191-1081-7 (perfect)

Library of Congress Catalog Card Number: 90-5382

To all the women and men throughout
the world struggling that the Church
be truly liberating, and in particular
to Gustavo Gutierrez, Beverley Harrison,
Bob Brown and Roger Shinn for their
encouragement and assistance with this
manuscript.

TABLE OF CONTENTS

Page

INTRODUCTION   ix

CHAPTER
 I. OVERALL TRENDS IN PAPAL
    TEACHING OF THE LAST CENTURY   1

    Papal Reliance on Thomas Aquinas:
        The Meaning of Justice.   1
    Justice and Charity in Papal Teaching.   3
    Papal Views of Historical Change . . .   6
        Pius XI and Change.   6
        Pius XII and Change 11
        John XXIII: A Shift in
            Papal Views of Change. 16
        Paul VI: The Shift Continues . . . 18
    Social Justice and the Status Quo. . . 21
        Social Justice and Peace. 22
        Social Justice and
            Commutative Justice. 29
        Social Justice and
            Distributive Justice 37

 II. THEOLOGICAL METHOD IN PAPAL TEACHING . 59

    Major Differences: Liberation The-
        ology and Current Church Teaching . 59
    Similarities Between Liberation
        Theology and the Vatican. 68
    Poverty and Theological Method
        in Papal Teaching 69
    Pius XI. 71
    Pius XII 75
    John XXIII 78

Paul VI. 79
Some Reasons for Understanding the
    Church's Task as Spiritual. 82
Inevitability of the
    Church's Partisanship 84
Recent Trends: The Challenge
    Remains Unmet 88

III. PRIVATE PROPERTY AND THIRD WORLD
DEVELOPMENT IN TWENTIETH CENTURY
PAPAL TEACHING 109

Private Property 112
    Pius XI 120
    Pius XII. 120
    John XXIII. 123
    Paul VI 124
Third World Development. 128
    Native Clergy and Culture 129
    Racism. 139
    Colonialism and Neo-Colonialism . . 145

IV. PAPAL TEACHING ON MARXISM. 167

Marxism and Liberation Theology. . . . 170
Background and Early Papal
    Teaching on Marxism 174
Pius XI on Marxism 180
Pius XII 205
John XXIII 217
Paul VI. 224
Conclusion 233

V. PAPAL TEACHING ON WOMAN. 249

Earlier Papal Teaching on Woman. . . . 256
Pius XI: On Woman 264
Pius XII: On Woman. 272
    The Nature of Woman 273
    Relation of Men and Women 277

Moral Considerations. 283
Women and Work. 286
Woman and the Church. 298
John XXIII: On Woman 302
Paul VI: On Woman. 312
Conclusion. 327

FINAL CONCLUSIONS. 341

BIBLIOGRAPHY 347

INDEX. 363

INTRODUCTION

Within the Catholic Church today there is a division over what is called liberation theology. Though most pronounced in Latin America, the division extends throughout the Third World, and, in the case of women's liberation theology, or feminist theology, to the First World as well. The Vatican is interested in this debate, as was demonstrated by Paul VI's part in the publication of the Declaration on the Question of the Admission of Women to the Ministerial Priesthood, and by John Paul II's announcement that he would attend the CELAM III meeting of the Latin American episcopacy in January 1979. But the popes are not only interested observers in the controversy over liberation theology. They have been, throughout the last century, some of the chief leaders and architects of those ideas and positions that liberation theologies in their various expressions now criticize.

This book is a study of the development of the papal position on selected themes in liberation theology through 1978. In its preparation I have consulted all the ordinary sources of papal documents: Acta Apostolicae Sedis, Acta Sanctae Sedis, Osservatore Romano, and collections of papal documents in English, French, and Italian, as well as many commentaries on papal documents. A claim to have read all Church documents of the last hundred years would be foolhardy. There are always private papal letters and transcribed speeches to visitors which evade the usual research techniques. But I do feel that no major works or ideas are neg-

lected, and that I have represented the common
papal positions on these issues.

In presenting the positions of the popes on
the issues under discussion I have often concentrated on the differences between papal formulations and between the popes and liberation positions. When I have contrasted papal views, I have
noted specific similarities also, but it is good
to remember that the discontinuities in the papal
tradition are remarkable against a usual background of intentional continuity on the part of
those persons charged with safeguarding the tradition of the Church. The attempt to highlight <u>de-
velopment</u> within a tradition inevitably tends to
give weight to changes and to minimize sameness.

Liberation Themes

In the following chapters the development of
papal social teaching on themes from liberation
theology are traced. Liberation theology is the
theology of the liberation movements of blacks,
Latin Americans, and women.

Neither these three movements nor the theologies they give rise to are in any way unitary.
The three movements themselves are collections of
smaller social and political groupings loosely
tied together by some shared goals, opponents, and
history. The theologies which arise from each of
these three movements are also diverse. Not only
does feminist theology, for example, differ from
Latin American and black theology, but there are
also numerous varieties of feminist liberation
theology, of Latin American liberation theology,
and of black liberation theology.

The diversity within these movements and
their allied theologies is so marked that it would

be misleading to attempt to define any one of them as a whole, without examining the various formulations in their particularity. The focus here is not on liberation theologies, but on certain issues in papal social teaching. The discussion of liberation theologies herein is limited to clarifying the more common objections of the varied liberation theologians to papal social teaching, so as to restrict the discussion of the social teaching to those specific issues and the course of their development. There is sufficient agreement among the theologians of each of the liberation movements, I think, to justify indicating some specific issues where liberation theologies and papal social teaching clash. The background treatment of the liberation theologies which is supplied herein is therefore limited to the information necessary for the comprehension of general liberation theology objections to papal teaching, and is not intended as adequate explanation of liberation theology itself.

Social Teaching

The bulk of the material to be examined is part of the papal corpus called "the social teaching." This term has become ambiguous in recent years; originally it referred to those aspects of Church teaching on the economic questions raised by industrial labor and addressed by Leo XIII in his encyclical Rerum novarum. In the almost ninety years since this encyclical many popes have issued "social teaching" documents commemorating Rerum novarum. But the range of topics presented in these documents has continually increased. By Paul VI's time there was basically no topical difference between the document commemorating Rerum novarum and much of Paul's other teaching. Whether John Paul II intends to have social questions dominate his papal teaching to the same extent remains to be seen.

Because of this trend of ever widening the scope of social teaching, it is impossible to retain the original understanding of "social teaching." The term "social teaching" has therefore come to be used to refer to the pronouncements of the popes on all social, political, and economic issues facing the human community.

Within this study there will be some use of documents outside the social teaching. These are largely documents on theology and on spiritual salvation. The very fact of this division of documents between spiritual and social says a great deal about the papal approach to both theology and social teaching, as we shall see in Chapter Two.

Popes To Be Examined

Although this study is designed to cover the entire twentieth-century social teaching on issues now debated between liberation theology and the Vatican, it will concentrate more on some periods and popes than on others. This study concentrates on the popes who developed the social teaching-- Leo XIII, Pius XI, Pius XII, John XXIII, and Paul VI, and less on Pius X and Benedict XV, neither of whom contributed significantly to the field of social teaching either in quantity or originality.

Though the bulk of the papacy of Leo XIII fell in the nineteenth century (1878-1903), no study of modern social teaching can fail to assign Leo a place of prominence. He was the first pope to tackle the problems of the modern industrial nation. Leo began the social teaching in the original economic sense, with his Rerum novarum. But Leo also produced major documents on other social issues, such as the place of marriage and family in society, the duties of Christian citizens, socialism, African slavery, Christian popular action,

Christian missions, relations between states, and human liberty. Leo is not only the originator of social teaching in the economic sense, but the father of the wider social teaching as well. One important reason that Leo's writings are so crucial to the work of Pius XI, Pius XII, John XXIII and Paul VI is that the two popes who followed Leo, Pius X and Benedict XV, did not deal with many social issues, thus leaving Leo's position unaltered.

Leo's immediate successor, Pius X, was chiefly occupied with combatting the Modernist movement. Modernism was the Church's encounter with the Enlightenment spirit in the theological field. The Modernist controversy ended in a declaration of heresy and a clerical purge involving the excommunication of theologians. Pius' remaining attention was devoted to the popularizing of the sacrament of the Eucharist by lowering the age at which it could be received and by urging daily communion.

Pius' successor, Benedict XV, expended the energies of his short reign (1914 to 1922) on war relief in Russia and Europe, and on urging the warring nations to submit to truce and negotiations. It was left to his successor, Pius XI, to address the new questions which arose immediately after the war and the Russian revolution. Since Pius XI, it has been impossible for the papacy to ignore the social and political issues confronting the world, regardless of pressing theological, liturgical, or sacramental matters. Pius X's successors have an impressive amount of literature devoted to the social teaching of the Church in the modern age.

On Translations

A further methodological matter to be explained is the area of translations. I have, whenever possible, used common English translations of for-

eign language originals. The largest part of the
documents are in Latin; a significant number are
in French or Italian, and a few are in Spanish and
German. All translations used have been checked
against the originals since some of the standard
English translations were found lacking. Correc-
tions, when I thought them warranted, are marked.

In checking the translations against the original document, a number of problems arose. Though
it was sometimes relatively simple to reject translations which were either incomplete, misleading,
or so literal as to be unclear, others were more
doubtful. There is a definite idiom in modern
Church Latin which must be learned: for example,
doctrina praecepta de rebus socialibus is translated "the social teaching." Because of such circumstances, and because the more contemporary
translations have been standardized under the direction of the U.S. bishop's conference, I did not
correct translations so long as: 1) I recognized
the idiom being translated, 2) nothing was omitted,
3) no ideas or interpretations were added which
could not be derived from the original, and 4) the
expansion into English (very necessary in older
texts, where one Latin sentence can be made into
three or four complex English ones) did not give a
radically different tone to the document or passage.

Since much of the translation, especially of
more recent documents, is fairly literal, the problems in translations were not insurmountable.
Classical Latin scholars may be uncomfortable with
some of the translations which I allowed to stand.
Especially difficult was the most famous line from
Populorum progressio: hodie nemo dubitat progres-
sionem idem valere ac pacem. This is always quoted in English as "development is the new name of
peace," whereas the literal translation from the
Latin is slightly different and even stronger:

"today no one doubts that development is the same as peace." But it is difficult to change the translation of the line which is often both title and subtitle for the encyclical, and which clearly carries the theme of the encyclical. That is, this line represents the encyclical itself to English-speaking people. Here I judged that the difference in meaning was not so large as to require a change, especially considered in context, for the line in question is part of a larger sentence: "For, if today no one doubts that development is the same as peace, who would not want to labour for it with all his powers?"

I wish to thank Dr. A. H. Franke for his irreplaceable help with the Italian translations. In all quotations whenever the source of the translation is not noted, the translation is my own. There are not many passages where I have done the translation; only in the absence of a relatively accurate translation (using the criteria above) of Latin or French passages.

Classification of Papal Documents

The papal documents from which I have excerpted are of various kinds. Vatican documents are classified by two systems. One is by the type of paper and seal used, and by the formality of the style. The other system is classification by content. Some of the more common types of documents are Pontifical letters (both encyclical letters to the whole Church and encyclical epistles to individual bishops or localities), apostolic letters, motu proprios, constitutions, chirographs, sermons, allocutions and radio addresses. Constitutions are important formal communications directed at the entire Church or a large part thereof on doctrinal or disciplinary matters of great import. Motu proprios are decrees of the pope issued of his own

accord (usually unsolicited, that is) on a disciplinary matter. Encyclical letters and epistles
are teaching instruments. Apostolic letters are
formal letters on administrative or executive matters. Sermons, chirographs, allocutions, and radio addresses speak for themselves as to purpose,
and are less weighty in status because of their
limited intended audience.

The question of the authority of each of
these types of documents is difficult to answer.
The pope is infallible when he speaks on matters
of faith and morals <u>ex</u> <u>cathedra</u>; this is, however,
a rare occurrence, though it could presumably oc-
cur in any of these different forms of document.
Among teaching documents, encyclical letters are
recognized as weightiest because they are so clearly intended to instruct the entire Church. Similarly with executive or disciplinary matters, the
type of document is a clue to the importance of the
content and to papal desire to be heard. It is
difficult to rank the various types of document,
then, because they do have varied content.

Non-Catholics may find it extremely difficult
to understand the status and authority of any of
the papal documents; Catholics themselves by no
means agree on this subject. Some hold that though
social teaching is not infallible, it is binding.

> Catholics are obliged to accept the <u>whole</u> body
> of doctrine proposed by the official teaching
> authority of the Church. Declarations which
> proceed from the ordinary, or noninfallible,
> teaching authority of the popes belong to that
> doctrine just as much as those proposed in-
> fallibly, though, of course, they do not ob-
> lige in quite the same way. That Catholics
> must accept and adhere to the noninfallible
> teaching of the Holy See is clear both from

reason itself and from authoritative declarations of recent popes.[1]

On the other hand, the pastoral letters of the national hierarchies of Belgium, the Netherlands, West Germany, Austria, Canada, Denmark and France following the publication of Paul VI's Humanae Vitae demonstrated that large groups of the hierarchy believe that Catholics are not obliged to accept and adhere to noninfallible papal teaching, so long as they dissent with full knowledge and in good conscience. Thus the Belgian bishops wrote on August 30, 1968:

> Someone, however, who is competent in the matter under consideration and capable of forming a personal and well founded judgment --which necessarily presupposes a sufficient amount of knowledge--may after a serious examination before God, come to other conclusions on certain points. In such cases he has the right to follow his conviction provided he remains sincerely disposed to continue his enquiry.[2]

And the Swiss hierarchy wrote on December 11, 1968:

> The faithful who cannot accept all the encyclical's instructions regarding birth control, when they are not motivated by selfishness or complacency and when honestly striving towards an ever better fulfillment of God's will, may be permitted to assume that they are not guilty before God.[3]

Not only is the exact authority of papal teaching in question, but the strictness of the classification system according to the purpose of the document is open to doubt. For Octogesima adveniens was a teaching document, not dealing with executive or administrative matters at all, and yet was issued not as an encyclical, but as an apostolic letter. This may be an indication that the system is rather flexible and that use of a particular type of document is simply meant to signal the degree of importance the pope attributes to the public consideration of the issue at hand.

Conclusion

Despite all these methodological problems I believe that the line of development of papal teaching on the issues traced here will withstand the scrutiny of those scholars in the field familiar with the documents. An understanding of the development detailed here seems to me essential for both sides in the current debate over liberation theology in the Catholic Church.

I ask the reader's patience in pursuing the subject herein. I recognize the difficulty of following the full line of explication through all the extensive quotations and references to the many papal documents. One cause of this difficulty is the poor stylistic quality of much papal writing. Due to the lack of development of the thought in papal texts, clarity is not common; obvious connection between the thought of one paragraph or sentence and the next is often missing. Nevertheless, I believe there is much to be gained through persistence in this undertaking.

NOTES

[1]Thomas J. Harte, C.Ss.R., <u>Papal</u> <u>Social</u> <u>Prin-</u><u>ciples</u> (Gloucester, Mass.: Peter Smith, 1960), p. 9.

[2]In Charles E. Curran and Robert E. Hunt, <u>Dissent</u> <u>In</u> <u>and</u> <u>For</u> <u>the</u> <u>Church</u> (New York: Sheed and Ward, 1969), p. 198.

[3]Ibid., p. 201.

CHAPTER I

OVERALL TRENDS IN PAPAL TEACHING ON JUSTICE OF THE LAST CENTURY

In the hundred years since Leo XIII so developed the social teaching as to make of it a separate area of study, the various popes have all placed slightly different emphases on the constituent elements of their predecessors' social teaching. But each of the popes who have elaborated papal teaching in this area has linked justice, charity, and peace in his writing. All have maintained that justice is an indispensable part of the charity which is the message of the Gospel.[1] All similarly agree that justice is a prerequisite for true peace.[2] The proposal of this chapter is that the linkage between these three-- justice, charity, and peace--has been so influenced by the popes' static view of human nature and society that the papal treatment of and understanding of justice, upon which the social teaching is built, has often tended to support the status quo.

Papal Reliance on Thomas Aquinas: The Meaning of Justice

Perhaps the most common definition of justice has been to "give to each what is due him." This is the papal understanding in Rerum novarum (May 15, 1891),[3] and in Quadragesimo anno (May 15 1931).[4] The popes take this definition from Thomas Aquinas, who defended this definition.[5] Such a definition leaves undetermined how one es-

1

tablishes what is due. As we shall see, this is
precisely where various papal teachings on justice
become problematic.

The general framework in which the popes deal
with the subject of justice is informed by this
Thomist perspective.[6] Thomas spoke of two kinds
of justice: general (literally, legal) justice
and particular justice. General justice has as
its direct object the welfare of the entire com-
munity--the common good.[7] Particular justice is
subordinate to general justice in that it consists
in individual determinations of justice which together make up general justice.[8] In Thomist
teaching the part (that is, particular justice) is
never allowed to endanger the whole (general justice).

There are, according to Thomas, two species
of particular justice. Commutative justice is a
justice typical of exchange.[9] It is a legal con-
tractual kind of justice whose conditions are lo-
cated in the implicit or explicit agreement of the
principles concerned. Distributive justice is
that proportional justice which a society accords
its members depending on the worth of the individual members to the whole society.[10]

These terms are used throughout the documents
of Pius XI as they had been under Leo XIII and
Pius X; in the work of more recent popes the same
concepts are implied but not referred to explicitly. The one technical term the popes use which is
not from Thomas is the term "social justice."
This term first appears in the writings of Pius
XI, where it was used in place of the term "general justice." Catholic apologists in the area of
social teaching, J. Y. Calves and J. Perrin, explain that Pius XI introduced the term "social

justice" for two reasons.[11] They state that the
first and major reason for its introduction was
the widespread tendency to confuse the Thomist
term "general justice" (literally, legal justice)
with the legal justice of the state. The second
reason, they claim, was that in the late nineteenth and early twentieth centuries the discussion of
justice centered on the "social problem" of the
day, which was, at heart, an economic one. The
term "social justice," then, was meant as the answer to the "social problem." It was that part of
the Church's teaching which dealt with economic
morality.[12]

Justice and Charity in Papal Teaching

The theoretical relationship between justice
and charity is much clearer in the twentieth-century documents of the popes than is the definition
of justice as such. For the popes, justice is indispensable to charity (caritas or carita). Both
are universal norms[13] and are necessarily inseparable, though clearly distinguishable.[14] Charity
is a higher virtue; it both motivates and com-
pletes justice.[15] The popes are careful to condemn attempts to downplay justice in the name of
charity, asserting that charity cannot legitimately substitute for justice.[16] They insist that
persons capable of doing justice are not justified
in preferring to do charity. From Leo XIII onward
there is a strong emphasis in papal social teaching on the need to incorporate justice in legal
and institutional structures so that a more just
society on the earth can be established.[17]

This view of the relationship of justice and
charity is the normative basis of the social
teaching for Leo XIII and his successors. But the
way in which this doctrine was applied in specific

3

areas is a much more complex story. Mingled with
this doctrinal strand are many other theological
strands which have influenced and often determined
papal teaching. Some of these strands stand in
tension, perhaps even contradiction, to this normative moral tradition.

Perhaps a passage from an encyclical best illustrates the mingling of this general doctrinal
strand with alien influences. The pope most explicit about the reprehensibility of preferring
works to charity before those of justice--Pius XI
--wrote in his first encyclical, Ubi arcano, December 23, 1922:

> Hence it follows that the true peace of
> Christ cannot deviate from the path of jus-
> tice because it is God Himself who 'judges
> justice' (Ps. iv, 5). Nor should such jus-
> tice be hard and inflexible, but it should
> be tempered with charity, whose peculiar
> virtue it is to establish peace among men.
> This is the peace which has come to us
> through Christ, or rather, He Himself is
> our peace, as St. Paul so pithily put it,
> for satisfying the divine justice in his
> own flesh on the cross, He 'has broken
> down the intervening wall of the enclosure,
> the emnity in his flesh' (Eph. ii, 14-16)
> and reconciled all men and all things to
> God. This Redemption itself St. Paul con-
> siders not so much a work of justice, as a
> divine work of charity: 'For God indeed
> was truly in Christ reconciling the world
> to Himself.' (II Cor. v, 19) 'God so loved
> the world that He gave His only begotten
> Son' (John iii, 16). Expressing the same
> thought, the Angelic Doctor with his usual
> felicity says: that 'true and authentic

4

peace emanates from charity rather than
from justice, since justice merely removed
the obstacles to peace, such as wrongs and
injuries, whereas peace is peculiarly an
act of charity.' (2a2ae 29:3,3)

.   .   .   .   .

Speaking of the Kingdom of God, St. Paul
used these words which apply equally to
that peace of Christ, offspring of charity,
whose habitation is the soul. For it is in
the soul that Christ reigns by charity:
'The Kingdom of God does not consist in
meat and drink' (Rom. xiv, 17). And Christ
Himself never wearied of bringing home to
this world and to men the pre-eminent excellence of this peace which rests not on
the transient things of this world, but on
the spiritual and eternal. Thus He hath
said, 'What does it profit a man if he gain
the whole world and suffer the loss of his
soul? Or what will a man give in exchange
for his soul?' (Matt. xvi, 26). And again
he taught us how constant and firm of mind
a Christian ought to be: 'Do not be afraid
of those who would kill the body but cannot
kill the soul; but rather fear him that can
destroy both body and soul in hell' (Matt.
x, 28; Luke xii, 4).

     Nor is he who deserves this peace called
upon to abjure the goods of this life; rather
shall he, as Christ Himself has promised, receive them in abundance: 'Seek first the
Kingdom of God and His justice and all these
things shall be given to you besides.'[18]

By the end of this passage, peace has been
redefined so that the earlier link between peace
and justice is less noticeable, and justice now
takes a position behind both peace and charity.

The passage's initial link between peace and justice carried the implication that action was ne-
cessary--that we should act justly but charitably.
By the end of the passage, attention has moved
from what we should do to the realm of heaven,
full attainment of which we are assured does not
rest upon actions such as abjuring material goods,
but upon our spiritual seeking. The spiritualization of the ultimate ends, peace and charity, is
so strong here that it is easily overlooked that
the papal point of origin here was justice, which
the popes noted must be valued as basic, since
neither of the others is possible without it. As
we shall see, this particular shift from the concrete to the spiritual is common in papal social
teaching in the twentieth century, especially before Vatican II, and is especially clear in <u>Summi</u>
<u>Pontificatus</u> and <u>Ad</u> <u>Patri</u> <u>Cathedram</u>.

<u>Papal</u> <u>Views</u> <u>of</u> <u>Historical</u> <u>Change</u>

At the root of many of the tensions and contradictions in the papal documents is the static
world view which has characterized the twentieth-
century popes. Their view of historical change
has been informed by, if not determined by, their
belief in the permanency and fixity of theological
truth.

<u>Pius XI and Change</u>

In his documents involving social teaching
Pius XI demonstrated a traditional view on the
permanency of truth. For Pius it was the Church's
possession of eternal truth--the whole of eternal
truth[19]--which was the basis of the Church's claim
to be "the perfect society, the leader of all
other societies."[20] Pius XI referred to the
teachings of the Church which contain these truths

as "eternal," "unchanging," and "unchangeable."[21]

Pius XI apparently felt that the age in which these eternal truths were best reflected was the Middle Ages, and demonstrated his attachment not only in allusions to that good order,[22] but also in his fascination with the theory of Catholic corporatism.[23] The Catholic corporatists opposed modern capitalism and the results of that system upon social relations.[24] They proposed a corporate model with many similarities to the earlier social structures of the Middle Ages. Pius found the corporate model attractive because it linked rights and power to social responsibility. The lack of this link in liberal capitalism was Pius' chief objection to the modern capitalist trends and the society they were shaping.

But despite Pius' fascination with corporatist theory, he withheld endorsement. One probable reason for this decision was reluctance to demand a return to the past and to renounce many of the advances which accompanied modern society. But his reservations about the system of Italian state corporatism which took shape during his pontificate were undoubtedly primary in his failure to endorse corporatist theory.[25]

Like all popes, Pius XI recognized the existence of change in the world. R. L. Camp quotes a May 16, 1926 letter of Pius XI to Italian Catholics which reads:

> My first reflection relates to the mutability of human affairs--not only the lesser ones but the greater ones as well, not only those which are contingent aspects of social life but also those which appear to be of its very essence and are usually considered im-

possible to conceive except as eternal. This
is truly a mutability from which no one can
escape, because this is the destiny of all
created things--in fact, this mutability is
inevitable.[26]

This was, as Camp maintained, a remarkable statement on historical change from any pope.[27] Camp
also asserted that this statement was characteristic of the openness of the first part of the papacy of Pius XI, an openness which ended with the
world depression. Beginning in the early thirties, Camp said, Pius XI became increasingly more
conservative, even more so than his predecessors.
This may well be the case. There is, however,
from the information which Camp provides,[28] another explanation for the discrepancy between the
idea expressed in the passage and those other
views of change Pius expressed. In this passage
Pius put forth the view that change is integral to
history and even affects essential aspects of human existence, such as property, labor, and the
family. But when he continued, after the above
passage, he asserted that the Church could live
with changes in the world.[29] What Camp missed was
an appreciation of the extent to which this was a
continuation of the traditional view that the
spiritual was primary, and the material secondary
because transient. Change in the world could be
accepted, insofar as it did not interfere with the
position of the Church, because it was not of importance theologically.

It is true that this passage was, nonetheless, much more accepting of change than any of
those of Pius XI's predecessors or even those of
his immediate successor. However, this sentiment
was not reflected in any of Pius' other writings.
This acceptance of change was entirely absent when

8

he considered particular historical development, such as in Pius' passage explaining how the good order of the Middle Ages gave way to the present order: •

> At one time there existed a social order, which, by no means perfect in every respect, corresponded nevertheless in a certain measure to the needs and conditions of the times. That this order has long since perished is not because it was incapable of development and adaptation to changing needs and circumstances, but rather to the wrongdoing of men. Men were hardened in excessive self-love, and refused to extend that good order, as was their duty, to the increasing numbers of people, or else, deceived by the attractions of a false liberty and other errors, they grew impatient of every restraint and endeavored to throw off every authority.[30]

This is the most characteristic explanation of change in the world for Pius XI: individual sin. And the most common particular sin responsible for such social changes was, for Pius XI as for the previous tradition, the sin of apostasy. The abandonment of the faith of the Church was the action which Pius saw responsible for all the evil besetting the modern world.[31] In his consideration of particular changes in the world, Pius XI's view of the social order of the Middle Ages as moral caused him to equate changes from that order with evil.

Pius' consideration of capitalism in Quadragesimo anno demonstrated that he did not view historical change as a continuous self-propelling process but as the result of human sinfulness.

Pius XI was the first pope to note that the character of capitalism had changed. In 1931 he observed that domination had replaced competition in the capitalist system.[32] He saw the concentration of wealth and power as a natural result of allowing unrestrained competition.[33] But despite his acute analysis of the concentration process,[34] Pius XI placed the blame for this change for the worse not on any natural direction of the system of capitalism, but on the lack of moral restraint of the individuals concerned.[35] He not only rebuked the State for having become involved in the economic controversy,[36] but praised Leo's attempt in _Rerum novarum_ to "adjust the capitalist economic system to the norms of right order" and declared:

> It is clear then that the system as such is not to be condemned. Surely it is not vicious of its very nature; but it violates right order whenever capital so employs the working classes as to divert business and economic activity entirely to its own arbitrary will. . . .[37]

Pius XI, then, left evidence that he viewed change in the world not as an essential element, but as the unavoidable result of human sin and the mark of the imperfection of all material things. Like the change from the medieval system, the change from competitive capitalism to monopoly capitalism was interpreted by Pius XI as the consequence of sin and not as a result of dynamic human history. That one change in human society could begin a chain of changes, each one influencing, though not determining the character of the following change --this idea was foreign to Pius XI.

10

Pius XII and Change

That the popes have rejected modern understandings of change in the world is most explicit in the teaching of Pius XII, ironically the twentieth century pope most interested in the modern world, its science, its communications, its technology, and its medicine.[38] Pius XII wrote an address on the Church and history, in which he said:

> The term 'historicism' describes a philosophical system; that which sees only change and evolution in every spiritual reality, in the knowledge of what is true, in religion, in morality and law, and rejects, in consequence, everything that is permanent, eternally of value, and absolute. Such a system is assuredly irreconcilable with the Catholic conception of the world, or, in general, with any religion which professes a personal God.[39]

In this passage Pius XII has picked up many of the points made by Pius XI--the permanency of the Church and her truths, the superiority of the eternal and absolute over the mutable--and applied them to a specific view toward change. This was written near the end of his pontificate (1955). But this understanding of change is also fou.id in his very first encyclical. In Summi Pontificatus Pius XII wrote:

> We are hoping for a new order of things, which shall govern the life of peoples and adjust their mutual relations, when these unnatural conflicts, these cruel butcheries, have died down at last. This new order must not be founded on the shifting standards of

right and wrong, treacherous as quicksands, which have been arbitrarily devised to suit public and private interest. It must stand firmly on the immoveable rock of natural law and divine revelation.[40]

Eleven years later Pius wrote his famous encyclical Humani generis to condemn the acceptance of evolution (especially polygenism or the belief in multiple first parents) and historicism. In that encyclical he declared:

Looking around at those outside the fold of Christ, one can easily discern the principal trends which now a few learned men follow. Some are imprudent and indiscreet enough to hold that the so-called theory of evolution, although not yet fully proved even in the domain of the natural sciences, explains the origin of all things, and they go so far as to support the monistic and pantheistic notion that the whole world is subject to continual evolution. Communists eagerly seize on this theory in the hope of depriving the souls of every idea of God and of defending and propagating more effectively their dialectical materialism.

The fictitious tenets of evolution, which repudiate all that is absolute, firm and immutable, have paved the way for the new erroneous philosophy which, a rival of idealism, immanentism, and pragmatism, has come to be called existentialism because, forgetful of the immutable essences of things, it concerns itself only with individual existence.

There is also a certain false historicism which, refusing to look beyond the random happenings of human life, undermines the

12

foundations of all truth and absolute law in the domain of philosophy as well as in that of Christian dogma.[41]

They also assert that such a change of Catholic doctrine would enable us to satisfy a modern need; for it would permit of a dogma being expressed in the categories of modern thought, whether of immanentism or idealism, or existentialism or any other ism. Some, more daring, affirm that this can and must be done for yet another reason; they claim that the mysteries of faith cannot be expressed by concepts that are adequately true, but only by approximate and ever changeable notions which vaguely hint at the truth, but also necessarily distort it. They do not consider it absurd, but altogether necessary that theology should substitute new concepts in place of the old ones in keeping with the variety of philosophies which it has used as its instruments; they think that theology could thus express in human language the same divine truths by different modes which though somewhat contradictory, may be called equivalent. Finally, they go on to say that the history of dogma consists in tracing the successive forms which were given to revealed truth in accordance with the various theories and speculations as they emerged in the course of centuries.

But it is obvious from all we said that such projects not merely lead to what is called dogmatic relativism, but already contain it. The contempt shown for the commonly accepted doctrine and the corresponding terminology is significant enough in this respect. To be sure, the terminology used in the schools and even by the Magisterium of the Church is susceptible of further improve-

13

ment and refinement; it is also well known
that the Church did not always keep to the
same identical terms; it is evident, too,
that the Church cannot tie herself to any
philosophy which enjoys a brief moment of
popularity. But what has been thought out
over the centuries and agreed upon by Catholic teachers in the effort to gain some
understanding of dogma, surely does not rest
on a flimsy foundation of that sort. It
rests on principles and conceptions which
are inferred from a just apprehension of
created things; and in the making of such
inferences divine revelation has, like a
star, illuminated the human mind through
the Church's agency. No wonder that General
Councils have not only used but also sanctioned some of these conceptions, so that it
would be wrong to discard them.

It would be wrong to neglect or cast
aside or rob of their meaning these precious
concepts which have been coined and polished
in order to express, with ever-increasing
accuracy, the truths of faith--a process that
has often cost centuries of labor and was
carried out by men of uncommon intelligence
and sanctity, with light and guidance, too,
from the Holy Spirit. To substitute for them
conjectural notions and the vague and fluid
diction of a new philosophy, which thrive today like the flowers of the field and wilt
tomorrow, would indeed be the height of imprudence; dogma itself would become no better
than a reed shaken by the wind. Disrespect
for the terms and concepts current among
scholastic theologians would take all the
force out of what is called speculative theology, which has no real validity, they say,
inasmuch as it rests on theological reasoning.

Worse still, the lovers of novelty easily
pass from disdain of scholastic theology to
the neglect of and even contempt for the
Magisterium of the Church which bestows high
authoritative approval on that branch of theology. They represent the Magisterium as a
hindrance to progress and an obstacle in the
way of science, while certain non-Catholics
look upon it as an unjust restraint which
prevents better qualified theologians from
reforming their science. Now it is true that
this sacred Magisterium must remain, in matters of faith and morals, the proximate and
universal criterion of truth for every theo-
logian, since to it has been entrusted by
Christ Our Lord the whole deposit of faith--
Sacred Scripture and divine Tradition--to be
preserved, guarded, and interpreted; but the
faithful are also obliged to flee those
errors which more or less approach heresy,
and accordingly, 'to keep also the constitutions and decrees by which such evil doctrines are proscribed and forbidden by the
Holy See.' This duty is sometimes ignored
just as if it did not exist.[42]

Here Pius XII obviously intended more than a defense of the truth of the faith or of the unchang-
ingness of God. For Pius XII, the Catholic God is
the true God, the Catholic Faith is the true
faith, and the Catholic Church the True Church
which pronounces the word of God for the world.
If God is unchanging, then his word is also immutable, and so the truths espoused by the Church
are unchanging. The Church, by association, must
also be unchanging. Pius XII was not only denying
that the truths of the faith take on different
manifestations in history, but he was also resisting the idea that change is integral to the world.

15

Both Pius XI and Pius XII refused to accept any theory of continual change, because for them permanency was the hallmark of all that was supremely valuable: God, truth, faith, theology, etc.

In this understanding, mundane historical reality and the teaching of the Church do not have any common meeting ground. They exist on different planes. The Church denies that the essence of things changes and does not, therefore, see the world as it is, in a state of ongoing alteration.

John XXIII: A Shift in Papal Views of Change

John XXIII modified to a degree the static understanding so characteristic of both Pius XI and Pius XII. John often spoke of truth, and identified truth with the Gospel and with the Church.[43] He claimed that this truth was eternal.[44] However, there was no nostalgia in John XXIII for a past age, as there was in Pius XI, nor was John concerned about the difficulty of an unchanging Church preserving eternal truth in a changing world, as Pius XII had been. John was conservative; historians and biographers agree that his position on the worker-priests, on the use of Latin in liturgy, on the preparations for the Council, and his theological understanding in general, all proclaimed him a conservative, if not a reactionary.[45] But John embraced the modern world in some ways, viewing it optimistically. He saw a world becoming more and more just,[46] and thus more receptive to the message of the Church:

> Finally, we notice in our time an opening in that people are arranging the coming together of entirely new nations and social and political arrangements. Because all peoples either have won or are on the way

16

to winning their liberty--for this reason
soon no people will exist who dominates
others or obeys the power of others.

For people everywhere are of groups
who either have already agreed in detail
on their civil freedoms as citizens, or
who are about to agree on this; no community wants to be called the home of another,
or to be subject to another. For in our
time attitudes have decayed which remained
fast for so many generations, by which some
classes of people accepted a position for
themselves inferior to others, and others
demanded the biggest part of that which be-
longed to others, all on account of economic and social status in the society, or
on account of sex, or because of civil
rank.

To the contrary, this widespread opinion pervades and holds: that all are equal
among themselves in the dignity bestowed by
nature. Because of this, discrimination
between people because of birth is in no
way acceptable, at least not by reason or
teaching.[47]

For John, change in the world was not self-
perpetuating, but the result of individuals heed-
ing the dictates of conscience and the Gospel.
The unchanging truth was being borne out in history. There was no need to examine the relation
between history and faith for John, for he thought
he saw his eternal truth being made manifest amidst all the change. John took an almost uncritical
attitude toward changes in the world. He disapproved of many aspects of modern life, but when he
considered the direction in which things were
changing, he was always able to identify encouraging signs.

17

Paul VI: The Shift Continues

In one of the episcopal documents of the
Second Vatican Council, _Gaudium et Spes_, which
Paul signed, we find even more modification:

> History itself speeds along on so rapid a
> course that an individual person can
> scarcely keep abreast of it. The destiny
> of the human community has become all of
> a piece, where once the various groups of
> men had a kind of private history of their
> own. Thus, the human race has passed from
> a rather static concept of reality to a
> more dynamic, evolutionary one. In conse-
> quence, there has arisen a new series of
> problems, a series as important as can be,
> calling for new efforts of analysis and
> synthesis.[48]

Here there is acknowledgment that history has
a force of its own, that the secular world is not
merely changing in the direction of the Kingdom,
as John thought, but that it takes on a new character, and that this character must be evaluated
as a different reality.

In _Octogesima adveniens_, May 14, 1971, Paul
wrote:

> The Gospel is not out of date because it was
> proclaimed, written and lived in a different
> socio-economic context. Its inspiration, en-
> riched by the living experiences of Christian
> tradition over the centuries, remains ever
> new for converting men and for advancing the
> life of society. It is not, however, to be
> utilized for the profit of particular tem-
> poral options, to the neglect of its univer-

sal and eternal message.[49]

This passage is a compromise between the traditional treatment of Gospel truth and an historicist understanding. It agrees that the inspiration of the Gospel is new in every age, but also
maintains that it has one universal and eternal
message. If we take the second part of this
statement seriously as far as theological method
goes, then the meaning of the first part is problematic. For if the Gospel is preached as if it
has only one universal and eternal (unchanging)
message, then its inspiration will fail to be new
in every age.

The passage quoted above continues:

Amid the disturbances and uncertainties
of the present hour, the Church has a specific message to proclaim and a support to
give to men in their efforts to take in hand
and give direction to their future. Since
the period in which Rerum novarum denounced
in a forceful and imperative manner the
scandal of the condition of the workers in
the nascent industrial society, historical
evolution has led to an awareness of other
dimensions and other applications of social
justice. The encyclical Quadragesimo anno
and Mater et Magistra already noted this fact.
The recent Council for its part took care to
point them out, in particular in the Pastoral
Constitution, Gaudium et Spes. We Ourselves
have already continued these lines of thought
in Our encyclical, Populorum progressio.[50]

Paul's understanding of historical evolution involved recognition that the application of principles changes, but made no room for recognition

19

that the evolution of human society and human nature entails a change in the principles themselves.
As a result this passage expresses elements of
both the traditional and the historicist position.
Paul spoke of historical evolution (the idea so
antithetical to Pius XII), but then he referred to
the "application" of social justice through the
social teaching.

A third example of Paul's position can be
noted in Populorum progressio, March 26, 1967:

> Founded to establish on earth the Kingdom
> of Heaven and not to conquer any earthly
> power, the Church clearly states that the
> two realms are distinct, just as the two
> powers, ecclesiastical and civil, are su-
> preme, each in its own domain. But since
> the Church lives in history, she ought to
> 'scrutinize the signs of the times and in-
> terpret them in the light of the Gospel.'[51]

There are some ambiguities here. It is not at all
clear how the two realms are to be kept separate
and each of the powers supreme if the Church is
active in history. How can she scrutinize the
signs of the times and interpret them in the light
of the Gospel without passing judgment on the
civil power? This matter will be more extensively
dealt with in Chapter Two.

The context in which this passage occurs suggests that what the Church is to do is to "carry
forward the work of Christ" who "entered this
world to give witness to the truth."[52] To do
this, Paul said, the Church "offers men what she
possesses as her characteristic attribute: a
global vision of men and the human race." This
vision, which it is the Church's duty to dissemin-

ate, is the vision upon which solutions to the
social problem must be based: "The present situation of the world demands concerted action based
on a clear vision of all economic, social, cultural, and spiritual aspects."[53] What the Church
offers to the world is her permanent truth concerning the unchangeable nature of human beings.
The changes in history are the context in which
she acts, not the context in which the truths
arise; for Paul, truth remained ahistorical.

Social Justice and the Status Quo

An important consequence of the influence of
the static papal world view appears in the papal
tendency to identify social justice, or what elsewhere is called general justice, with the social
and political order of the status quo, and with
the institutions which preserve that order. One
common way of doing this has been to associate justice with peace, as we saw above in the passage
from Ubi arcano.

Another aspect of this identification of social justice and the status quo is the papal use
of a particular understanding of the concept of
commutative justice in the formulation of social
justice. Because commutative justice is that justice which characterizes exchange,[54] it is exact,
is often characterized by an agreement or contract,
and is dependent upon just circumstances surrounding the exchange. As we shall see, the papal use
of the concept of commutative justice presupposes
the justice of the surrounding circumstances, and
thereby of the status quo. The identification of
this use of commutative justice with social justice implies an identification between social justice and the social order, between social justice
and the institutions which preserve that order.

A third way that the concept of social justice gets linked to the status quo in papal teaching is through the use made of the concept of distributive justice[55]: that is, by assuming that what is due to each is determined by rank in society. Natural inequality, an assumption of a static world view, then becomes a background against which social justice is determined. This assumption has a long history in the Christian Church, and continues up until the present, as we shall see by examining each of these papal approaches to social justice.

Social Justice and Peace

In the use of the Thomist framework by the popes through John XXIII, there is a continuing tendency to relate social justice to peace and order in society. This is to say that for them the common good was often defined in terms of the presence of peace and order, and the absence of strife and controversy.[56] Peace is also a Christian virtue, one to which the popes are sincerely attached. The peace of Christ should prevail on earth, they say.[57] But though all of them recognize explicitly from time to time that peace can only be built on justice, the assumed static view of society, of history and of human nature made it difficult for them to accept that each new approximation of justice necessitates controversy.[58] Consequently there is a tendency, such as was observed above in _Ubi arcano_, to de-emphasize justice because of the great stress put on peace. This stress on peace seems a subtle response to the social unrest and demands for change in the contemporary social and political order.

It is undeniable that the history of the nineteenth and early twentieth centuries offered the popes little incentive either to recognize the faster pace of change or to adapt to a new modern reality. The popes considered that the modern world refused to recognize the responsibilities that devolved upon human beings, both as individuals and as members of human society. A constant theme of Leo XIII's, often echoed in the writings of his successors, was the onesidedness of the modern view of freedom; freedom and rights, he said, were for a purpose, and that purpose was the exercise of responsibility and the fulfillment of duties.

Nor had the modern world been kind to the temporal authority of the Church, and her unwillingness to embrace modernity was to some extent an understandable reluctance to submit to more attacks. The popes were determined to retain those aspects of the world which were familiar and acceptable, and to resist changes which threatened either the Church's power or the understanding of human nature upon which her structure and theology were predicated. The popes themselves realized that theirs was a basically reformist position.[59] The basic structures of society were not called into question by the popes who saw them as supports of that peace and order which had reigned in the past and could again if all would uphold the traditional institutions: the Church, the family, private property, and the (Christian) state.[60] All the popes have either identified the cause of social problems with apostasy from God and the Church, or identified the solution of the social problems with the return of the entire flock to the Shepherd, the Church.[61] But though the popes saw all social problems linked to this sin of apostasy, they did not see them linked to one another. They envisioned them as self-contained,[62] not as evidence of social sin, of structural problems in

23

society.

In paragraph 29 of _Rerum novarum_ Leo XIII set
forth a principle which, elaborated by Pius XI as
the principle of subsidiarity, was highly influential in later social teaching on this point. Leo
XIII wrote that:

> If by a strike, or other combination of
> workmen, there should be imminent danger of
> disturbance to the public peace; or if the
> circumstances were such that among the labor-
> ing population the ties of family life were
> relaxed; if Religion were found to suffer
> through the workmen not having time and
> opportunity to practice it; if in workshops
> and factories there were danger to morals
> through the mixing of the sexes or from any
> occasion of evil; or if employers laid bur-
> dens upon the workingmen which were repugnant
> to their dignity as human beings; finally, if
> health were endangered by excessive labor, or
> if work were unsuited to sex or age,--in
> these cases, there can be no question that,
> within certain limits, it would be right to
> call in the help and authority of the law.
> The limits must be determined by the nature
> of the occasion which calls for the law's
> interference--the principle being this, that
> the law must not undertake more, nor go fur-
> ther, than is required for the remedy of the
> evil or the removal of the danger.[63]

As we shall see, this is the first of a series of
papal documents in which it is assumed, if not
stated, that justice is to be _restored_ after a
disturbance of the peace. Presumably, a disturbance alerted authorities to the existence of an
injustice, which, when remedied, ended both the

disturbance of the peace and the specific injustice. The papal discussion seems to begin with peace, called here the fruit of justice, moves to an equation of peace and justice, and finally assumes that where peace is, there is justice. Thus when wage disputes broke the peace, one remedied the obvious cause of the disturbance and raised wages, thereby doing justice. But since the <u>principal</u> objective was to restore peace, no investigation or analysis of the justice of the total social situation was ever done. In fact, Leo above denied that the civil authority had the right to do more than restore peace by rectifying the particular evil which threatened or disturbed the peace.

This restriction on the civil authority was formulated by Pius XI as the principle of subsidiarity[64]:

> It is indeed true, as history clearly shows, that owing to the change in social conditions, much that was formerly done by small bodies can nowdays be accomplished only by large organizations. Nevertheless, it is a fundamental principle of social philosophy, fixed and unchangeable, that one should not withdraw from individuals and commit to the community what they can accomplish by their own enterprise and industry. So, too, it is an injustice and at the same time a grave evil and a disturbance of right order, to transfer to a larger and higher collectivity functions which can be performed and provided by lesser and subordinate bodies. Inasmuch as every social activity should, by its very nature, prove a help to members of the body social, it should never absorb or destroy them.

The state authorities should leave to
other bodies the care the expediting of
business and activities of lesser moment,
which otherwise become for it a great dis-
traction. It will then perform with greater
vigor, freedom, and effectiveness, the tasks
belonging properly to it, and which it alone
can accomplish: directing, supervising, encouraging and restraining as circumstances
suggest or necessity demands. Let those in
power, therefore, be convinced that the more
faithfully the principle of 'subsidiarity' is
followed and a hierarchical order prevails
among the various organizations, the more
excellent will be the authority and efficiency of society, and the happier and more
prosperous the condition of the commonwealth.[65]

Pius XI and Leo XIII were both reacting a-
gainst the modern trend of the State to absorb all
the powers of former intermediate institutions
"leaving virtually only individuals and the
State."[66] They maintained that this was a dangerous situation for the State, which had its energies diverted from its real task, which was not
business or commerce, but the general overseeing
of the fabric of society. But the popes were also
aware that this newly empowered State was dangerous for the Church as well, as recent history had
well proved. This state challenged not only the
privileges of the Church, but the rights of individuals, who could not stand against the power of
the state and were left without intermediate institutions under which to shelter. As a result,
the limitation of the rights of states has been a
central theme of papal teaching.[67] Pius XI's
statement was a characteristic example of that
teaching which sought to delimit the powers of

the state.

This principle of subsidiarity raised questions about the legitimacy of state attempts to tackle structural problems in its society (industrial, agricultural, financial, political structures), even though the presupposition underlying the principle of subsidiarity was that there were no other powers capable of attacking structural problems. Pius XII relied on this same formulation of the principle of subsidiarity in his address, La solennita (June 1, 1941) on the anniversary of Rerum novarum.[68] He denied the state's power to reconstruct itself or to restructure any part of itself, because to Pius XII it seemed that the group demanding that power was atheistic communism. In his view communism made false promises of a greater justice to lure people into supporting its program for revolution. Pius XII would not give communism the legitimacy it claimed for the use of state authority against individuals.

By contrast, John XXIII in Mater et Magistra quoted the first of the two paragraphs above from Pius XI on the principle of subsidiarity, and then qualified their application:

> Indeed, as is easily perceived, recent developments of science and technology provide additional reasons why, to a greater extent than heretofore, it is within the power of public authorities to reduce imbalances, whether these be between various sectors of economic life, or between different regions of the same nation, or even between different peoples of the world as a whole. These same developments make it possible to keep fluctuations in the economy within bounds and to provide effective measures for pre-

venting mass unemployment. Consequently, it is requested again and again of public authorities responsible for the common good, that they intervene in a wide variety of economic affairs, and that, in a more extensive and organized way than heretofore, they adapt institutions, tasks, means and procedures to this end. Nevertheless, it remains true that precautionary activities of public authorities in the economic field, though widespread and penetrating, should be such that they not only avoid restricting the freedom of private citizens, but also increase it, so long as the basic rights of each individual person are preserved inviolate.[69]

John has here softened the effect of Pius XI's teaching, first, by omitting the specific prohibitions against the state interfering in business, and, second, by approving the state as the overseer of the economy. His warning that in doing these things the state should take care not to infringe on individual rights radically changes the sense of Pius' statement. Pius had said that the state could not do these things without infringing on these rights, and therefore it was not licit to do them. John XXIII further modified the use of the principle of subsidiarity two years later in Pacem in terris:

Just as it is necessary, moreover, in each state that relations which the public authority has with its citizens, families, and intermediate associations be controlled and regulated by the principle of subsidiarity, it is equally necessary that the relationships which exist between the world-wide public authority and the public authorities of individual nations be governed by the

28

same principle. This means that the world-
wide public authority and the public authorities of individual nations must tackle and
solve problems of an economic, political, and
cultural character which are posed by the
universal common good. For, because of the
vastness, complexity and urgency of those
problems, the public authorities of the individual states are not in a position to tackle
them with any hope of a positive solution.
The world-wide public authority is not
intended to limit the sphere of action of the
public authority of the individual state,
much less to take its place. On the contrary,
its purpose is to create, on a world basis,
an environment in which the public authorities of each state, its citizens and intermediate associations can carry out their
tasks, fulfill their duties, and exercise
their rights with greater security.[70]

The principle of subsidiarity, then, prior to
John XXIII tended to support the status quo. What
had been a principle that denied to the state the
authority to regulate the economy and associated
aspects of social life became a mandate for the
creation of overarching authorities to deal with
problems of injustice that could be tackled by
nothing less.

Social Justice and Commutative Justice

In addition to often identifying social justice with the status quo through their connection
of social justice and peace, the popes have sometimes made this identification of social justice
and the status quo through linking social justice
with a particular understanding of commutative
justice.

29

Commutative justice is the justice characteristic of exchange, of trade. It calls for a one-
for-one exchange, a trade of equal though different commodities. In a trade situation justice depends upon both the freedom of both parties to the
exchange and to their having just title to the
goods they offer for exchange. In the absence of
just title one party could be unjustly enriched by
trading goods stolen from another (perhaps even
stolen from the party to whom they are being trad-
ed). In the absence of freedom of the trading
partners one party could be forced to make unfavorable exchanges which enrich the more powerful
partner, ensuring that further contracts of exchange are even more unfavorable to the weaker
party. For commutative justice to be reflected in
any specific exchange or contract, therefore, the
social situation in which the exchange takes place
must approximate social justice. The fact that
both parties are prepared to exchange is not evidence either of free choice or of just title.

The difficulty with the papal use of commutative justice is that the social situation was
assumed to reflect social justice. Except for the
papal insistence that just contracts pay a living
wage, neither the freedom of the parties to the
exchange nor just title to the goods of those parties was questioned. The present ownership situation was accepted by the popes; the history of how
some came to be owners and others did not was not
questioned. Therefore the papal stress on commutative justice in the creation of social justice
reinforced the status quo insofar as ownership was
concerned.

Pius XI was very explicit as to the centrality of commutative justice to social justice in
the areas of poverty and labor. In a discussion

30

of social justice in Quadragesimo anno he wrote:
"It belongs to what is called commutative justice
to respect faithfully private ownership, and not
to encroach on the rights of another by exceeding
one's own property." And later in Quadragesimo
anno we find: "The mutual relations between capital and labor must be determined according to the
law of the strictest justice, called commutative
justice."[71]

Calves and Perrin claim that what Pius meant
in demanding, in the name of commutative justice,
that private property be strictly respected was
that "where legitimate ownership has been determined" there were strict obligations on all to
observe them.[72] But in none of Pius' documents
did he discuss either who should make such determinations, or what standards should be used in
making them. He rather seems to have assumed that
de facto ownership was legitimate ownership.

Similarly, the insistence upon one-for-one
exchange in the labor-capital situation was mean-
ingless in the absence of alternative means for
the laborer to exist and to support his family.
He was not free to refuse any contract of exchange. The power relationship between the trading partners was unequal. The trade of equal
amounts of commodities (wages and labor) requires
some equalization of the respective situations of
the traders.

A similar understanding of the relationship
of social justice and commutative justice was implicit in the work of Pius XII. In La solennita,
his commemorative address on the anniversary of
Rerum novarum, Pius presented a somewhat contradictory position. This address was brief and cursory as compared to others written for the anni-

31

versary of <u>Rerum</u> <u>novarum</u>, for example, its predecessor, <u>Quadragesimo</u> <u>anno</u>, and its successors,
<u>Mater</u> <u>et</u> <u>Magistra</u> and, in a different style, <u>Octo-
gesima</u> <u>adveniens</u>. Perhaps if the work had been
further developed it would have been less ambiguous. In it, Pius maintained that:

> It is the right and duty of the individu-
> al workers and employers to work out their
> agreements as to labor, because the duty and
> the right to labor is imposed on the indivi-
> dual by nature, and not by society.[73]

This statement seems to imply that employers and
employees should enter into one-to-one agreements.
But in other contexts Pius had defended the right
of laborers to organize, so we may assume that he
was not here denying that right. What he seems to
have urged was that any agreement be a contract of
exchange, that the sustenance of the workers and
their families be obtained through an exact trade
for labor time. This certainly casts justice in
the labor situation in the form of commutative
justice. Therefore, the following affirmation
from the same document is much qualified:

> Likewise, the national economy as it is the
> produce of men who work together in the com-
> munity of the state, has no other end than
> to secure without interruption the material
> conditions in which the individual life of
> the citizens may develop.[74]

Pius XII maintained, then, that the national
economy was to be built upon agreements of exchange between capital and labor, and that this
national economy's purpose was to secure the material conditions in which the life of the citizen
might thrive. The end of social justice--the com-

mon good--can be expressed in terms of "material conditions in which the life of the citizens may develop." The implication suggested by the juxtaposition of these two passages is that the labor system created by free market capitalism is the basis of social justice.

That this is the thrust of Pius XII's understanding was clear in the following passage from the same document:

> Hence, it follows that the care of such a common good does not imply a power so extensive over the members of a community that in virtue of it the public authority can interfere with the evolution of the individual activity which we have just described, decide directly on the beginning or (excepting the case of legitimate capital punishment) the ending of human life, determine at will the manner of his physical, religious, and moral movements in opposition to the personal duties or rights of men, and to this end abolish or deprive of its efficacy his natural right to material goods.[75]

Here is a part of what was clearly meant to be a repudiation of the Marxist stance on property and labor. If, as we must suppose, the "his" in the above passage refers back to "members,"[76] then we have here a claim that the state cannot legitimately redistribute its material goods. A common example of this papal condemnation of state redistribution was the prohibition on taxation designed to fall so heavily on the wealthy that maintenance of large estates was difficult.[77] Thus Pius insured that within the social teaching of his time, social justice would be interpreted in terms of commutative justice. Only labor and employer were

33

to be parties to the labor agreement, and the civil authority in society was forbidden to redistribute wealth so as to create the possibility of change in the relative power of the bargaining parties.

None of this is to imply that for any pope since Leo there were no limits on the validity of mutually entered contracts. One of the radical points Leo made for his own time was that since the preservation of life is the duty of all, workers cannot make valid contracts for less than a living wage.[78] This was upheld by every pope since Leo.[79] But this position merely justified workers' right to a bare minimum of wages. It counseled improvement of a situation in which a worker totally lacked protection, but it did not encourage change in the relative power of the worker and employer in the negotiating of work agreements.

This interpretation of social justice exclusively in terms of commutative justice in property and labor theory did not continue in the work of either John XXIII or Paul VI. While John resembled Pius XI and Pius XII in his identification of social justice with peace and order, he did not follow their lead in the prominence given to commutative justice, any more than he followed their lead in the meaning of the principle of subsidarity. Paul VI reflected even greater change. In fact, one would be hard pressed to prove that Paul assumed the traditional association of social justice and the order of the status quo.

Gaudium et Spes, the Pastoral Constitution of Vatican II (which Paul signed), broke new ground for the social teaching in demanding a reconstruction of human institutions which do not minister

34

to the dignity and purpose of humanity.[80] While earlier popes, especially Pius XI, condemned the domination of capital and criticized the structures of society, they clearly thought these structures basically sound and capable of reform, as we saw earlier. Paul, in both _Populorum progressio_ and _Octogesima adveniens_, was also critical of the existing social and economic order and of the modern mentality which justified and supported it. The following passages are examples of this critical attitude which seems, in contrast to John XXIII, tinged with pessimism:

> Yet once this is admitted that colonizers brought some skills and advantages to the Third World it remains only too true that the resultant situation is manifestly inadequate for facing the hard reality of modern economics. Left to itself it works rather to widen the differences in the world's level of life, not to diminish them: rich people enjoy rapid growth while the poor develop slowly.[81]
> However, local and individual undertakings are no longer enough. The present situation of the world demands concerted action based on a clear vision of all social, economic, cultural and spiritual aspects.[82]
> But it is unfortunate that on these new conditions of society a system has been constructed which considers profit as the key motive for economic progress, competition as the supreme law of economics, and private ownership of the means of production as an absolute right that has no limits and carries no corresponding social obligations.[83]
>
> Development demands bold transformations, innovations that go deep.[84]

35

Thus it is necessary to have the courage to
undertake a revision of the relationships
between nations, whether it is a question of
the international division of production, the
structure of exchanges, the control of profits, the monetary system. . . .[85]

Thus many people are reaching the point of
questioning the very model of society. The
ambition of many nations, in the competition
that sets them in opposition and which carries them along, is to attain technological,
economic, and military power. This ambition
then stands in the way of setting up structures in which the rhythms of progress would
be regulated with a view to greater justice,
instead of accentuating inequalities and living in a climate of distrust and struggle
which would unceasingly compromise peace.[86]

While these statements reveal certain similarities to those of Paul's predecessors (who also
saw the solution in ever greater efforts to turn
the present system around), they also resemble
those of liberation theologians and other critics
of development policy. Paul envisaged no alternative to the capitalist system, though he recognized
clearly that a great deal of manipulation of that
system would be necessary for real development to
occur. Paul was much stronger in his criticism of
capitalism, and not nearly so optimistic about its
possible reform as his predecessors. Paul condemned the relationship between First and Third
World countries in _Populorum progressio_, which he
referred to in paragraph 52 as "neo-colonialism".
This condemnation was more than a deliberate balance to his condemnation of socialism and more
than a purely theoretical critique of capitalism.
The statement seems rather based on the data

gathered by the social sciences on the operations
of present economic structures, such as on the
growing gap between rich and poor, and between
rich and poor nations.[87]

Perhaps the point which best conveys the
difference between Paul and the previous tradition concerning the relationship between social
justice and the status quo is the famous phrase
from _Populorum progressio_: "development is the
new name for peace" (_hodie_ _nemo_ _dubitat_ _progres-
sionem_ _idem_ _valere_ _ac_ _pacem_, literally translated
"today no one doubts that development is the same
as peace").[88] Clearly Paul had turned the usual
attitude on its head: justice was no longer a
return to a former set of arrangements, or the
elimination of disruptions to the general status
quo; rather, justice now demanded thoroughgoing
changes. This was a significant shift in theory;
whether this theoretical change will be continued
and implemented in specific teaching reversing the
traditional tendency to legitimize the status quo
is, of course, another question.

Social Justice and Distributive Justice

The last point of importance to the way social justice was identified with the prevailing
order in social teaching concerns the papal understanding of distributive justice and its relationship to social justice. For their understanding
of distributive justice the popes again followed
Aquinas:

> . . . distributive justice, which apportions
> proportionately to each his share of the com-
> mon stock.[89]
> We have said that distributive justice
> gives something to a private person insofar

37

as something belonging to the community is due to a part. This is so much the more considerable in correspondence with the greater importance of the part to the whole. Consequently, so much the more is given from the common stock as the recipient holds more responsibility in the community.[90]

Because the popes understood distributive justice in this way, as proportional to rank (and rank depended upon function in society), they did not object until very recently to the existence of inequality in society. Pius XII illustrated this in his encyclical epistle to the American hierarchy, Sertum laetitiae:

> One point stands out in demanding attention: the good things which God has created for the benefit of all men should find their way to all alike in a just proportion . . . God in his excellent disposition of our fortunes has thus ordained that there be rich and poor in the world, for the better exercise of our human virtues, the better trial of our human worth . . .[91]

This passage makes clear the erroneousness of Calves' and Perrin's contention that distributive justice was not utilized in the papal discussion of social justice questions because the popes realized that it was a political, not an economic, concept.[92] There is considerably more evidence on this point than this one passage. In the writings of Pius XI (as in Leo XII before him) the idea of distributive justice was the basic concept from which the papal position on capital was developed.[93] The right of capitalists to control business enterprises was, for these popes, based on the importance of capital to the modern economy.[94]

Not only did the popes until John never consider
that labor might have a right to management equal
to capital's, but the just wage was never considered pegged to any standard of profits. The only
limit on profits was that the laborers were not to
be paid less than a living wage. This is another
example of preferential treatment (power and
wealth) for those considered to be of more service
to the entire society.

In fact, in all the popes up to Paul VI, if
not including Paul himself, we find insistence
upon both proportional equity[95] and general condemnations of more egalitarian conceptions of justice. Such condemnations are a consistent part of
the popes' treatment of socialism and communism.
Egalitarianism can denote more than just one kind
of justice, and can even be combined with proportionality in some social justice schemes. Thus
the strict egalitarianism of a given social plan
may reside in the proposed goal for all the members
of the society--equal pay, equal education, equal
responsibility and power. But the means of arriving at that proposed goal may be based upon proportion, since some may be far ahead of others at the
very start. But there is no place for equality in
a social justice scheme which looks to proportionality as the goal of the society, and therefore
mandates ongoing inequality of power, material
benefits, and rights. The popes were led to maintain just such proportionality by their view of
nature as containing a hierarchy. Thus Pius XI
wrote in _Divini Redemptoris_:

> It is not true that all have equal rights in
> civil society. It is not true that there ex-
> ists no lawful social hierarchy.[96]

Pius XII, in his first encyclical, _Summi Pon-_

<u>tificatus</u>, wrote: "Mankind, by a divinely appoint-
ed law, is divided into a variety of classes."[97]
In his Christmas message he continued this same
thought:

> In a nation worthy of the name, inequalities
> among the social classes present few or no
> obstacles to their brotherly union. We re-
> fer, of course, to those inequalities which
> result not from human caprice but from the
> nature of things--inequalities in intellec-
> tual and spiritual growth, with economics,
> with differences in individual circumstances,
> within, of course, the limits prescribed by
> justice and mutual charity.[98]

Similarly, John XXIII, in his first encyclical, <u>Ad petri cathedram</u>, quoted both the above
passage by Pius XII and Leo XIII's <u>Rerum novarum</u>
on the inevitability of classes. He then continued: "Anyone, therefore, who ventures to deny
that there are differences between social classes
contradicts the very laws of nature."[99]

Beginning with Paul VI one might say that
there is some ambivalence on the subject of human
equality. The bishop's documents, both <u>Gaudium et
Spes</u> and <u>De Justitia in Mundo</u>, are outspoken about
the equality of all persons, not merely in the
eyes of God (as all the traditions had maintained),
but socially and politically as well. In <u>De Justitia in Mundo</u> we find the following:

> Never before have the forces working for
> bringing about a unified world appeared so
> powerful and dynamic; they are rooted in the
> awareness of the full basic equality as well
> as of the human dignity of all.[100]

<u>Gaudium</u> <u>et</u> <u>Spes</u> was very clear on this point:

> Since all men possess a rational soul and are
> created in God's likeness, since they have
> the same nature and origin, have been redeem-
> ed by Christ, and enjoy the same divine call-
> ing and destiny, the basic equality of all
> must receive increasingly greater recogni-
> tion.
>   True, all men are not alike from the
> point of view of varying physical power and
> the diversity of intellectual and moral re-
> sources. Nevertheless, with respect to the
> fundamental rights of the person, every type
> of discrimination, whether based on sex,
> race, color, social condition, language or
> religion, is to be overcome and eradicated
> as contrary to God's intent.[101]

The first sentence of the second paragraph in
this passage, especially the phrase "diversity of
intellectual and moral resources," is reminiscent
of the traditional viewpoint. In the traditional
view, because of the heavy emphasis on reason, the
diversity of intellectual resources was the basis
for claiming diversity of moral resources, which
then became a proof of natural inequality. Here
the overall message seems to affirm equality. The
traditional phrase may have been intended to demonstrate some affinity with the past by acknowled-
ging empirical differences, though these are no
longer considered related to moral value. Neither
the hierarchy nor the popes like to appear innovative, but prefer to appear to remain in some kind
of continuity with past tradition.[102]

However clear the episcopal documents seem to
be about the stance of the Church on the issue of
equality, we cannot assume that such expressions

are given clear and consistent application. They are, however, indicators of some pressure for change at work in the Church. We need to be aware that in writings actually authored by Paul (and not merely signed by him, like the episcopal documents) he said much less than his bishops or his predecessors on the subject of human equality. Where most of his predecessors denounced egalitarianism as inappropriate in many areas, especially any which related to communist claims, Paul's only denunciation of it occurred in the context of the role of women. In _Octogesima adveniens_ Paul condemned discrimination against women on the basis of sex as well as the "false equality" popular today. He insisted that equality understood as sameness destroys the God-given order.[103] Men and women are called to different tasks, he said, and to ignore this is to ignore nature.

This was the same argument which has been used to justify inequality (not only between the sexes, but in economics and politics as well) in the tradition for centuries. The presence of this understanding in any form throws doubt on the security of the overall shift from a reliance on natural inequality. This issue will be discussed at length in Chapter Five.

The question of the papal position on equality is of critical importance for understanding the papal pronouncements on justice. Gene Outka, in his examination of the relationship between justice and charity,[104] noted that definitions of justice differ on the basis of whether justice is understood to be based on notions of merit, effort, need, or sameness (i.e., to each the same thing). He concluded that justice and charity correspond best when justice is egalitarian in the latter sense. If we look at the development of papal social teaching in this century, we can observe that some papal stands, taken originally in the name of charity, came to be defended in the name of justice as the popes, moved by a compassion for the plight of the poor, became increasingly more egalitarian in their understanding of the demands of justice. This is most noticeable in papal treatment of ownership of the means of production.

Leo XIII had advised workers, through frugality, to save from the just wage they were to receive. Such saving of funds would, he suggested, allow them to become owners of property.[105] By the time of Pius XI, it was plain to all that the condition of wage laborer was inescapable; through frugality the worker could acquire property, but not _productive_ property, as Leo had assumed. Pius denied that the wage contract was unjust,[106] and insisted that Leo had never implied that it was. However, he added that in the present time he deemed it _advisable_ that, whenever possible, the wage contract be modified to a contract of partnership.[107] Pius XII often emphasized that this was not a requirement of justice[108] but he nonetheless urged that large scale enterprises be modified by partnership agreements.[109] John XXIII, in _Mater et Magistra_, _began_ with the assumption of partnership in industry and crafts, and elaborated the rights of participation and control which accrue to workers in industry.[110] He demanded that collaboration be the model used in the workplace, because it is in accordance with the dignity of humanity.[111] This point was reiterated in _Pacem in terris_.[112] This was a long road from Leo XIII's claim that "To suffer and endure, then, is the lot of humanity"[113] to John XXIII's claim that both employment and insurance against sickness, old age, and unemployment are natural rights of human beings.[114] The movement is unmistakable and often remarked.[115]

This development of a more egalitarian understanding of justice within the social teaching has
not been due solely to the workings of charity in
the minds of the popes. As the inequality recognized in the world broadened beyond those class
and sex inequalities to which the popes had been
accustomed, they increasingly questioned the justice of social inequalities.

The popes have defended the class system
within specific countries as a natural, God-given
order, legitimate so long as the workers were
accorded both the dignity of human beings and the
living wage that dignity required. But as it became increasingly clear that the class system
operated among societies and nations, such that
entire societies were second-class world citizens,
papal sensibilities were offended. We shall see
in Chapter Three that the very popes who defended
inequality with regard to domestic classes denounced it in the missions and among the clergy of
the various areas of the world.

Pius XI, Pius XII, and John XXIII all tended
to place increasing stress on justice for workers
within a national economy while denying natural
equality. John stated that all that was necessary
to rise within the class structure was capability
and diligence.[116] This was in itself a shift from
the static view of classes which had prevailed at
the end of the nineteenth century. Paul VI, who
seems to have picked up the thread of change in
John's view of the need for international justice,
elaborated on and altered this theme. He made it
clear that in his view the reality of the world
economy was incompatible with upward mobility. It
was not lack of capability or diligence which pre-

vented prosperity in the Third World; it was the relationship with the First World which doomed the citizens of the Third World to inequality and misery. For the first time in the papal tradition, Paul connected justice with freedom of determination: the injustice done the Third World is the result, he said, of their inability to control their own economies.[117] The episcopal document De Justitia in Mundo places great stress on this point.[118]

This is not the same issue as equality within a society, once the sole concern of former popes. On this issue, equality of classes, Paul was silent. The direction of the papal position on the international level, however, is clear through the end of Paul's pontificate, and may signify a shift on the domestic level as well: the Church may not be accepting empirical inequality as evidence of natural inequality. Contradictions between narrow interpretations of legal or commutative justice and a justice consistent with Christian charity are explicitly recognized. Both Populorum progressio and Octogesima adveniens gave evidence of an inquiry into justice in which natural inequality was not a presupposition. The possibility of socially created inequality--injustice--could therefore appear.

NOTES

[1]Some examples of this are: Quadragesimo anno, para. 137, Acta Apostolicae Sedis (hereafter AAS) 23 (1931):223-224; Divini Redemptoris, para. 49, AAS 29 (1937):91; Summi Pontificatus, AAS 31 (1939):441; Quoniam Paschaliam, April 9, 1939, AAS 31 (1939):149-150; Pacem in terris, para. 35, 37, AAS 55 (1963):265-266; Populorum progressio, para. 73, 76, AAS 59 (1967):292-293, 294; Octogesima adveniens, para. 43, AAS 63 (1971):431-432.

[2]Some examples are: Summi Pontificatus, AAS 31 (1939):441; Quoniam Paschaliam, AAS 31 (1939): 149; Pacem in terris, para. 167, AAS 55 (1963): 202-203; Populorum progressio, para. 5, 45, 55, 76, AAS 59 (1967):279, 259, 284, 294; and Octogesima adveniens, para. 43, 45, AAS 63 (1971):431-432, 433.

[3]Acta Sanctae Sedis (hereafter ASS) 23:649.

[4]AAS 23 (1931):197, 198, 217.

[5]Summa Theologiae, ed. Black friars Dominicans (New York: McGraw-Hill Book Co., 1964), 60 vols., 2a2ae 58:11.

[6]Both Pius XI and Pius XII were explicit about their reliance on Thomas: Officiorum omnium (August 1, 1922), AAS 14 (1922):449-458; Nous nous souhaitons (September 4, 1955), AAS 47 (1955):683-691. Major commentators, such as Pierre Bigo, in his La doctrine sociale de l'Eglise (Paris: Presses de Universitaires de France, 1965) spend

entire chapters on Thomas before treating papal
social teaching. (Chapter 4, "Thomas D'Aquin,"
pp. 35-44)

[7]*Summa*, 2a2ae 58:5.

[8]*Ibid.*, 2a2ae 58:12 and 7: this is the meaning of *non differunt solum secundum multum et pau-
cem* (emphasis mine) in article 7. Also J. Y.
Calves and J. Perrin, *Eglise et société economique*,
vol. 1, translated: *The Church and Social Justice*
(London: Burns and Oates, 1961), pp. 145-147.

[9]*Summa*, 2a2ae 61:2.

[10]*Ibid.*

[11]*Church and Social Justice*, pp. 153ff.

[12]Thus the original title of Calves' and Perrin's book was *Eglise et société economique*.

[13]*Church and Social Justice*, p. 169; Pius
XII, *AAS* 31 (1939):149-150, *Quoniam Paschaliam*.

[14]*Mater et Magistra*, May 14, 1961, para. 39,
AAS 53 (1961):410; *La solennita*, June 1, 1941, *AAS*
33 (1941):199.

[15]*Evangelii praecones*, June 2, 1951, *AAS* 43
(1951):518, para. 71; *Quadragesimo anno*, May 15,
1931, *AAS* 23 (1931):223-224, para. 137; *Pacem in
terris*, April 11, 1963, *AAS* 55 (1963):302-303,
para. 167.

[16]*Divini Redemptoris*, March 19, 1939, *AAS* 29
(1937):91; *Quadragesimo anno*, May 15, 1931, *AAS* 23
(1931):178, 224, para. 4, 5, 138.

[17]Rerum novarum, May 15, 1891 (hereafter ASS) 23:655-656, para. 25, 26; Quadragesimo anno, AAS 23 (1931):202-207, para. 76-90; Summi Pontificatus, October 22, 1939, AAS 31 (1939):435; Mater et Magistra, AAS 53 (1961):441-442, 448, para. 163-165, 201; Gaudium et Spes, AAS 58 (1966):1049-1050, para. 30, 31; Populorum progressio, AAS 59 (1967):273-275, 276, 277, 281-282, para. 33-35, 38, 40, 49-51; De Justitia in Mundo, AAS 63 (1971): 938-941.

[18]AAS 14 (1922):685-686; translation: J. Husslein, ed., Social Wellsprings: Pius XI (Milwaukee: Bruce, 1942), pp. 14-15.

[19]Divini illius Magistri (also known as Rappresentanti in terris), AAS 22 (1930):55.

[20]Ubi arcano, AAS 14 (1922):689-690.

[21]Quadragesimo anno: "immutata prorsus atque immutabilis," AAS 23 (1931):183; Divini illius Magistri: "aeternas," AAS 22 (1930):83.

[22]Quadragesimo anno, AAS 23 (1931):209; Ubi arcano, AAS 14 (1922):689; Divini illius Magistri AAS 22 (1930):53-54. Pius XI was not alone in his nostalgia for the Middle Ages: cf., Rerum novarum, ASS 23:663-664.

[23]Quadragesimo anno, AAS 23 (1931):207-208; R. L. Camp, The Papal Ideology of Social Reform (Leiden: Brill, 1969), pp. 38-40.

[24]Karl Otmar von Aretin, The Papacy and the Modern World (New York: McGraw-Hill, 1970), pp. 191-192.

[25]Church and Social Justice, pp. 422-423;

Papal Ideology, pp. 36-40.

[26]Papal Ideology, pp. 37-38.

[27]Ibid., p. 37.

[28]This letter is not in the Acta, and I find no other references to it.

[29]Papal Ideology, p. 38.

[30]Quadragesimo anno, AAS 23 (1931):209; translation: Seven Great Encyclicals (New York: Paulist Press, 1963), p. 152.

[31]Ibid., pp. 180, 181, 218, 219, 222-223 and 219-220; Divini Redemptoris, AAS 29 (1937):85, 86, 104-105.

[32]Quadragesimo anno, AAS 23 (1931):211.

[33]Ibid.

[34]Ibid.

[35]Ibid., p. 212.

[36]Ibid., p. 211.

[37]Ibid.; translation: Seven Great Encyclicals, p. 152.

[38]Pius XII's addresses and letters are on every subject in the modern world, especially on various technical and scientific vocations. He reveals knowledge of a great deal of technique used in mining, medicine, banking, and various manufactories.

[39]AAS 47 (1955):673; translation: The Pope

Speaks, Vol. 2, No. 3, p. 206.

[40]October 20, 1939, AAS 31 (1939):440; translation: The Pope Speaks: The Words of Pius XII (New York: Harcourt, Brace and Co., 1940), p. 180.

[41]August 12, 1950, AAS 42 (1950):562-563; translation: A. C. Cotter, The Encyclical "Humani Generis" (Weston, Mass.: Weston College Press, 1952), para. 5-7.

[42]Ibid., pp. 565-567, para. 15-18; translation from A. C. Cotter, The Encyclical "Humani Generis".

[43]Especially in his first encyclical, Ad petri cathedram, AAS 51 (1959):498-502.

[44]Mater et Magistra, AAS 53 (1961):453: "Quam Catholicam Ecclesia doctrinam tradit et pronunciat de hominum convictu ac societate, ea sine vila dubitatione vi pollet.

[45]Papacy in the Modern World, p. 227.

[46]Ringrazia di vero, November 15, 1958, AAS 50 (1958):998; Ad petri cathedram, AAS 51 (1959): 506-507; Mater et Magristra, AAS 53 (1961):412-413, 418, 424-425, 441-442.

[47]Pacem in terris, AAS 55 (1963):268.

[48]Gaudium et Spes, AAS 58 (1966):1029, para. 5; translation: Renewing the Earth: Catholic Documents on Peace, Justice and Liberation (Garden City: Image Books, 1976), p. 182.

[49]Octogesima adveniens, AAS 63 (1971):403-

404, para. 4; translation: <u>Renewing the Earth</u>, p. 354.

[50]<u>Octogesima adveniens</u>, <u>AAS</u> 63 (1971):404; para. 5; translation: <u>Renewing the Earth</u>, pp. 354-355.

[51]<u>Populorum progressio</u>, para. 13, <u>AAS</u> 59 (1967):264; translation: <u>Renewing the Earth</u>, p. 317.

[52]Ibid.

[53]Ibid.

[54]<u>Summa Theologiae</u>, 2a2ae, 58.

[55]Ibid.

[56]For example, see <u>Quadragesimo anno</u>, para. 45, <u>AAS</u> 23 (1931):191-192; <u>Rerum novarum</u>, para. 15, <u>ASS</u> 23:648-649; <u>Casti connubi</u>, December 31, 1930, <u>AAS</u> 22 (1930):568; <u>Quoniam Paschaliam</u>, April 9, 1939, <u>AAS</u> 31 (1939):149.

[57]Two major encyclicals, <u>Ubi arcano</u> and <u>Pacem in terris</u>, are devoted solely to this theme.

[58]It is significant that a continual note in the papal documents is the gradualism which the popes urge as the proper method for dealing with injustice. Speedy changes, they say, destroy the order which prevents total injustice. <u>Meminisse juvat</u>, July 16, 1958, <u>AAS</u> 50 (1958):449-459; <u>In plurimis</u>, May 5, 1888, <u>ASS</u> 20:545-559; <u>Mater et Magistra</u>, <u>AAS</u> 53 (1961):433, <u>Populorum progressio</u>, <u>AAS</u> 59 (1967):272-273; <u>Ad petri cathedram</u>, <u>AAS</u> 51 (1959):527; <u>Pacem in terris</u>, <u>AAS</u> 55 (1963):301.

[59]Quadragesimo anno, AAS 23 (1931):202-203, 205, 207, 210, 218, 225-226, para. 77, 78, 90, 101, 126, 142; Divini Redemptoris, AAS 29 (1937):84, para. 36; Populorum progressio, AAS 59 (1967):273, 296, 297, para. 32, 81. These are instances of the popes' labelling their own proposals as reforms. But perhaps John and Pius XII were the most reformist in that they were the more optimistic about the worth of the present structure.

[60]Rerum novarum, ASS 23:642-646; Quadragesimo anno, AAS 23 (1931):191-194, 218-222; Mater et Magistra, AAS 53 (1961):426-431; Casti connubi, AAS 22 (1930):553, 560; Pacem in terris, AAS 55 (1963):262, 269, 280.

[61]Quadragesimo anno, AAS 23 (1931):180, 181, 218, 219, 222-223, 230; Divini Redemptoris, AAS 29 (1937):85, 86, 104-105; Christmas message 1939, AAS 32 (1940):11; Ad petri cathedram, AAS 51 (1959):525.

[62]Rerum novarum, ASS 23:658; Quadragesimo anno, AAS 23 (1931):210; Populorum progressio, AAS 59 (1967):287. Such an understanding is implied in the writings of all the popes, in their insistence on gradualism, the need for preserving order, and in their lack of attack on the system itself.

[63]ASS 23:658; translation: Seven Great Encyclicals, pp. 17-18.

[64]Pius XI presented this as a traditional philosophical idea which had always been in force, in keeping with the papal dislike of innovation.

[65]Quadragesimo anno, AAS 23 (1931):203, para. 79-80; translation: Seven Great Encyclicals, pp. 147-148.

[66]Quadragesimo anno, AAS 23 (1931):203, para. 78; translation: Seven Great Encyclicals, p. 147.

[67]Leo did this in Arcanum, ASS 12:385-402; Diuturnum, ASS 14:3-14; Immortale Dei, ASS 18:161-180; Libertas humana, ASS 20:593-613; Sapientiae Christianae, ASS 22:385-404; and Graves de communi, ASS 33:385-396. Pius XI continued to place limits on the action of the state: Mit brennender sorge, AAS 29 (1937):145-167; Divini Redemptoris, AAS 29 (1937):65-106; Casti connubi, AAS 22 (1930):539-592; Divini illius magistri, AAS 21 (1929):723-762; Non abiamo bisogno, AAS 23 (1931):285-312. Pius XII was much less systematic, but took up the question in his Summi Pontificatus, AAS 31 (1939):413-454; Sertum laetitiae, AAS 31 (1939):650-651; In questo giorno, AAS 32 (1940):5-14; and La solennita, AAS 33 (1941):195-205 (Italian), 216-227 (English). There is a break with John XXIII. Although John and Paul both wrote about the rights and restrictions of states, there is a completely new spirit at work, as we shall see later in this chapter.

[68]AAS 33 (1941):222.

[69]AAS 53 (1961):414-415, para. 54-55; translation: Renewing the Earth, p. 63.

[70]Pacem in terris, AAS 55 (1963):294, para. 140-141; translation: Renewing the Earth, p. 158.

[71]Quadragesimo anno, AAS 23 (1931):192, 212, para. 47, 110.

[72]Church and Social Justice, p. 156.

[73]AAS 33 (1941):223.

[74]Ibid., p. 222.   [75]Ibid.

[76]The original Italian is no help here, for the English is a literal translation: suo-his, memri-members.

[77]Rerum novarum, ASS 23:663, Quadragesimo anno 23 (1931):194.

[78]Rerum novarum, ASS 23:661-662, para. 34.

[79]Rerum novarum, AAS 23 (1931):194-195, 200; La solennita, AAS 33 (1941):223; Mater et Magistra, AAS 53 (1961):419; Octogesima adveniens, AAS 63 (1971):411.

[80]Gaudium et Spes, AAS 58 (1966):1049.

[81]Populorum progressio, AAS 59 (1967):261, para. 8; translation: Renewing the Earth, p. 315.

[82]Ibid., pp. 263-264, para. 13.

[83]Ibid., p. 270, para. 32.

[84]Ibid., AAS 59 (1967):273, para. 32; translation: Renewing the Earth, pp. 324-325.

[85]Octogesima adveniens, AAS 63 (1971):431-432, para. 42; translation: Renewing the Earth, p. 376.

[86]Ibid., p. 433; translation: Renewing the Earth, p. 377.

[87]The annual food deficit of underdeveloped countries is expected to jump from 36 million metric tons in 1978 to between 120 and 145 million metric tons in 1990. (Source: Bread for the World

publication "Can Food Aid and Development Aid Promote Self-Reliance?"). The World Bank estimates
that the outstanding external public debt of underdeveloped countries rose from $40 billion in 1967
to nearly $140 billion in 1974, and has continued
to rise sharply since then. The inclusion of indebtedness to private entities (banks and commer-
cial companies) would greatly increase that figure
--in 1977 underdeveloped countries owed the U.S.
$29 billion in public debt, but $42 billion to
private U.S. banks. Such indebtedness can only
enrich those nations wealthy enough to lend money
at interest and impoverish those who must pay on
such large debt.

[88]AAS 59 (1967):299, para. 86.

[89]Summa, 2a2ae 61:1.

[90]Summa, 2a2ae 61:2.

[91]AAS 31 (1939):642, emphasis mine.

[92]Church and Social Justice, p. 159.

[93]Rerum novarum, ASS 23:647, 654, especially
648-649 and 657; Quadragesimo anno, AAS 23 (1931):
91, para. 53.

[94]Quadragesimo anno, AAS 23 (1931):195-196.

[95]This concept was left fairly ambiguous in
all their writing.

[96]Divini Redemptoris, March 19, 1937, AAS 29
(1937):81.

[97]AAS 31 (1939):437; translation: The Pope
Speaks: The Words of Pius XII, p. 176. (A better

translation than the incoherent, literal translation in the Acta.)

[98]AAS 37 (1945):14.

[99]Ad petri cathedram, June 29, 1959, AAS 51
(1959):506.

[100]De Justitia in Mundo, AAS 63 (1971):924;
translation: Renewing the Earth, p. 391.

[101]Gaudium et Spes, AAS 58 (1966):1048; translation: Renewing the Earth, p. 203.

[102]E.E.Y. Hales, Pope John and His Revolution
(Garden City, New York: Doubleday, 1966), p. 39:
"Popes always show a great deal of respect for
their predecessor's teaching, frequently quoting
the words of the previous occupant of St. Peter's
Chair. They don't want to seem original; they prefer not even to seem to innovate. When discussing
matters of faith they like to give chapter and
verse from the Bible. And in their political and
social teaching, too, they look for a precedent,
as do British judges or civil servants . . ."

[103]AAS 63 (1971):410-411.

[104]Chapter Three, "Agape and Justice," in
Agape: An Ethical Analysis (New Haven: Yale University Press, 1972), p. 92.

[105]Rerum novarum, ASS 23:662-663, para. 35.

[106]AAS 23 (1931):199, para. 64.

[107]Ibid., para. 65.

[108]J. Y. Calves, Eglise et société economique,

Vol. II (Paris: Aubier, 1963), pp. 55-56.

[109]AAS 36 (1944):254, Radio broadcast, September 1, 1944, quoted in Mater et Magistra, para. 84.

[110]AAS 53 (1961):423, para. 91.

[111]Ibid., para. 92.

[112]AAS 55 (1963):262, para. 20.

[113]ASS 23:648, para. 14 (Rerum novarum).

[114]AAS 55 (1963):259-260, 261, para. 11, 18 (Pacem in terris).

[115]J. L. Segundo, The Liberation of Theology (New York: Orbis, 1976), p. 93; J. Y. Calves, Eglise et société economique, Vol. II, pp. 42-43, 50-51.

[116]Ad petri cathedram, AAS 51 (1959):507; Mater et Magistra, AAS 53 (1961):442, para. 167-168.

[117]Populorum progressio, AAS 59 (1967):287, para. 61.

[118]De Justitia in Mundo, AAS 63 (1971):926.

CHAPTER II

THEOLOGICAL METHOD IN PAPAL TEACHING

This chapter examines the challenge put to
the papal teaching by the method of liberation
theology. The difference between the varieties
of liberation theology with regard to method are
negligible compared to the differences between the
method of traditional and liberation theology.
Though differences in method do exist between the
various liberation theologies, they will not be
highlighted here. The purpose of this chapter is
to examine the method of liberation theology only
insofar as is necessary to illustrate the points
at which it exerts pressure on the official theology and social teaching of the Catholic Church.

Major Differences: Liberation Theology and Current Church Teaching

The first difference, though not the primary
one, between liberation theology and traditional
Catholic theology concerns the definition of theology. The accepted definition of theology among
liberation theologians is Gustavo Gutierrez':
theology is critical reflection on praxis in the
light of the Word.[1] Praxis itself is the primary
difference between liberation theology and the
theology current in the Church. Praxis is not
merely "practice," in the sense of applying in
action the principles of one's belief in whatever
one happens to do. Praxis is the commitment of
oneself to the struggle for liberation. The relationship of theology and praxis is a spiral one in

liberation theology. Theology is critical reflection on praxis in the light of faith. This reflection is then used to guide continuing praxis
in new channels. Further reflection on this altered praxis results in new theology, which then
continues to correct and guide praxis.

Latin American liberation theologians understand Christian praxis to aim at liberation. This
Christian praxis is liberative insofar as it involves commitment to and action on behalf of the
poor and oppressed of the world.[2] This commitment
to action on behalf of the poor and oppressed of
the world entails both striving to eliminate poverty in the world, and adopting the "poverty perspective."[3] Striving to eliminate poverty in the
world is not enough. The presidents of multina-
tional corporations maintain that they do this by
working for a new economic order controlled by
these corporations, which will break down national
barriers preventing progress. Some evangelists
claim to work for the end of poverty and oppression by the preaching of charity and brotherhood.
Real, effective striving to eliminate poverty is,
say the liberation theologians, linked to the
"poverty perspective." Affluent liberals who
speak of the perspective of the poor have not,
according to liberation theologians, adopted the
poverty perspective.

Gutierrez and others maintain that the poverty perspective is the perspective of the poor engaged in the struggle for liberation. They claim
that it is the Christian perspective.[4] The poor
who are engaged in the struggle for liberation
have a clear understanding of the faith and of
the world--a truer interpretation of what faith
means and what the world is really like.[5] This
is one reason why the poverty perspective is the

perspective of those <u>within</u> the movement of the poor for liberation--only the poor within the struggle can see what needs to be struggled against, and what faith really means clearly enough to give shape to real liberation.

Poverty is an integral part of the method of liberation theology. It is the inescapable presence of overwhelming poverty in the Latin American context which causes the liberation movement to use social class analysis. Since liberation theology is critical reflection on the praxis of this liberation movement, social class analysis is also a part of the method of liberation theology. In the Latin American context social class analysis is necessary to prevent the cooptation of the term "oppressed"--to insure that the liberation to be won is <u>real</u> liberation from the real oppression, material poverty. The use of social class analysis from within engagement in the liberation struggle therefore prevents the "spiritualization" of the term "poverty" and the deflection of the liberation movement.

Liberation theologians deny that theology can be done apart from liberative action and commitment to political struggle.[6] This political struggle, praxis, is toward the construction of a new "historical project" indicated by Christian faith.[7] This historical project is not identical with the Kingdom of God, in that the Kingdom cannot be completed or finally realized through human efforts alone. But through construction of the historical project we do participate in the creation of the Kingdom by bringing about the liberation of humanity in history. This is a necessary part of and precondition for a liberation of humanity from sin and for the communion of humanity with God which will signal the existence of the

Kingdom of God.

This historical project, in which humanity moves from social and political liberation to liberation in history, that is, to psychological liberation to self-creation and responsibility, is utopia, the creation of a new type of human being.[8] One of the Latin American liberation theologians wrote of this utopia:

> We must remember that Jesus' project is a utopia. But 'utopia,' according to modern sociology, psychology, and anthropology, does not have the negative meaning of illusion or flight from the conflictive reality of the world. It possesses a positive depth and signifies the capacity to transcend, a creative fantasy, the dialectical reason of man. Man can rise above his own historical construction and project a not-yet-experienced but still possible reality. From this moment on, historical expressions are relativized, criticized, and placed in a process of liberating conquest. The utopia of the kingdom of God does not mean the construction of a particular kind of world and a certain kind of future. Rather it surpasses the totality of the concrete forms of the world in function of another, more human and more open to the coming of God. Jesus, with the announcement of the Kingdom of God did not postulate another world, but rather a new world; this old and broken world would be totally transfigured.[9]

Liberation theology views the commitment of the Christian to the building of the historical project, utopia, through action in solidarity with the poor as the initial step. Theology, critical

reflection on this praxis, is the second step, dependent not only upon theological commitment but
upon this political commitment.[10]

The implications of such an understanding of
theology are critical for the Church. Understanding theology as liberation theologians do, as mo-
ments of critical reflection in a life of action
in faith, entails new visions. The Latin American
vision of a liberative God, acting throughout history in the political struggles of the oppressed--
a God of conflict--challenges the Church's view of
God. The Church's traditional view of salvation
is challenged by liberation theology's rejection
of a split between the spiritual and the material.
Salvation can no longer refer to another realm,
separate and distinct from the material world.[11]
The human person is seen to be both material and
spiritual. A distinction is made between the
spiritual and the spiritualistic,[12] a term used
to refer to a false level of abstraction divorced
from the real material conditions of human life.
The spiritual is another dimension of real lived
life, the dimension of "religious experience."
Salvation, then, in liberation theology, begins
here on earth in the construction of the historical project.[13] The implications for sacramental
theology and for Christology are also a distinct
challenge to the tradition, as is the understanding of sin which results from this conception of
the human condition and the mission of the Church.
The liberation theologians' understanding of theology also diverges from the traditional understanding in the matter of religious authority. A
more traditional Catholic definition of theology
would stress reflection on revealed truths as interpreted by the Church. Not only does the liberation definition move the spotlight to the world
of action, away from an understanding of faith as

dogmatic, but in so doing the traditional emphasis upon the Church as the interpreter of faith and overseer of all Catholic praxis has been omitted. Presumably it is the individual Catholic who now does his/her _own_ critical reflection on his/her praxis in the light of his/her experience of the Word. This is not to deny the importance of the Church in structuring and informing that individual's experience of the Word. However, there is no room here for the kind of total control the popes claimed for the hierarchy in the various forms of Catholic Action.

It is important to note that even in this instance of departure from the traditional emphasis on the Church as sole interpreter of the faith and overseer of all praxis, the liberation theologians are critical. They do stress a measure of individualism in the understanding of praxis and theology, but they also stress that praxis entails joining with others in action, and advocate using the social weight of the Church to attack social problems rather than simply the efforts of individual Christians. It is, therefore, a selective individualism.

Traditionally the Church has understood her mission in terms of calling humanity to salvation in another world. If life on earth and salvation are no longer distinct, but rather intimately connected, then the Church's view of the appropriate approach to social and political entities of the world must be re-evaluated. The Church cannot ignore the world and its events in her concentration on the next life, but must recast herself as an agent in the political struggle in the world. To this end she requires a new set of tools for working in the world.

For there is a leap between faith and the

commitment to the historical project. That leap
is bridged by the use of the tools of social
science--of sociology, economics, psychology,
and political science--to analyze the world in
order to determine how God is acting in the world
and where lies the appropriate commitment which
puts us on the side God has chosen. The historical project is to be built in the world for, by,
and with human beings. Therefore the real world
and its people need to be understood by all
Christians who face commitment to the historical
project. It is not enough to understand the
Church's concept of unchanging human nature.
Political struggle involves concrete conditions
which work on human nature and create differing
situations which need to be understood in their
differentness. This requires social scientific
analysis.

Because these tools of social science, so
necessary for determining particular praxis, do
not always lead to the same analysis of reality,
the political options of Christians, even of
Christians committed to liberation, may not be
identical.[14] Hugo Assman writes that since human
experience is the starting point for theology,
and the secular (social) sciences have the first
word about it, liberation theology takes a decisive step toward these sciences.[15]

Juan Luis Segundo distinguishes between
the sciences of the past, which theology has embraced, and the sciences of the present, from
which theology asserts its independence.[16] Though
it is true that traditionally theology has preferred the sciences of the past, this statement
of Segundo's is misleading. Even in its use of
the sciences of the past the Church has resisted
and refused to develop a scientific mentality.
She has rejected the idea that the results of

social scientific endeavor could call into question any of her past understanding of theology or society or require some new understanding of either. In short, she has not been open to changes indicated by social scientific work. Her refusal to allow the socialist political option is one example, say liberation theologians, of her refusal to use the social sciences to analyze reality which is often criticized by liberation theologians, as we shall see in Chapter Four.

Thus it is clear that there are many points at which liberation theology contests the method of traditional Church theology. Some of these contested issues are: the mission of the Church, the definition of theology, the relation of the Church to the world, the character of God, the nature of truth, and many others. It is not possible to examine the social teaching and theology of the popes for each of these in turn, for these are found in different combinations in varying contexts in the writings of each of the twentieth-century popes. But as we examine the teaching of each one of the popes in turn, it will become obvious that the same themes recur.

Before beginning this examination it may be helpful to observe the difference between theology and social teaching in the tradition of the Church. Within the social teaching there is much theology. But this is dogmatic theology, and in many cases a kind of applied theology, rather than the fundamental theology from which it is distinguished. Fundamental theology is usually less concrete, more abstract or spiritual. It deals with questions such as the existence of God, and how we know what we think we know about God. Fundamental theology deals more explicitly with method; dogmatic theology deals more with the conclusions of fundamental theology. Much of what the popes have to say about theological method, then, is not found in the social teaching on human beings and their world, but in addresses and letters on what for them are less "worldly" things.

Despite a great deal of change in the social teaching of this century--change in the general direction of what is now liberation theology--the Church's social teaching and theology have little common meeting ground with liberation theology insofar as method is concerned. The change in the social teaching, which largely occurred in the pontificate of Paul, has not up to John Paul II changed the way the popes conceive the basic relationship between theology and social teaching. Liberation theology assumes that the mission of the Church requires her to take a political position, to engage in the struggle for the liberation of the poor and oppressed. The traditional understanding of the relationship between theology and social teaching, however, is built upon the presupposition that the Church acts in the world only through her various members. The Church, it is assumed, draws from her theology and teaches rules and principles authoritative for all which relate directly and immediately to the material world. The social teaching, then, because based on a true understanding of human nature and derived from authoritative sources, is always true and authoritative. But the Church does not act as a social institution to embody these principles and rules; her action ends with the teaching of these principles to her individual members who are expected to put them into effect in the world.

Gutierrez has spoken of his hopes for an end of the Church's social teaching.[17] What he means

is that he looks for the end of this division of
theology and social teaching and of the reliance
of the Church on the individual action of her members to bring about needed change in the world.
He hopes for the beginning of political engagement
on the part of the Church on the side of the poor
and oppressed, for a "Church of the poor." These
hopes draw upon a completely different vision of
the relationship between the Church and the world
than the traditional Church view.

Similarities Between Liberation
Theology and the Vatican

Twentieth-century development of the social
teaching has tended toward the adoption of some of
the language of liberation theology, though it has
not adopted the assumptions regarding liberation
praxis or the perspective from which praxis might
come. Segundo wrote of the 1968 Medellin Conference of Latin American bishops:

> The fact is that the reaction will come when
> the bishops, taking their own general state-
> ment seriously, move into the realm of real
> facts and happenings and take a stance vis-a-
> vis them. This is the novel and scandalous
> element in the magisterium of the Church.
> The general principles were tolerable enough
> so long as it was left to each believer to
> take up the task of reaching a concrete deci-
> sion on the basis of those principles. ...[18]

In both the perspective of the 1968 Medellin Conference and the general themes of the 1971 Synod
of Bishops we see concern for the poor, and desire
that the Church be committed to the liberation of
the poor and oppressed. Though liberative action
by the Church on behalf of the poor is not forth-

coming at the papal level, some aspects of liberation theology's methodological use of poverty
appear in papal teaching.

Poverty in Papal Teaching

Within the tradition as expressed in the
papal documents the notion of the clear sight of
the poor, and their advantage in the life of
faith, is not new. Pius XII in _Sertum laetitiae_
(November 1, 1939) wrote of how "readily the poor
abound in supernatural graces."[19] In _Populorum
progressio_ Paul VI devoted paragraph 10 to this
idea,[20] and returned to it in paragraph 68:

> It is painful to think of the numerous young
> people who come to more advanced countries
> to receive the science, the competence and
> the culture which will make them more quali-
> fied to serve their homeland, and who cer-
> tainly acquire there a formation of high
> quality, but who too often lose the esteem
> for the spiritual values which often were to
> be found, as a precious patrimony, in the
> civilization where they had grown up.[21]

John XXIII wrote in paragraph 176 of _Mater et
Magistra_:

> For among the citizens of these latter [poor-
> er] nations there is operative a general
> awareness of the higher values on which the
> moral teaching rests--an awareness derived
> from ancient traditional custom which pro-
> vides them with motivation.[22]

Nevertheless, there is, in the understanding
of these popes, no sense that this awareness on
the part of the poor is the result of struggle, or

69

resisting oppression. There is also no attempt in
the tradition to relate these isolated statements
to theological method. The clear religious and
moral insight of the poor is never seen as valuable for the entire Church to emulate; rather, it
is viewed as a kind of compensation to the poor
for their material deprivation.

That poverty is not methodologically a part
of the Church's theology or social teaching is
manifest in that, as we shall see, there has been
no mention of poverty in the many passages in
which the popes explicitly address theological
method and the purpose of theology. While it is
true that the temporal welfare of humanity was
proposed by the popes as a proper, though secondary, concern of the Church, poverty was not the
temporal condition which historically prompted
this claim. As we shall see, papal documents reveal that it was rather the ideological commitment of the political structure which the popes
claimed the right to judge.

This is certainly not meant to imply that the
popes have not been concerned with the suffering
caused by poverty in the world. The social teaching of the Church was itself a response to the
plight of the poor, first in Europe and more recently in the Third World. Chapter Three will
examine the social teaching in the light of the
content of liberation theology, and will demonstrate that the popes have spoken at great length
on the causes, remedies and consequences of poverty. But these popes have not deemed poverty to
have anything to say to theological method. They
have not recognized any difference between Christians working to alleviate poverty for the benefit of the poor, and the Church working to abolish
poverty from within a commitment with the poor ex-

70

pressed in political terms. Hence, the "poverty perspective" in the sense in which Latin American theologians mean that term, is not recognized.

John XXIII gave an address on the subject of the Church in Latin America to the bishops of Latin America in which no mention was made of poverty.[23] Certainly the bishops of Latin America do not need to be told that theirs is a poor continent. But John considered it possible to address the spiritual welfare of the Catholics of Latin America without reference to the material conditions in which the vast numbers of Catholics live out those spiritual lives. There was nothing in that address which in any way distinguished it from an address on the Church in any other area of the world.

Paul VI demanded that all recognize that poverty is an evil, not only for those who suffer it, but for all of humanity.[24] He wrote more on poverty than any other pope in the world. But the importance of the subject of poverty within the social teaching did not, for Paul, involve a connection with theological method. He wrote an entire address on the purposes and method of theology without mentioning poverty (Libentissimo sane animo, October 1, 1966[25]). There still remains a variance between traditional and liberation theology as to the role of poverty in theology.

Pius XI

In general, the language and concepts of the popes have been very different from those of liberation theology. Pius XI, in his most famous encyclical, Quadragesimo anno (May 15, 1931), harked back to the beginning of the social teaching, Leo XIII's Rerum novarum. Pius wrote:

Rerum novarum, however, stood out in this, that it laid down for all mankind unerring rules for the right solution of the difficult problem of human community, called the 'social question,' at the very time when such guidance was most opportune and necessary.[26]

Basing his teaching only on the unchanging principles drawn from right reason and divine revelation, he [Leo] indicated and proclaimed with confidence 'as one having authority' what are 'the rights and duties whereby the wealthy and the propertyless, those providing capital and those who labor, should be mutually united and restrained,' and furthermore, what should be the role of the Church, of the public authorities, and of the parties themselves.[27]

Pius XI listed as one of the purposes of his own encyclical "to expose the root of the present social disorder, and to point out the only way to salutary renewal, namely, a Christian reform of morals."[28]

In this same document Pius XI reflected on the authority of the Church in social and economic matters:

But before proceeding to discuss these problems, We lay down the principle long established by Leo XIII that it is Our right and Our duty to deal authoritatively with social and economic questions. It is not, of course, for the Church to lead men to transient and perishable happiness only, but to that which is eternal. Indeed, 'the Church believes it to be wrong for her to interfere without just cause in such earthly concerns;' but she can

72

never relinquish her God-given task of inter-
posing her authority, not indeed in technical
matters, for which she has neither the equip-
ment nor the mission, but in all those which
have a bearing on moral conduct. For the deposit of truth entrusted to us by God, and
our weighty office of propagating, interpret-
ing and urging in season and out of season
the entire moral law, demand that both social
and economic questions be brought within Our
supreme jurisdiction, insofar as they relate
to moral issues.[29]

These passages taken together express a number of ideas important to Pius XI's understanding
of the relationship between the Church and the
secular realm. He viewed the two realms as distinct, each having its own authority. The Church
was the spiritual authority and did not normally
interfere in the secular realm. The dependence of
human spiritual welfare upon moral activity did,
however, necessitate the interference of the
spiritual authority in those secular matters which
concerned the moral. The position of the Church
as the possessor of eternal truth, as interpreter
of right reason and divine revelation, indicated
that in those secular matters which involved the
moral, the Church was the supreme authority. Depending upon the breadth of one's understanding of
the moral, therefore, there might not really be
two distinct realms--the Church could claim to be
supreme in all secular matters by recognizing in
them a moral component. This is an important
point to observe in later social teaching. Two of
Pius' basic assumptions here, (1) the eternal and
unchanging truth of Church teaching and (2) the
supreme authority of the Church in the secular
realm in matters concerning morality, are common in
much of his teaching, especially in _Casti connubi_,

<u>Divini illius</u> <u>Magistri</u>, <u>Ubi</u> <u>arcano</u>, and <u>Divini</u> <u>Re-</u>
<u>demptoris</u>.[30]

In <u>Divini</u> <u>Redemptoris</u> Pius XI affirmed not
only the superiority of the spiritual over the
eternal, but the Church's subordination of the
material needs of mankind to its spiritual
needs.[31] With this understanding of the primary
task of the Church as spiritual, it is not surprising that Pius XI insisted that the mission of
the Church was evangelization, the spread of the
truths of the Gospel.[32] This evangelical approach
on the part of Pius XI was in accordance with the
tradition. The solution for the ills of the world
was moral and spiritual renovation, i.e., the return of all to the Church and her teaching. Leo
had insisted on this in <u>Rerum</u> <u>novarum</u>:

> But we affirm without hesitation that all
> the striving of men will be in vain if they
> leave out the Church. It is the Church
> which proclaims from the Gospel those teach-
> ings by which the conflict can be brought
> to an end, or at least made far less bit-
> ter.[33]

Pius XI referred to Leo when he wrote in <u>Quadra-</u>
<u>gesimo</u> <u>anno</u>:

> 'And if society is to be healed now'--We use
> the words of Our predecessor--'it cannot be
> healed save by a return to Christian life
> and Christian institutions,' for Christian-
> ity alone can apply the successful remedy
> for the excessive attention for transitory
> things, which is the origin of all vices.
> When people are fascinated and completely
> absorbed in worldly things, it alone can
> draw their attention and raise it to heaven.

And who does not see that this remedy is urgently needed by society?[34]

The efficacy of the Word was clearly not doubted by Pius XI. The solution to social problems lay not in attention to them, but in the religious renewal implied in a return to the Gospel and the Church. There is an implicit idealism underlying most of Pius' writings, a belief that right belief is primary. This is idealism, the direct opposite of Marxist materialism. It is a preference to work with ideas rather than material reality in the consideration of theology and social problems. Such idealism was made explicit in the following passage:

> Even today the authority of Church doctrine is greater than it seems; for the influence of ideas is surely of predominant importance.[35]

This is what Assman referred to when he wrote: "In essence, the precise term 'liberation' subverts the magical and proclamatory structure of 'action through the word' (Ger. Worttat) and replaces it with 'the word of action' (Ger. Tatwort)."[36]

Pius XII

This "action through the word" concept did not end with the papacy of Pius XI, but continued in the works of his successors. The writings of Pius XII[37] reveal the same general understanding of the task of the Church as we found in Pius XI. For Pius XII the duty of the Church is to spread the Gospel. This is a spiritual task, but it does, for Pius XII also, involve the material world. For the only hope for improvement in the

material world is the changing of the hearts of
human beings through contact with the faith.[38]
Thus for Pius XII the task of the Church was to
teach the Gospel and to indicate the principles
in the Gospel under which a better social order
could be built. These principles comprise the
social teaching of the Church, but the task of
doing the building belongs to individuals, not to
the Church as such. The Church, therefore,
stressed the social group insofar as <u>future goals</u>
were the object--the Christian society was ideal
for all and secular power should be directed at
achieving it--but action was viewed as individual
action, unless hierarchically directed by one individual placed over others (as in Catholic Action).

The following passages reveal this understanding on the part of Pius XII:

> There is no duty more urgent, Worshipful
> Brethren, than to bring the unfathomable
> riches of Christ to the men of our own time.
> There is no nobler ambition than to unfurl
> the standards of our divine king and let
> them take the wind, before men who have en-
> rolled themselves under false colors; than
> to rally, in the joyful service of the tri-
> umphant cross, those who have had the mis-
> fortune to abandon it.[39]
>
> At the moment when new structures are
> being sought in Africa--while some run the
> risk of abandoning themselves to the false
> seductions of a technical civilization--the
> Church has the duty to offer them, as much
> as possible, the substantial riches of her
> doctrine and her life as animators of a
> Christian social order. Any delay would be
> full of serious consequences.[40]

It is absolutely necessary that correct social principles as taught by the Church be reduced to action with forethought, diligence and zeal. It is absolutely necessary that all men should be shielded from those baleful errors which propose present earthly enjoyment as our sole objective in this earthly world. It is also absolutely necessary to liberate those who have been infected with such error from its ruinous consequences. For according to it everything is to be owned and controlled by the power and dictates of the state. Hence the dignity of the human person is so degraded as to become almost zero.

It is then indispensable to proclaim privately and publicly that all of us are, like exiles, trying to reach our everlasting homeland; that eternal life and eternal happiness are our destiny; that we should provide for the attainment of this goal by accepting truth and preaching virtue. Christ is the sole protector of human justice. He is, too, the most satisfying consoler in the inescapable sufferings of this life. He alone points out our haven of peace, of justice, of unending happiness, where all of us, redeemed by his divine blood, must find shelter after our voyage on this earthly globe.[41]

The Church, for Pius XII, was to aid human beings to achieve this heavenly destiny. She did this through teaching of the Gospel and the social teaching, in that these taught principles of right action. The interest expressed in the state of the social order is explicitly linked to the task of saving souls, and not to an interest in the social order because of concern for the material well-being of Church members and other inhabitants

of the world. Even so, her interest in the social
order made teaching the Church's distinctive mode
of action; individuals are to apply the principles,
"reducing" them to action.

John XXIII

In John XXIII's Mater et Magistra the task
of the Church was considered in much these same
terms. John wrote:

> Hence, though the Church's first care must
> be for souls, how she can sanctify them and
> make them share in the gifts of heaven, she
> concerns herself too, with the exigencies
> of human daily life, with human livelihood,
> education and general temporal welfare and
> prosperity.[42]

The Church demonstrated this care for body and
soul, John claimed, through charity:

> There is small wonder, then, that the
> Catholic Church, in imitation of Christ and
> in fulfillment of His commandment, relies
> not only upon her teaching to hold aloft the
> torch of charity, but also upon her wide-
> spread example. This has been her course
> now nigh onto two thousand years, from the
> early ministrations of her deacons to the
> present time. . . .[43]

In the first passage John included concern
for the material life of Church members in the
task of the Church, though this was secondary to
spiritual concern for those members. In the
second passage John referred not only to the
Church's task of teaching, but to her task of
giving example of charity. In the succeeding

78

paragraph he explained of what this example consists.

> An outstanding instance of this social teaching and <u>action</u> carried on by the Church throughout the ages is undoubtedly that magnificent encyclical on the christianizing of the conditions of the working classes.
> . . . [44]

Here John made a distinction between the possession of the social teaching by the Church, and her action in presenting that teaching to the world for the benefit of all. John at no time referred to the <u>Church</u> putting the principles into effect. Her task was to present them to the world. Though it is somewhat difficult to see that the Church has a double task here, this particular formulation was taken from Leo XIII's <u>Rerum novarum</u> (paragraph 22):

> But the Church, not content with pointing out the remedy, also applies it. For the Church does its utmost to teach and to train men, to educate them; and by means of its bishops and clergy, it diffuses its salutary teachings far and wide. [45]

Paul VI

This view of how the Church acts on social ethics was not only present before John; it continued after him. Paul VI, in the apostolic letter <u>Octogesima adveniens</u> of May 14, 1971, wrote:

> In the social sphere, the Church has always wished to assume a double function: first to enlighten minds in order to assist them to discover the truth and to find the

right path to follow amidst the different
teachings that call for their attention; and
secondly to take part in action and to spread,
with a real care for service and effectiveness, the energies of the Gospel. Is it not
in order to be faithful to this desire that
the Church has sent out an apostolic mission
among the worker priests who, by sharing the
condition of the worker, are at that level
the witnesses to the Church's solicitude and
seeking?[46]

It is interesting that Paul referred here to the
worker-priest experiment, which occupied a middle
ground between traditional social teaching and
present liberation theology. That experiment began after the fall of France in World War II, when
large numbers of French workers were conscripted
to work in labor camps in Germany.[47] Priests followed these workers, taking on the life of the
workers, laboring alongside them in the factories.
Through their work these priests and others became
convinced of the need to reclaim the vast majority
of the French working class which had been lost to
the Church during the previous century. This re-
claiming was to be done by clergy sharing the life
and concerns of the workers.

This work was at least severely restricted by
Pius XII in 1953-54. Some sources say that he effectively ended this ministry.[48] But interest in
this new departure was high in some circles of
Europe, and the question was still alive at the
time of John's ascension to the papacy. In 1959
John so restricted worker-priests as to virtually
end the program;[49] he forbade priests to work full-
time on the grounds that their spiritual (as distinct from their material) life would suffer from
a lack of time devoted to it. Only under Paul was
the experiment restored.[50]

Paul's reference to this experiment as the action of the Church applying her remedy in the world implied some alteration in the traditional relationship between the Church and the world. Not only did the Church, through the industrial missions, bring the Gospel into specific world situations, but she further mixed the spiritual and the material when, in the person of the worker-priests, the Church became involved in unions and political organizations of workers.

Even so, using the worker-priest experiment as evidence of the Church's engagement in and commitment to social and political problems is questionable for two reasons. The first is the historical fact that though the socio-political situation itself radicalized many of the priests involved so that they did come to view their social and political work as a part of their ministry, the program was so designed that any such activity was undertaken only in order to meet the workers where they were. The second reason that use of the worker-priest example of the Church's commitment is questionable is that the New Catholic Encyclopedia rightly calls this an "experiment." Though now over thirty years old, this "experiment" has not changed the conception of ministry in the Church as a whole; the worker-priests remain an anomaly. This is partly because, in taking on political activity for temporal goals as an important part of the primary task of the Church and of ministry, the experiment went beyond its design and intent. This step is not generally accepted in the hierarchy.

The traditional approach to social change, that it depends upon the spiritual evangelization of the world, was still apparent in Paul's 1966 address in CELAM, the conference of Latin American

bishops, in the sharp distinction he continued to
draw between social problems and the supernatural
order:

> In the face of the vast field of specific
> action, you pastors of souls will readily
> conclude that the Church is not called to
> become a specialist in one or the other field
> of sociology or economics, but to contribute
> to the solution of grave contemporary pro-
> blems with something that is all her own--
> that is, with the resources of a religious
> and supernatural order which she has received
> from her divine founder, Christ the Lord.[51]

Some Reasons for Understanding the Church's Task as Spiritual

Though the papal documents since John assigned more emphasis to material life than previously,
the above selections make clear that usually this
concern for human material well-being was separated
from concern for spiritual life, and that the popes
continued to assume that the action of the Church
was especially involved with the spiritual task.

There are at least two different reasons for
this continuing position on the part of the popes.
One, of course, is the body/soul dualism with which
the Christian tradition has operated for centuries,
in which the material is always subordinate to and
distinct from the spiritual. This tradition was
especially clear in the passage above from Pius
XII's Evangelii praecones.[52]

The other reason, however, is more political.
The popes have seen their affirmation that the task
of the Church is spiritual and not political as an
assurance to the political powers that the Church

will not interfere in their concerns. On the basis of this assurance the popes have demanded that the Church be guaranteed freedom to conduct her ministry. In his letter Ehrwurdige Bruder! of September 2, 1956, Pius XII stated the minimum rights demanded by the Church in order to fulfill her ministry:

> The Catholic Church constrains no one to belong to her ranks. She does, however, demand for herself the freedom to be able to live in a country according to her own constitution and law, and minister to her faithful and to preach the Gospel of Jesus Christ faithfully. This is, indeed, in her view, the necessary basis of any sincere coexistence. In the meantime she continues to fight, not in the field of politics and economics, as she has always been falsely charged, but with her own weapons: the steadfastness of her faithful, prayer, truth, and love.[53]

There is real fear on the part of the popes that the Church's entry into the political realm could initiate another era of persecution from the state, a persecution which could endanger or prevent the fulfillment of what the Church regards as her primary mission, the spreading of the Gospel. Particularly under the repressive regimes of the world, the Church has been afraid to provoke hostility against the Church by taking political sides.[54] And the Church has good reason to be concerned that taking up this cause would lose her privileges and bring her crosses to bear. Segundo wrote of this very thing happening now in Latin America,[55] and current in the news is a situation along similar lines in the Philippines.[56]

Inevitability of the Church's Partisanship

Regardless of all this, a study of history in the twentieth century makes clear that even under the popes who spoke of the task of the Church as spiritual, the Church has been involved in world politics and has not been non-partisan. In effect, the Latin American liberation theologians who urge that the social weight of the Church be used in the cause of the liberation of the poor and oppressed are not calling for a revolutionary departure from Church practice; the only revolutionary element would be the use of the Church's power on a new side--that of the poor. One of the best known examples of the Church attempting to use her social weight to influence temporal affairs will be further discussed in Chapter Four--Pius XII's support for the Hungarian revolt of 1956.

The actual involvement of the Church in politics should not be seen as a contradiction of the statement of the popes concerning the separation of the spiritual and temporal powers, for each of them has excepted those situations in which they judged that the spiritual and temporal are joined. In these situations the spiritual authority, the Church, has been viewed as higher than the temporal authority precisely because the spiritual takes precedence over the temporal plane. One formulation of this superiority of the spiritual is that of Pius XII quoted by John XXIII in Mater et Magistra. John wrote of Pius' broadcast commemoration of Rerum novarum:

> In that broadcast message the great Pontiff claimed for the Church 'the indisputable competence' to 'decide whether the bases of any given social order are in accord with the unchangeable order which God Our Creator and

Redeemer has shown us through the Natural
Law and Revelation.'[57]

In the case of Pius XII, this statement[58] and
the idea it expressed were a justification for the
political partiality he exhibited. Pius XII, however, was only exceptional in that his political
partisanship was more pronounced and more public
than other modern popes, partly because of the
times in which he lived. Many have criticized
Pius XII for his partiality for Germany up to and
into World War II, and for his resulting silence
about the Nazi atrocities as well. But most sources agree that the main reason for his partiality
for Germany (which they distinguish from partiality to Naziism) was his fear of and opposition to
Communism, which he always saw as the primary enemy of both the Church and European civilization.[59]
This fear, combined with the responsibility he felt
for preventing reprisals against the Church's members and personnel, kept him silent despite his
knowledge of the atrocities.[60]

Nor have the popes been alone in this attitude
within the Church. Segundo cited the example of
the bishops of Chile. During the Allende period,
the bishops issued a long statement which began
with the assertion that the Church could not take
sides for or against Allende. But this was followed, in the same document, by the bishops' declaration that, in Chile, socialism was not a real alternative to capitalism. The two statements were
not perceived by the bishops as contradictory; they
are no more contradictory than the statement of
Pius XII above, that the Church has a spiritual
task and spiritual authority, but has the right to
judge whether the bases of any social system accord
with those of God. This particular position of
Pius XII in La solennita was not only quoted by

John in _Mater et Magistra_[61] but seems to have built upon a similar formulation by Pius XI in _Quadragesimo anno_, paragraph 41.[62]

This papal position on politics is a result of what is sometimes called the "Christendom mentality." Gutierrez remarked of it:

> In the Christendom mentality, and in the point of view which prolongs it, temporal relations lack autonomy. They are not regarded by the Church as having an authentic existence. It therefore uses them for its own ends. This is a sequel of the so-called 'political Augustinianism.' This plan for the Kingdom of God has no room for a profane, historical plan.
> The Church is regarded substantially as the exclusive depository of salvation: 'Outside the Church there is no salvation.' Because of this exclusiveness, notwithstanding certain qualifications which do not change the overall picture, the Church feels justified in considering itself as the center of the economy of salvation and therefore presenting itself as a powerful force in relation to the world. This power will spontaneously and inevitably seek to express itself in the political arena. Under these circumstances, participation in temporal tasks has a very precise meaning for the Christian: to work for the direct and immediate benefit of the Church.[63]

Until the separation between the spiritual and the material is eliminated so that the moral dimensions of all human activity can be recognized, it is difficult to escape the Christendom mentality. This mentality leads individual Christians for the most part to understand the end of their political action as the advancement of the interests of the Church. And the Church herself is led to consider her welfare as the proper object of all action in the world because of the dependence of all good in the world on the teaching of the Church. In practice, of course, these two attitudes reinforce each other. The Church is thus led to perceive those who oppose her as the enemies of the world, and to use the forces of the world against these enemies. Pius XI exemplified this clearly in his encyclical on atheistic communism, _Divini Redemptoris_, in which he asserted the duty of the Christian state to aid the Church against communism with all the means at its command.[64]

The papal positions against both democracy and socialism in the late nineteenth and early twentieth centuries also illustrated this particular perception and response by the Church. Both democracy and socialism threatened the authority and power of the Church. According to the popes, democracy threatened, and ultimately destroyed, the temporal authority of the Church, and together with socialism was responsible for much of the anticlericalism which manifested itself in legal attacks on Church property and rights. The popes, however, in countering the claims of democracy did not use democratic anticlericalism as the primary reason for refusing to sanction democracy. Instead, they deplored the inability of democratic governments to be strong enough to preserve order and to protect the Christian civilization and the rights of the Church.[65] That is, they attacked the ability of democracy to govern well, rather than the fact that democracy threatened their own position.

While they deplored socialism's attacks on the

87

Church and religion in general, their chief objection was that in choosing atheism socialism manifested an inadequate understanding of human nature, which prevented its programs from achieving any of its professed goals. In their opposition to these movements the popes perceived no difference between their enemies and the enemies of the secular order, and therefore did not hesitate to demand and to use the secular power against socialism and democracy. Though the popes seem to have a higher opinion of democracy since World War II, the traditional attitude toward socialism is still influential within the Church, as we will see in Chapter Four.

What liberation theologians demand of the Church is more than the extension of Pius XII's claim that the Church can authoritatively judge the bases of any social system. For they do not agree that it is only the bases of any social system which need to be judged by the standards of the Gospel. The total conditions of a people's life deserve such judgment. There is a step between the principles (bases) which are espoused within a system and the consequences of the decisions that are supposedly based on them. The Latin Americans point out that they live under some of the most liberal constitutions in the world, as well as some of the most dehumanizing economic and political situations. But the Church's concern with the atheism of communism has prevented it from seeing that Christian words do not always indicate Christian realities, and atheist words do not always cloak realities worse than the "Christian" ones.

Recent Trends: The Challenge Remains Unmet

The traditional way of doing theology has not

been entirely abandoned by the popes by any means. In John's _Mater et Magistra_ he wrote:

> There are three stages which should normally be followed in the reduction of social principles into practice. First, one reviews the concrete situation; secondly, one forms a judgement on it in the light of these principles; thirdly, one decides what in the circumstances can and should be done to implement these principles. These are the three stages that are usually expressed in the three terms: look, judge, act.
> It is important for our young people to grasp this method and to practice it. . . . Needless to say, when the hierarchy has made a decision on any point, Catholics are bound to follow their directive.[66]

This is in keeping with the tradition, in that these are steps to be followed by individual Catholics, not by the Church as a body. Even for individuals, the sense of the entire passage is weakened by the last sentence, in that in the presence of a hierarchical decision, none of the three stages is appropriate, only obedience. This is entirely in keeping with the teaching of the popes on Catholic Action, which both Pius XI and Pius XII insisted was to be directed entirely by the hierarchy.[67]

But concerning theological method, if we look to the first sentence, we find in the original: _Iamvero, doctrinae praecepta quae sunt de rebus socialibus, plerumque per tres hos gradus ad effectum adducuntur._ The use of the word "adducuntur" here is significant. Its translation above as "reduction" is misleading, though common.[68] The translation "reduction of social principles into effect" is more appropriate (and was commonly used) for passages in which Pius XI and Pius XII spoke of

the application of social principles using the
verb deduco.[69] John's use of the verb adduco in
this connection in Mater et Magistra (paragraphs
236 and 238) and in Pacem in terris (paragraph
160)[70] was a significant shift in itself, for
adduco means to lead out, to bring into effect.
The change from "reducing principles into effect"
to "bringing principles into effect" reflects a
subtle lessening of the hold of the idealist philosophical position on the papacy. The fact that
none of the translators consistently reflects this
change in John's writing testifies not only to the
strength of the traditional idealism, but also to
the subtlety of the shift. John still stood
clearly within the idealist position.

   The "review of the concrete situation" of
which John spoke in the above passage was not by
any means an analysis of the real situation, but
was a recognition that the doctrinae praecepta ad
effectum adducuntur (the principles of the doctrine
are brought to effect) in a concrete situation.
There was no sense in which the concrete situation
could ever be important enough to influence the
understanding of the principles themselves, much
less to stand the principles on their heads. Liberation theologians do believe that in their situation the principles are so stood on their heads
that their interpretation is often the reverse of
the traditional interpretation of principles derived from Christian faith.[71] For example, the
principle of respect for the sanctity and dignity
of human life was traditionally interpreted to prohibit violence and require obedience to legitimate
authority. Liberation theologians reinterpret the
principle of respect for human life to demand resistance to that socio-political and economic order
which violates the sanctity of human life and denies
its dignity. Such resistance can encompass even
violent response.

Paul VI made many changes in the emphasis put on the various areas of the content of the social teaching, but retained the traditional view of theology and the task of the Church. In *Libentissimo sane animo* (October 1, 1966) his address to the International Congress on the Theology of Vatican II, he said:

> Both Theology and the magisterium seek to further the same purpose: to preserve the sacred deposit of revelation; to look more deeply into it; to explain it, to teach it, and to defend it. In short, they both seek to shed the light of divine truth on the life of the Church and mankind, so that all men might be led to eternal salvation.
>
> But theology and the magisterium have different duties and are endowed with different gifts. Sacred theology uses reason enlightened by faith; and it receives no little light from the divine paraclete, to which the theologian must pay heed. Its duty is to examine and comprehend the truths of revelation more thoroughly, to bring the fruits of its labor to the attention of the Christian community, and in particular, to the attention of the magisterium itself, so that the whole Christian people may be enlightened by the doctrine which the ecclesiastical authority hands down; and finally to lend its efforts to the spreading, clarifying, confirming and defending of the truth which the magisterium authoritatively propounds.[72]

An examination of this passage makes clear that in seeking to "shed the light of divine truth on the life of the Church and mankind" theology and theologians use *only* reason and the enlightenment of the paraclete to examine and comprehend the truth of revelation. They do not look to the life of the

Church and humankind; rather they come to their
conclusion in the abstract, at the conceptual
level. The theory is to be imposed on practice,
not developed through and in the light of the suc-
cesses and failures of that practice. This implies
an understanding of "the truths of revelation"
which does not recognize the possibility of present
revelation in history. Without a sense of ongoing
revelation, the Church will not look to present
history to determine where her liberative action
should be.

At no time in this statement did Paul intimate
that the Church's purpose ever goes beyond the task
of enlightening people as to doctrine. And yet
five years later, only ten years after John's Mater
et Magistra insisted on the three steps for the
application of social principles, Paul wrote:

> In the face of such widely varying situa-
> tions it is difficult for Us to utter a uni-
> fied message and to put forward a solution
> which has universal validity. Such is not
> Our ambition, nor is it Our mission. It is
> up to the various Christian communities to
> analyse with objectivity the situation which
> is proper to their own country, to shed on it
> the light of the Gospel's inalterable words,
> and to draw principles of reflection, norms
> of judgement, and directives for action from
> the social teaching of the Catholic Church.
> This social teaching has been worked out in
> the course of history and notably, in this
> industrial era, since the historic date of the
> message of Pope Leo XIII on 'the condition of
> the workers' and it is an honor and a joy for
> us to celebrate today the anniversary of that
> message. It is up to these Christian communi-
> ties, with the help of the Holy Spirit, in
> communion with the bishops who hold responsi-

bility and in dialogue with other Christian
brethren and all men of good will, to discern
the options and commitments which are called
for in order to bring about the social, political, and economic changes seen in many
cases to be urgently needed.[73]

The language of this statement from <u>Octogesima</u> <u>ad-</u>
<u>veniens</u> signals a shift in papal thinking. No
longer did Paul refer to obedience to the decisions of the hierarchy as the required action, or
stress applying principles from the social teaching to concrete situations. Instead he spoke of
Christian communities coming to decision (in communion with the bishops and the paraclete), and of
the need to analyze the concrete situation objec-
tively. This, especially, is a far cry from previous teaching, which called more for obedience
than analysis and judgement.

    <u>Octogesima</u> <u>adveniens</u> represents a break in
the tradition on a wide number of issues. The
context in which Christian communities exist has
assumed some importance between John's time and
Paul's. It was no longer assumed that the principles always lead to the same response regardless
of the context, or that the method to be followed
is only to impose the principle on the individual
situation.

    <u>Octogesima</u> <u>adveniens</u> is interesting on sever-
al counts. There is a break between this statement and previous commemorations of <u>Rerum</u> <u>novarum</u>
not only in terms of papal purpose, but in the
type of document used. In 1941 Pius XII had ex-
cused himself for giving only a short radio broadcast rather than a major document on the grounds
that the war took up most of his attention, and
because Pius XI had given a complete treatment of
the issue only ten years previously. Both Pius XI

and John XXIII had issued encyclical letters. Paul's document, though roughly similar in size and scope, did not carry this same force because it was, for unknown reasons, issued as an apostolic letter and not as an encyclical.[74]

The change in the form of Octogesima adveniens was matched by a significant change in style. Octogesima adveniens did not attempt to set forth principles and solutions in the authoritarian style of earlier teaching. It discussed the current issues at stake in the economic, political, and social problems of the day rather than setting forth papal conclusions. Paul indicated the direction in which the Church teaching moved and the Church's general understanding of human nature and the social situation in present history. The "principles" with which he dealt are much more general than those of which his predecessors spoke. Where they referred to more or less hard and fast regulations (that Catholics were forbidden to join or work for Marxist organizations, that all Catholic Action activity be controlled by the hierarchy, or that use of violence was forbidden in all social justice struggles within a society)--Paul, in contrast, referred to the general principles of past social teaching. He found it important, for example, that John had insisted on the right to participate in decision-making as a human right. Paul emphasized not the particular conclusions to which John had come, but rather the general principle which had implications far beyond the labor situation John discussed. All of this may signal a shift away from the classic social teaching.

Paul might have written Octogesima adveniens to liberation theologians. In it he took up many of the major themes of liberation theology without, however, mentioning liberation theology by

name. Paragraphs 7 through 21 dealt with the problems of modern society, especially as these relate to the Third World. In paragraph 22 Paul
stated: "legislation is necessary but is not sufficient for setting up true relationships of justice and equality." This was certainly a shift
for a tradition which relied on "action through
the word."[75]

Paul then spoke of two human aspirations, to
equality and to participation, which "seek to promote democratic society."[76] Political society
should be, he said, "the projection of a plan of
society which is consistent with its concrete
means and in its inspiration, and which springs
from a complete conception of the total vocation
of human beings and of their differing social expressions." The question here arises: how similar is this "projection of a plan of society" to
the historical project of liberation theology?

Next Paul took up the idea of utopia so important in liberation theology. Previous references
to utopia in papal writings of the twentieth century had been pejorative, dismissing utopian
thought as unrealistic. Some examples of this are
found in Quadragesimo anno, Divini Redemptoris,
and Populorum progressio.[77] In Octogesima adveniens Paul condemned those who adopt utopia as a
convenient excuse to escape from concrete tasks to
refuge in an imaginary world. But he recognized
the power of utopia to "provoke imagination, to
direct the world to a fresh future, and to sustain
social dynamism."[78]

When Paul turned to the subject of the role
of the human sciences in Christian understanding,
he stated that the human sciences give promise of
a positive function which the Church recognizes
and so urged Christians to play an active part in

scientific work. Science could assist Christian morality, he said, which

> will no doubt see its field restricted when it comes to suggesting certain models of society, while its function of making a critical judgement and taking an overall view will be strengthened by its showing the relative character of the behavior and values presented by such and such a society as definitive and inherent in the very nature of humanity.[79]

Paul maintained that these sciences are a condition at once indispensable and inadequate for a better discovery of what is human.[80] This was a giant step toward the position occupied by liberation theology. Nevertheless, recognizing the importance of the social sciences for the information they provide is not the same as recognizing that ultimately the social sciences lead to conclusions which influence and shape the very theological principles from which Paul assumed that social teaching and decision-making in the world proceed.

Perhaps the passage in Octogesima adveniens which most clearly revealed the influence of liberation theology was that concerning the dynamism of the Church's social teaching. Here Paul clearly adapted elements (especially language) of the liberation message. In paragraph 42 of Octogesima adveniens he wrote:

> It is with all its own dynamism that the social teaching of the Church accompanies men in their search. If it does not intervene to authenticate a given structure or to propose a ready made model, it does not thereby limit itself to recalling general principles. It

develops through reflection applied to the
changing situations of the world, under the
driving force of the gospel as the source of
renewal, when its message is accepted in its
totality and with all its demands.[81]

For liberation theologians, however, this must be
seen as an adaptation of their position, not yet
an adoption. In fact, some liberation theologians
might label this a co-optation of their position.
Paul did not read the Gospel as they do, to demand
commitment first. Only from the other side of
active commitment, say the liberation theologians,
can the Gospel be understood. For Paul, the
Church possessed the truthful message regardless
of its commitment.

Similarly, while Paul claimed that the social
teaching develops through reflection applied to
the changing situations of the world, he did not
suggest that this reflection must be upon participation in the liberation struggle. Paul spoke as
if the development of the social teaching comes
through passive reflection on something happening
"out there." For liberation theology the problem
with the social teaching, and with theology in
general, is misunderstanding the demands of true
praxis.

When the report on liberation theology was
made in September 1977 by Paul's hand-picked[82]
International Commission on Theology, this misunderstanding of praxis was still very much the case.
Though the report did agree that liberation was the
true message of the Bible and of the Christian tradition, and did not condemn liberation theology in
any way, it issued many warnings as to the dangers
of theology which was too political, and involved
the Church too far in the workings of the world.[83]

Ainsi donc la pratique de la foi ne saurait
se reduire à l'effort d'amelioration de la
société humaine. Cette pratique de la foi
comporte, en effet, à côté de la dénoncia-
tion de l'injustice, la formation de la
conscience, la conversion des dispositions
intimes, l'adoration du vrai Dieu et de
Jésus-Christ Notre Sauveur en opposition
à toutes les formes d'idolâtrie. Aussi la
'foi comme praxis' ne doit-elle pas être
comprise de telle façon que l'engagement
en matière politique embrasse et dirige de
façon totalitaire et 'radicale' toutes les
activités de l'homme.[84]

NOTES

[1]Gustavo Gutierrez, A Theology of Liberation (New York: Orbis, 1973), p. 13. See also Juan Luis Segundo, The Liberation of Theology (New York: Orbis, 1976), pp. 71-81 and Hugo Assman, Theology for a Nomad Church (New York: Orbis, 1975), p. 59.

[2]Theology for a Nomad Church, pp. 53-54.

[3]A Theology of Liberation, pp. 287-308.

[4]A Theology of Liberation, pp. 287-308; The Liberation of Theology, pp. 83-87.

[5]The Liberation of Theology, pp. 83-87; Gustavo Gutierrez, "Freedom and Salvation," in Liberation and Change, by Gustavo Gutierrez and Richard Shaull (Atlanta: John Knox Press, 1977), p. 75.

[6]The Liberation of Theology, pp. 98-101; Theology for a Nomad Church, p. 83.

[7]Theology of Liberation, p. 236.

[8]Theology of Liberation, p. 236; Theology for a Nomad Church, pp. 67-68.

[9]Leonardo Boff, "Statement of Leonardo Boff," Theology in the Americas, ed. by Sergio Torres and John Eagleson (New York: Orbis, 1976), p. 295.

[10]A Theology of Liberation, pp. 11-13; The Liberation of Theology, pp. 75-90; Theology for a

Nomad Church, pp. 74-83.

[11]A Theology of Liberation, pp. 71-72.

[12]Ibid., p. 290.

[13]"Freedom and Salvation," p. 86; Theology for a Nomad Church, p. 67.

[14]This is why Gutierrez in an April 1977 article in The Witness said: "my personal option for the socialist way is not a conclusion drawn from Evangelical premises. It comes from my socio-political analysis, which is the starting point for this option." "Terrorism, Liberation and Sexuality," The Witness, April 1977, p. 11.

[15]Theology for a Nomad Church, p. 64.

[16]The Liberation of Theology, p. 7.

[17]Personal conversation, December 1977, at Union Seminary.

[18]The Liberation of Theology, p. 72.

[19]AAS 31 (1939):642.

[20]AAS 59 (1967):262.

[21]Ibid., p. 290; translation: Renewing the Earth, p. 337.

[22]AAS 53 (1961):443; translation: Renewing the Earth, p. 93.

[23]Ringrazia di vero, November 15, 1958, AAS 50 (1958):997-1005.

[24]Nous nous appris, Osservatore Romano, June

8, 1966; Nous voudrions d'abord, Osservatore Romano, June 26, 1966.

25Osservatore Romano, October 2, 1966.

26AAS 23 (1931):178, para. 2; translation: Seven Great Encyclicals (New York: Paulist Press, 1963), p. 125.

27AAS 23 (1931):180, para. 11; translation: Seven Great Encyclicals, p. 127.

28AAS 23 (1931):181, para. 15; translation: Seven Great Encyclicals, p. 128.

29AAS 23 (1931):190, para. 41; translation: Seven Great Encyclicals, pp. 135-136.

30Divini illius Magistri, December 31, 1929, AAS 22 (1930):65-67 and 22 (1930):58; Ubi arcano, December 23, 1922, AAS 14 (1922):690; Divini Redemptoris, March 19, 1937, AAS 29 (1937):82-83; Casti connubi, December 31, 1930, AAS 22 (1930): 541, 550-552, 579-580.

31Divini illius Magistri, AAS 22 (1930):53-56.

32Divini Redemptoris, AAS 29 (1937):82-83.

33ASS 23:654.

34AAS 23 (1931):219, para. 129 (also p. 218, para. 127-128).

35Divini Redemptoris, AAS 29 (1937):85.

36Theology for a Nomad Church, p. 47.

37These writings include no major social

teaching documents such as Pius XI, John XXIII, or Paul VI issued. Pius XII's 19 year reign did, however, produce myriad documents which touch on different aspects of the social teaching.

[38]*Summi Pontificatus*, October 20, 1939, AAS 31 (1939):421-422; Easter broadcast, March 24, 1940, AAS 32 (1940):149; Christmas message, December 24, 1939, AAS 32 (1940):5-14; December 7, 1939 letter to Italian Ambassador in The Pope Speaks: The Words of Pius XII, pp. 222-223.

[39]*Summi Pontificatus*, AAS 31 (1939):415-416.

[40]*Fidei donum*, April 21, 1957, para. 30, AAS 49 (1957):231.

[41]*Evangelii praecones*, June 2, 1951, AAS 43 (1951):517-518.

[42]*Mater et Magistra*, May 14, 1961, AAS 53 (1961):402, para. 3.

[43]Ibid., pp. 402-403, para. 6.

[44]Ibid., p. 403, para. 6 (emphasis mine).

[45]ASS 23:653-654; translation: Seven Great Encyclicals, p. 13.

[46]*Octogesima adveniens*, AAS 63 (1971):437-438, para. 48; translation: Renewing the Earth, pp. 379-380.

[47]New Catholic Encyclopedia (New York: McGraw-Hill, 1967), Vol. 14, pp. 1019-1020.

[48]Ibid., Vol. 7, p. 1017.

[49]Ibid.; Karl Otmar von Aretin, The Papacy

and the Modern World (New York: McGraw-Hill, 1970), p. 227.

[50]New Catholic Encyclopedia, Vol. 11, p. 17.

[51]Osservatore Romano, October 14, 1966; translation: The Pope Speaks, Vol. 12, No. 1, pp. 50-51.

[52]Supra, p. 77.

[53]AAS 48 (1956):625-626; translation: The Pope Speaks, Vol. 3, No. 3, p. 236.

[54]This is the crux of the debate in Latin America today over the stance to be taken at the Puebla Episcopal Conference: "Taking on the Vatican," Time, May 8, 1978.

[55]The Liberation of Theology, p. 4.

[56]Philippino clergy and hierarchy are experiencing some repression as a result of their championing of the poor against the Marcos regime. Leon Howell, "Chavez for the Defense," Christianity and Crisis, Vol. 37, No. 17, November 14, 1977.

[57]AAS 53 (1961):410; translation: Renewing the Earth, p. 59.

[58]La solennita, June 1, 1941, AAS 33 (1941): 196.

[59]Carlo Falconi, The Popes in the Twentieth Century (Boston: Little, Brown, 1967), pp. 259-262; The Papacy and the Modern World, p. 196; Paul Johnson, Pope John XXIII (Boston: Little, Brown, 1974), pp. 91-92; Pius XII, December 24, 1939 Christmas message, In questo giorno:
As the war monster progressively acquires,

swallows, and demands more and more of the
materials available (in Europe) all of which
are inexorably put at the disposal of its
ever increasing requirements, the greater
becomes the danger that the nations directly
or indirectly affected by the conflict will
become victims of a sort of pernicious anemia
--and the inevitable question arises: How
will an exhausted or attenuated economy continue to find the means necessary for economic and social reconstruction at a time when
difficulties of every kind will be multiplied,
difficulties which the disruptive and revolutionary forces now holding themselves in read-
iness will not fail to take advantage, in the
hope of striking a decisive blow at Christian
Europe?
AAS 32 (1940):9; translation: The Pope Speaks:
The Words of Pius XII, p. 230. This same idea was
expressed by Pius in a January 7, 1940 letter to
President Roosevelt, AAS 32 (1940):45 (The memorable message).

[60]Popes in the Twentieth Century, pp. 251-
262.

[61]Supra, pp. 84-85.

[62]AAS 23 (1931):190.

[63]This statement of Gutierrez' in A Theology
of Liberation, pp. 53-54, was used with reference
to the Church in Africa by P. A. Kalilombe in
"The Presence of the Church in Africa," in The
Emergent Gospel, edited by Sergio Torres and Virginia Fabella (New York: Orbis, 1977).

[64]Divini Redemptoris, AAS 29 (1937):103, 105,
para. 73, 77.

[65]*Papacy and the Modern World*, pp. 167-181; *Popes in the Twentieth Century*, p. 187.

[66]*AAS* 53 (1961):456-457, para. 236-239; translation: *The Encyclicals and other Messages of Pope John XXIII* (Washington, D.C.: The Pope Speaks Press, 1964), p. 308.

[67]*Chers fils*, September 3, 1950, *AAS* 42 (1950):639; *Dequelle consolation*, October 14, 1951, *AAS* 43 (1951):784; *Se a tempere*, September 4, 1940, *AAS* 32 (1940):362; *Divini Redemptoris*, March 19, 1937, *AAS* 29 (1937):100, 102; J. W. Poynter, *The Popes and Social Problems* (London: Watts and Co., 1949), p. 31; *The Popes in the Twentieth Century*, pp. 195-196.

[68]See *The Gospel of Peace and Justice: Catholic Social Teaching Since Pope John*, edited by Joseph Gremillion (New York: Orbis, 1976), p. 93, para. 238; *Seven Great Encyclicals*, p. 268, para. 238; *Renewing the Earth: Catholic Documents on Peace, Justice, and Liberation*, edited by David O'Brien and Thomas Shannon (Garden City, N.Y.: Doubleday, 1977), p. 107, para. 238.

[69]Pius XI used the phrase "reduction of social principles into effect" in *Divini Redemptoris*, *AAS* 29 (1937):85-86 and *Quadragesimo anno*, *AAS* 23 (1931):212. Pius XII used the phrase in *Evangelii praecones*, *AAS* 43 (1951):517-518. These passages use *deduco*.

[70]*AAS* 55 (1963):301, para. 160.

[71]This is the meaning of some recent titles and phrases in liberation theology: the absent of history, the subversion of history, history written with a white hand (Gutierrez, "Freedom and Salvation," pp. 75, 92). James Cone and Gustavo

Gutierrez offered a seminar entitled "Theology from the Reversal of History." And Sergio Torres and Virginia Fabella have a book entitled The Emergent Gospel: Theology from the Underside of History (New York: Orbis, 1977).

[72]Osservatore Romano, October 2, 1966; translation: The Pope Speaks, Vol. II, p. 345.

[73]AAS 63 (1971):403-404, para. 4; translation: Renewing the Earth, pp. 353-354.

[74]In the classification of papal documents by content litterae encyclicae rank first. Epistulae encyclicae are second, and epistulae apostolicae (the category of Octogesima adveniens) rank third. (Index Documentorum of Acta Apostolicae Sedis.) This ranking of the documents is explained by Thomas Harte, in Papal Social Principles (Gloucester, Mass.: Peter Smith, 1960), p. 7; he described apostolic letters as concerning affairs of the executive or administrative order, and encyclicals as teaching instruments which explain, instruct, or admonish.

[75]Theology of a Nomad Church, p. 47.

[76]Here Paul demonstrated the new attitude toward participation and democracy which John began in Mater et Magistra, para. 82-99, AAS 53 (1961): 421-425.

[77]Quadragesimo anno, AAS 23 (1931):180, para. 14; Divini Redemptoris, AAS 29 (1937):69, para. 8; and Populorum progressio, AAS 59 (1967):295-296, para. 79.

[78]AAS 63 (1971):426-427, para. 37.

[79]Ibid., pp. 428-429, para. 40; translation:

Renewing the Earth, p. 373.

[80]Ibid.

[81]Ibid., p. 431; translation: Renewing the Earth, p. 375.

[82]Le Monde, 7 Septembre, 1977.

[83]Commission Theologique Internationale, Declaration Sur Le Promotion Humaine et Le Salut Chretien, La Documentation Catholique, Septembre 4-8, 1977, No. 1726, pp. 762 (b,2); 763 (c); and 765 (4,b).

[84]Ibid., p. 762, 2a.

CHAPTER III

PRIVATE PROPERTY AND THIRD WORLD DEVELOPMENT

IN TWENTIETH CENTURY PAPAL TEACHING

Within the debate between liberation theologians and the forces aligned with the Vatican there
are various levels of disagreement. Chapters Two
and Four, on theological method and Marxism, are
examples of issues in which one or the other side
more or less rejects the position of the other in
toto. Liberation theologians refuse to use traditional theological method and to accept its presuppositions; the Vatican and allied hierarchy reject the integration and use of Marxism in theology and Church practice. On the issues to be examined in this chapter, however, the disagreements
are more subtle. The direction of papal teaching
on private property and Third World development
since Leo XIII has been in the general direction
of the liberation theology position. In the case
of private property this movement represents not
only an affirmation of the liberation theology
position, but a return to the classical position
of Thomas Aquinas. The case of Third World development is different, since this issue is a relatively modern one. On this issue, liberation theologians accept many aspects of the papal teaching
and use these aspects to criticize others in the
papal teaching with which they seem to conflict.

On these two issues, therefore, we do not find
the total rejection of the opposing position characteristic of either the Vatican and its supporters
or the liberation theologians. Rather, we find

agreement and disagreement on various points within the issues. In general, the papal treatment of private property and Third World development is criticized by the liberation theologians on the grounds that some aspects of the teaching make it irrelevant to the solution of the poverty in the Third World. Since the popes have, until recently, continued to maintain that the social teaching of the popes, especially that on private property and Third World development, offered the only possible solutions to the problem of poverty in the world, there are still clear issues in contention between them.

The fundamental, widespread condition of poverty is the primary fact to which liberation theologians address themselves. They understand poverty as the deprivation of the material necessities required for literacy, education, social and political participation and decision-making, all of which are preconditions for truly human existence. This deprivation constitutes the condition of the vast majority of the people of the Third World, the condition out of which liberation theologians speak. Poverty, for them, is a theological matter because these liberation theologians view the historical project of creating a new, truly human person as a theological task, the task to which faith commits us. The creation of this truly human person entails the elimination of poverty since it prevents the realization of free, responsible participation in social and political activity and decision-making on the part of human beings. Gutierrez has said that poverty is the entire basis of liberation theology.[1]

Liberation theologians assert[2] that their own attitude toward poverty accords with the Biblical attitude. They maintain that Scripture not only refers to poverty as an affront to God, but it presents God as one who delivers human beings not only from sin, but also from material oppression in the world.

As we observed in Chapter Two, poverty is also a major theme in the papal social teaching. But in the social teaching the focus is not on poverty as the occasion for struggle of the poor for liberation, but only upon God's special love for the poor. As we saw in Chapter Two, the social teaching maintains that the poor have a clearer than usual grasp of spiritual values, that they abound in supernatural graces and have an awareness of the higher values on which the gospel is based. The social teaching, therefore, affirms the epistemological privilege of the poor unconditionally while liberation theologians deny that the condition of poverty without struggle against it confers any privilege. It is the engagement of the poor in the struggle for liberation which confers their epistemological privilege. The difference here is the difference between a focus on poverty from outside the condition itself, and the adoption of the poverty perspective. The poverty perspective, as we suggested in Chapter Two, is the perspective of the poor from within the struggle for liberation. Again, engagement, praxis, is the crucial difference between the papal stance and that of liberation theology.

The social teaching of the popes came into being because of the severity and epidemic proportions of poverty in Leo's day. His first two paragraphs of Rerum novarum clearly identify poverty as the chief factor which motivated the composition of the pronouncement which initiated modern papal social teaching.[3] However, Leo identified a further reason for the need for papal social teaching in 1891: the danger that "crafty agitators constantly make use of these economic disputes to pervert men's judgements and stir up the people to sedition."[4] This dual emphasis on the fact of poverty and the presence of agitators proposing false solutions is central to more recent social teaching as well.[5]

The popes in the course of this century have proposed and endorsed several "solutions" to the problem of poverty. The status of private property and Third World development are central to these proposals. The still significant differences between the Vatican and liberation theologians on these issues will become clearer as we trace the papal positions on these issues.

Private Property

Until recently the popes have maintained that the preservation of private property was of first priority in any solution of the social problem. The first section of Rerum novarum, following the explanation for the necessity for the document, focuses on private property. This section, paragraphs 4-12, ends: "Our first and most fundamental principle, therefore, when we undertake to alleviate the condition of the masses, must be the inviolability of private property. This laid down, we go on to show where we find the remedy we seek."[6]

Pius XI opened Quadragesimo anno with an extensive account of Rerum novarum, its origin, its purpose, and its consequences in many spheres. After then asserting the authority of the Church in these matters, Pius immediately took up the subject of private property: "Descending now to individual aspects of the matter, we commence with ownership, or the right of property."[7] Pius then defended the Leonine teaching on property, equating it with the Catholic conception.[8]

Pius XII included a defense of private property in La solennita,[9] and in other addresses
often included short references to the communist
error according to which "everything is to be
owned and controlled by the power and dictates of
the State."[10] Like Leo XIII and Pius XI, Pius
XII defended private property as the only material
distribution arrangement which accorded with human
nature and dignity, the good of the community, and
the will of God. For all of these popes, there
seemed no alternative to private property.

Pope John XXIII explicitly defended this position of his predecessors in his Mater et Magistra:
"For the right of private property, including the
right of goods devoted to productive enterprises,
is permanently valid."[11] John XXIII further elaborated the right of private property into a major
topic of part II of Mater et Magistra. With Paul
VI came a substantive break in the papal attitude
toward private property, one which we will examine.
Even so, it is a mistake to ignore the very real
differences between Paul's predecessors as so many
commentators do. Calves and Perrin insisted that
the change between Leo XIII and Pius XII (with
whom their study ended) was merely a verbal
change.[12] Bigo similarly minimized the differences between the popes through the pontificate
of John (with whom his volume concluded).[13] We
will see that the papal documents demonstrate
major differences between the popes of the twentieth century. These differences are not so easily
explained away as those who prefer to see continuity rather than change assume.

An examination of the writings of these popes
in the area of private property must begin with
two ideas taken from Thomas Aquinas, whose writings form the basis of the theology and philosophy
for these popes.[14] The first is the concept of

113

natural law and natural law right, and the second
is the distinction between the right to possess
property and the right to use property as one
wills.[15] The Thomist position is quite clear on
these points. Thomas explicitly denied that private property was a part of primary natural law
because the distribution of property was by jus
gentium (human law) rather than from creation:

>Community of goods is said to be part of the
>natural law not because it requires every-
>thing to be held in common and nothing to be
>appropriated to individual possession, but
>because the distribution of property is a
>matter not for natural law, but rather, hu-
>man agreement, which is what positive law is
>about, as we saw above.
>   You speak of something according to na-
>tural right in two ways. The first is because
>nature is set that way; thus the command that
>no harm should be done to another. The second
>is because nature does not bid the contrary.
>Thus we might say that it is of natural law
>for man to be naked, for nature does not give
>him clothes; these he has to make by art. In
>this way common ownership and universal lib-
>erty are said to be of natural law, because
>private property and slavery exist by human
>contrivance for the convenience of social
>life, and not by natural law.[16]

Thomas did support the institution of private
property, and considered it the rational course for
societies to follow.[17] But he did this because he
thought that material goods could best be cared for
and of benefit to all through the institution of
private property:

>Man has a twofold competence with regard
>to material things. The first is to care for

and distribute the earth's resources. Understood in this way, it is not merely legitimate for a man to possess things as his own, it is even necessary for human life, and this for three reasons. First, because each man takes more trouble to care for something that is his sole responsibility than what is held in common or by many, for in such a case each individual shirks the work and leaves the responsibility to someone else, which is what happens when too many officials are involved. Second, because human affairs are more efficiently organized if each person has his own responsibility to discharge; there would be chaos if everybody cared for everything. Third, because men live together in greater peace where everyone is content with his task. We do, in fact, notice that quarrels often break out between men who hold things in common without qualification.

Man's other great competence is to use and manage the world's resources. Now in regard to this, no man is entitled to manage things entirely for himself, he must do so in the interests of all, so that he is ready to share with others in case of necessity.[18]

Leo XIII was responsible for establishing Thomism as the basis for all philosophy and theology in the Catholic Church.[19] Leo was a well educated pope and can be held responsible personally for the documents released in his name as much as or more than any pope of this century. He is often assumed to have written his own documents.[20] Yet Leo held that private property was a natural law right, therefore permanent, despite Thomas' assertions to the contrary.[21] Thomas and Leo clearly meant different things by natural law.

It is from this fact that the differences be-

tween other twentieth century popes arose. Both
Thomas and Leo agreed that property distribution
is from _jus gentium_, and not from creation. But
while this excluded private property from natural
law for Thomas, it affirmed private property as
natural law for Leo. Thomas understood natural
law as the unchanging order written into human
hearts by God at the time of creation. This order
was shared by all human beings and was knowable to
all, to various extents. For Leo, natural law was
an unchanging, universal order discerned through
reason to comply with the nature and purpose of
human beings. If, on the basis of present univer-
sality and reasonableness, the magisterium declared something of natural law, historical universal-
ity and fixity were presumed with regard to both
past and future.

There seems little difference between these
understandings of natural law. But in the _use_ of
these understandings the differences become apparent. For Leo, anything that appeared to the magisterium as reasonable, generally universal, and
in accord with the end and purpose of human beings
was a part of natural law. As a part of natural
law it was unchangeable because always necessary.
The check which had operated for Thomas--the necessity that the institution or precept have been a
part of original creation--was not regarded. There
were virtually no restraints on what could be declared dictated by natural law, since the reasonableness of a thing depended upon the person or
group determining it, and any exceptions to the
universal acceptance of an institution or precept
could be dismissed as unnatural, and as _violations_
of natural law.

Leo's formulation of natural law and private
property was one response to the strong attack being made on the institution of private property in

116

his day by the socialists. Another response to
this attack can be viewed in another Leonine departure from the Thomist position on private property. Thomas had maintained that the duties of
private property ownership took precedence over
the right of ownership itself. The chief duty was
to use property in the interests of all. Leo
stressed the rights of ownership much more than
the duties of ownership. Even when affirming
Thomas's view that owners should not consider property as their own, Leo elaborates this to mean
that excess wealth not required to maintain the
owner becomingly in his/her station should be given
to the indigent.[22] This obligation to do charity
with excess wealth was acknowledged by Thomas, but
for him this obligation is not synonymous with the
use of property in the common good; that obligation
is more rigorous and basic in the Thomas teaching.

In the works of Pius XI there is another position on private property. Pius XI agreed with Leo
that private property was both natural and right,
and referred to it as a part of natural law.[23]
But he also explained that property had been, in
the course of history, held in very different systems.[24] This is a distinct undermining of the
reasoning Leo used to declare private property
part of natural law. Where Leo assumed that individual ownership of property was reasonable and
universal throughout all history and societies,
and therefore a part of natural law, Pius claimed
it both part of natural law and a fairly recent
development among the people of the world. Here
we have evidence against the claim of Calves and
Perrin that there were no substantive differences
on private property between the papacies of Leo
and Pius XII.[25] The claim of both Bigo's book and
that of Calves and Perrin that Thomas and the popes
were in agreement[26] is clearly not supported by the
documents.

Calves and Perrin asserted that all these popes considered private property a secondary natural law right.[27] But if they had done so, they would have been in agreement with Thomas, whose answer to the question as to whether natural law could change left little doubt that private property _is_ a secondary natural law institution, which can, therefore, change under certain conditions.[28]

As noted, Leo explicitly named private property a natural law right, and claimed it not only from reason, but from nature.[29] Because he considered that the root of private property lay in an unchanging human nature, he deemed the institution eternal and unchanging.

The statements of Pius XI and his successors can be read on both sides of the issue. It is impossible, therefore, to support the claim that they regarded private property as a secondary natural law right. Pius XI's Quadragesimo anno passage (paragraph 49) on the varied forms of property through the ages would accord well with the secondary natural law explanation, but in other passages he affirmed, with Pius XII and John XXIII, that private property was an eternal institution,[30] as well as referred to it as a part of natural law. Now permanency is a trait of primary natural law, not secondary natural law. It is impossible to solve the dilemma as Calves and Perrin indicated.

Despite these differences between the popes on the issue of private property, they were in agreement on the value of private property for human beings. They insisted, from Leo XIII through Paul VI, that the value of property ownership for human beings was so great that the goal insofar as property was concerned must be universal family ownership.[31] (It is not clear how this family ownership would apply to women, since much of the discussion regarded the necessity of property for men as "paterfamilias" (heads of families).[32]

It was not until the pontificate of John that universal family ownership was considered a real possibility; as we observed in Chapter One, Leo XIII, Pius XI, and Pius XII all viewed economic classes and poverty as inevitable.[33] These popes nevertheless insisted that the value of property for the growth of the human personality, and for the security this growth required, made universal ownership desirable. They thought this insistence necessary to keep open the possibility for indi- viduals, if not classes, to escape from poverty into property ownership.

In Rerum novarum Leo claimed that all (not just owners) have a right to own property.[34] For Leo, the best way to implement this goal of univer- sal property ownership seemed to include: (1) de- fending the principle of private property in the strongest terms, (2) opposing those who threatened it, and (3) encouraging a just wage and labor or- ganizations to support it. The just wage was to be sufficient to allow workers of a thrifty nature to save toward ownership.[35] To Leo's mind, such a policy seemed designed to eliminate both the suf- ferings of the workers and the unrest which threa- tened the peace and order.

Leo XIII indicated in Rerum novarum that the property for which workers were to save was land.[36] This was not an extraordinary thought for an old man writing from an unindustrialized country in 1891. But this agrarian view (which continued to be verbalized through Pius XII[37]) may account for the general failure of the twentieth century popes to distinguish between private ownership of con- sumer goods and private ownership of means of pro-

119

duction. (Paul comes closest to distinguishing the two, but does not deal with the issue directly, as we shall see.) The popes' knowledge of and response to Marxism will be dealt with in Chapter Four, but it is important here to note that if the popes visualized workers saving from their wages to buy farmland, they were not likely to embrace a distinction between consumer and productive goods which would preclude individual ownership of land.

Pius XI

Pius XI accepted most of the Leonine position on private property, with the exception discussed above. He agreed that the misuse or non-use of property was not cause for the forfeiture of the right of ownership. He agreed that private property was in accordance with nature. The major modifications in Leo's position inaugurated by Pius XI were: (1) his recognition of the various historical forms of property distribution, (2) his allowance of the possibility of the civil authority adjusting ownership in the interest of the common good,[38] and (3) his insistence that for any distribution of private property to conform to social justice it must promote the common good.[39] These are important points because they indicate a significant shift from the position of Leo. Pius was at least as interested in defining the obligations of ownership as he was in explaining the rights of ownership. The principal obligation of ownership for Pius XI was to use property in the best interests of the common good.

Pius XII

Pius XII brought two fundamental emphases to the subject of private property: (1) that all persons in society should be allowed to develop their personalities in the way in which property permits,[40] and (2) that property owners have clear social obligations. In this latter regard he continued the emphasis of his predecessor. Pius XII seemed to imply that he did not agree with Leo and Pius XI that the misuse or non-use of property did not cause forfeiture of property: "We remind employers that while the Church condemns every unjust violation of the right of ownership, it warns that this right is neither illimitable nor absolute, that it carries with it clear social obligations."[41]

Pius XII related private property to both human nature and human reason, as had Leo XIII, maintaining that private property was natural for human beings because it was reasonable for them, and that God's natural order demanded private property.[42] While universal property ownership was also the ideal for Pius XII, he felt called upon to deny more than once that his predecessor had ever indicated that justice or charity, much less the Church, demanded partnership agreements for workers.[43] He opposed demands that workers were entitled to some kind of co-management.[44] These were not forbidden, but were not necessary, since the wage contract was not inherently unjust. In his June 3, 1950 address, Nous nous addressons, Pius XII warned that insistence on economic co-management could not insure re-integration of the economy and the stability of productivity which was essential for full recovery.[45] In general he implied a wariness of co-management. In Nous nous addressons he went on to express support for "collaboration" between labor and management, as opposed to co-management schemes. This support for "collaboration" was reiterated the following year in a March 11, 1951 speech.[46]

Pius XII looked more favorably than his predecessors on state intervention in ownership in the

121

interests of the common good,[47] though he was
known to have emphasized the disadvantages of nationalization. In his letter, _C'est un geste_, of
July 10, 1946, Pius noted the advantages of corporative units over nationalization and insisted
that nationalization accentuated the mechanization
of life and labor.[48] Pius looked to a middle way
between state capitalism and irresponsible private
ownership of powerful industries. In so doing he
implied an abandonment of the papal policy: to
foster the good chiefly by stressing to the powerful the obligations they have to others, as both
Christians and human beings.

In Pius XII's _La solennita_ there was a significant alteration in the expression of the limitations on private ownership. For previous popes,
the limitation had been the interest of the common
good; for Pius XII it was primarily the interests
of the individual. That is, he affirmed the right
of every individual to make use of the goods of
the earth, and elaborated: "This individual right
cannot in any way be suppressed, even by other
clear and undisputed rights over material goods."[49]
This oft demonstrated concern of Pius XII that the
freedom and rights of the individual be protected
against encroachment was formulated in the context
of his opposition to communism. The result was
that his concern for individual rights was expressed not in terms of the state adjusting ownership so
as to prevent the oppression of the poor by the
propertied, not in terms of the necessity for nationalization, but in a translation of the Thomist
position into modern, individualist, terms. The
common good which had precedence over the rights
of ownership in Thomas was no longer expressed in
corporative terms, but in terms of the individual
good of all members of the society. This shift was
important for the work of Pius's successors, who
continued to elaborate individual rights and there-

by limit "other clear and undisputed rights."

John XXIII

John XXIII retained many of the points which
characterized his predecessor's stances on private
property. He saw private property as natural because necessary for the exercise of the freedom,
and for the growth of which human beings were capable.[50] Private property, he said, was a right of
each person bestowed by nature.[51] John expanded
his predecessors' explanations of the benefits of
private property for the individual into a demand
for not only partnerships for workers in the financial aspects of enterprises, but partnerships in
control and management also. If the ownership of
property were a human right because it allowed personality to grow through increased opportunities
for decision-making, then such decision-making was,
for John, a part of the partnership which nature
intended.[52]

The right of the state to collectivize and
nationalize upon occasion in the interests of the
common good was recognized as necessary by John
XXIII.[53] This was a shift from the stance of Pius
XII. John was more concerned with the morals of
the administrators, and the way in which their
power would be used, than he was in prohibiting or
limiting the state's activity in this area.[54] He
acknowledged that modern times required such col-
lectivization more than previous times.[55]

More than any previous pope, John concerned
himself with the possibility of universal property
ownership.[56] The age in which John reigned was
one of the most prosperous ages in modern history
(1958-63). Such prosperity seemed to have combined
with John's optimism about the direction of history
(toward the equality and independence of all na-

123

tions,[57] the end of poverty,[58] the equality of
women,[59] etc.), to have produced a conviction that
the ideal was not far from realization.[60]

During his pontificate John also expanded on
Pius XII's interest in the individual and concentrated on the individual personality, its growth
and development in freedom. To this end John i-
dentified a new field of human rights with regard
to property and labor; the right to employment, to
insurance for sickness and old age, and the right
to unemployment compensation. All of these were
defended on the same grounds as the need for private property had been defended: as necessary for
safeguarding the rights of the person and for the
common good of society, right order.[61]

Paul VI

The Pastoral Constitution of Vatican II, Gaudium et Spes, which Paul VI signed, considered
private property within the context of the basic
rights of human persons. It declared:

> God intended the earth and all that it
> contains for the use of every human being and
> people. Thus, as all men follow justice and
> unite in charity, created goods should abound
> for them on a reasonable basis. Whatever the
> forms of ownership may be, as adapted to the
> legitimate institutions of people according
> to diverse and changeable circumstances, at-
> tention must always be paid to the universal
> purpose for which created goods are meant.
> In using them, therefore, a man should regard
> his lawful possessions not merely as his own,
> but also as common property in the sense that
> they should accrue to the benefit of not only
> himself but of others.
> For the rest, the right to have a share

of earthly goods sufficient for oneself and one's family belongs to everyone. The Fathers and the Doctors of the Church held this view, teaching that men are obliged to come to the relief of the poor, and to do so not merely out of their superfluous goods. If a person is in extreme necessity, he has the right to take from the riches of others what he himself needs.[62]

This paragraph went on to observe that since so much of the world exists in hunger, all should observe the obligation to provide, through sharing, the nations and individuals of the world with the means for helping themselves.

This necessity for sharing the goods of the world was here also defended on the grounds of the growth of human personality, as we saw above under John, and even under Pius XII:

> Ownership and other forms of private control over material goods contribute to the expression of personality. Moreover, they furnish men with an occasion for exercising their role in society and in the economy. Hence it is very important to facilitate the access of both individuals and communities to some control over material goods.
> Private ownership or some other kind of dominion over material goods provides everyone with a wholly necessary area of independence, and should be regarded as an extension of human freedom. Finally, since it adds incentives for carrying on one's function and duty, it constitutes a kind of prerequisite for civil liberties.
> The forms of such dominion or ownership are varied today and are becoming increasingly diversified. They all remain a source

of security not to be underestimated, even in
the face of the public funds, rights, and
services provided by society. This is true
not only of material goods, but also of in-
tangible goods, such as professional
skills.[63]

These passages demonstrate the significant
changes between the positions of Leo XIII and Paul
VI. By the time of Paul the Vatican stance had
abandoned Leo's denial of any change in the institution of private property, and shifted the emphasis from the rights of ownership to an emphasis on
the obligations and limitations of ownership. A
new flexibility concerning the forms of ownership
was not due only to Pius XI's recognition of other
historical forms of ownership, nor merely to Pius
XII's concern for the rights of the individual.
John's reinterpretation of the principle of subsidiarity[64] combined with the changes by Pius XI
and Pius XII. This principle of subsidiarity,
once used to deny delegating the power of smaller
bodies to larger ones, had come to be used to demand collective ownership of enterprises too large
and powerful to be safely owned by individuals.
The stance we see in _Gaudium et Spes_, and in Paul's
individual writings as well, is not, then, due to
any one individual pope, but represents the cul-
mination of a movement continuing throughout the
twentieth-century papacy.

Paul wrote in _Populorum progressio_:

If the world is made to furnish each individual with the means of livelihood and the
instruments for his growth and progress, each
man has therefore the right to find in the
world what is necessary for himself. The recent Council reminded us of this: 'God intended the earth and all that it contains for

126

the use of every human being and people.
Thus, as all men follow justice and unite in
charity, created goods should abound for them
on a reasonable basis.' All other rights
whatever, including those of property and of
free commerce, are to be subordinated to this
principle. They should not hinder, but on
the contrary, favor, its application. It is
a grave and urgent social duty to redirect
them to their primary finality.[65]

In _Populorum progressio_ Paul, in his use of
the phrase "and of free commerce," further extended the declarations of Vatican II in _Gaudium et
Spes_. The rights of all to the goods of the earth
supersede not only property rights, but also the
right of free commerce. In saying this, Paul gave
provisional approval to nations which, in order to
feed their people, not only seized the mines and
factories of foreign companies, but failed to re-
pay loans, or to honor their contracts with other
companies or countries. The possibilities are
endless.

Paul took the position that "What must be
aimed at is complete humanism. And what is that
if not the fully rounded development of the whole
man and of all men?"[66] This was "integral development." _Populorum progressio_ went on to describe
the course of this development in humanism:

Less human conditions: the lack of material necessities for those who are without
the minimum essential for life, the moral deficiencies of those who are mutilated by self-
ishness. Less human conditions: oppressive
social structures whether due to abuses of
ownership or to abuses of power, to the exploitation of workers or to unjust transac-
tions. Conditions that are more human: the

passage from misery toward the possession of
necessities, victory over social scourges,
the growth of knowledge, the acquisition of
culture.[67]

The statement of the 1971 Synod of Bishops
revealed the same understanding of the relationship of human development to those rights such as
property, though it did not mention private property by name:

The right to development must be seen as a
dynamic interpenetration of all those fundamental human rights upon which the aspirations
of individuals and nations are based.[68]

Substantively, the Church has so changed her
stance on private property between the pontificates
of Leo XIII and Paul VI that remaining differences
between the official position and that of liberation theologians are no longer major ones. In
fact, the latest papal teaching on private property
is similar enough to the position elaborated by
liberation theologians that it has been, at times,
useful against those who cling to older papal formulations.

Third World Development

"Development" is a term usually used to desig-
nate an economic and social goal for the Third
World. The reasons for this being a contested
issue between papal teaching and liberation theology chiefly revolve around the presuppositions and
method of the policy used to achieve the development of the Third World. The direction of that
policy--prosperity--is not disputed. The underlying assumption of dominant development policy is
that all nations grow and develop along a continu-
um, some being more advanced than others. The

Third World is considered a slow area, due, in
time, to prosper in the same manner as the First
World. The objection to this assumption is that,
in the opinion of liberation theologians and
others, the underdevelopment of the Third World is
the cause and the result of the development of the
First World. They maintain that the Third World
cannot take the same path to prosperity because
there is no longer an area of the world to exploit.
The Third World exists in a dependency relationship with the First World while her exploitation
continues and her dependency increases. The normal course of events will not bring development,
but further dependency, they say.

Development is primarily a social scientific
term used by economists and political scientists.
Though first mentioned by Pius XII,[69] "development"
became prominent in the social teaching of John
XXIII, whose writing also reflected certain assumptions about development policy; the issue has dominated the social teaching of Paul VI. Before examining the writings of John XXIII and Paul VI on
development, we will examine the background to
this policy. Consistency to our method of treating these issues as they arose in the papal corpus
dictates that we begin with the mission encyclicals. Until the 1960's the mission encyclicals
were the papal documents which chiefly dealt with
papal teaching on and attitude toward the Third
World. Three issues which need to be examined
within the mission encyclicals, and need to be
traced in more recent papal teaching, are native
clergy and culture, racism, and colonialism and
neocolonialism.

Native Clergy and Culture

We will begin with the issue of native clergy,
as this is the aspect of the papal teaching on the

129

Third World which has the longest history. An
obvious question here is: What is the reason for
including native clergy in a discussion of economic development? Its relevance is only clear when
the papal documents are consulted. It is then
obvious that not for the first time does recent
papal teaching insist that: "Development cannot
be limited to mere economic growth. In order to
be authentic, it has to promote the good of every
man and of the whole man."[70] For the earlier
twentieth century popes the only aspect of the development of the Third World which was of concern
was the development of the Church in these lands.
The mission encyclicals, especially Benedict XV's
Maximum illud, Pius XI's Rerum ecclesiae, and Pius
XII's Evangelii praecones and Fidei donum make
this clear. Native clergy was the surest sign to
these popes that the Church was becoming established, that the Third World was being truly developed
--spiritually developed. The papal teaching on
native clergy, then, forms an important part of
the background to the teaching on development.

     This is especially so since the popes, in
treating the subject of native clergy, often discussed Third World culture and its relationship to
Christianity, an issue that proved very important
both for the discussions of racism by the popes,
and later for colonialism and neocolonialism.

     The insistence of the Church on the importance
of native clergy is very old. The Church has pointed to the fact that by the seventh century all the
monks and abbots of England were native born.[71] In
the work of St. Patrick ordaining native clergy in
Ireland in the fifth century and through the response of Pope Gregory VII to the King of Norway's
request for missionaries--Gregory demanded natives
who could be trained and sent back--the Church has
demonstrated the high value it placed upon native

clergy to carry out her work.

Undoubtedly one reason for the prominence of
the affirmation of the importance of native clergy
in the twentieth century is that the Church did
not act according to her earlier conviction and
tradition during the colonial period in the West.
Especially during the Spanish and Portugese colonial periods the various popes of the Church were not
effective in promoting native clergy because they
had surrendered to the crowns of these countries
immediate control over both political and religious activity in the Americas. This had been done
in the hope that a centralized effort would benefit the coordination and pace of the evangelization
program. In other areas of the world, especially
in the Far East, the popes and the Sacred Congregation for the Propagation of the Faith systematically urged native clergy beginning in the seventeenth
century.[72]

In more modern times, Leo XIII strongly urged
the bishops of India to ordain Indians in his apostolic letter of June 24, 1893, Ad extremas Orientis
oras:

> The preservation of the Catholic faith in
> India will be insecure, and its propagation
> uncertain, as long as there is wanting in the
> ranks of the clergy a select group of natives,
> who do not merely serve as helpers to foreign
> missionaries, but are able by themselves to
> administer to Christian bodies well in their
> own territories. . . .[73]

Benedict XV in his apostolic letter Maximum
illud of November 30, 1919 also demanded a native
clergy in the mission lands:

> The main care of those who rule the mis-

sions should be to raise and train a clergy
from amidst the nations among which they
dwell, for on this are founded the best hope
for the Church of the future. Linked to his
compatriots as he is by the bonds of origin,
character, feelings and inclinations, the
indigenous priest possesses extraordinary
facilities for introducing the faith to their
minds and is endowed with power of persuasion
far superior to those of any other man. It
thus frequently happens that he has access to
where a foreign priest might not set foot.[74]

In Rerum ecclesiae Pius XI expanded the reasons for supporting the formation of a native
clergy. He agreed with his predecessors that "unless you provide to the best of your ability for
native priests, your apostolate will remain crippled and the establishment of a fully organized
Church in your territories will encounter still
further delay."[75] But Pius XI went beyond the
pragmatic reasons for a native clergy, even beyond
Church tradition which had referred to apostolic
practice as revealed in the Bible.[76] Pius XI asked:

Why should the local clergy be prevented from
cultivating their own vineyard, or from govern-
ing their own people?[77]

This question was asked only with reference to the
Church and her government, not with reference to
political government and the colonial system. Nevertheless, within this narrow range Pius continued
to the heart of the problem and attacked the racism
which undermined the Church's position on native
clergy:

If anyone considered these indigenous
people inferior, gifted with only limited

132

intelligence, he is seriously mistaken. For
experience has proved that the peoples who
inhabit the distant areas of Asia and Africa
acquit themselves quite well in the pursuit
of education, and in general are our intellectual equals. If you do find the students
from the very heart of an undeveloped terri-
tory are slow in their studies, this is readily explained, as you can examine for your-
selves, in the fact that their very simple
habits of living have made few demands on
their intelligence. We know of many seminarians in the various colleges of Rome of
whom we can say that in every branch of
learning they not only equal the achievements
of the other students but frequently surpass
them. Wherefore, you should not permit your
local priests to be regarded as inferior to
the foreign clergy, or employed in only the
more menial ministries, as though they were
not adorned with the self-same priesthood and
did not share the same apostolate. Rather
you should keep in mind that one day they
should head both the communities established
by your sweat and toil already, and future
communities as well. Therefore let there be
no discrimination or caste distinction between European and native clergy, but let
them all cooperate with each other, united by
ties of mutual respect and charity.[78]

Pius XII continued this new equal rights theme
in his first encyclical, Summi Pontificatus:

Those who enter the Church, whatever their
race or speech, can be sure that they have
equal rights as children in the House of God,
in which all live by the law in the peace of
Jesus Christ. That this principle of equitable treatment is brought gradually to be, the

133

Church is choosing candidates from the various races to fill up the episcopal and priestly ranks of their own countries.[79]

In the twenty-five years between Pius XI's Rerum ecclesiae and Pius XII's Evangelii praecones which celebrated it, Pius XI and Pius XII had appointed 88 native bishops.[80] Pius XII had the distinction of overseeing the development of the native clergy of most of Africa. In fact, during the 1950's all living Negro bishops were appointees of Pius XII.[81]

That papal pronouncements have stressed the importance of native clergy in the last century is clear. For the most part the popes have agreed that the Gospel is most convincingly preached by a representative of the ranks of the audience, after proper training, of course. Pius XII, however, in an attempt to defend the work of and use of foreign missionaries, wrote in an address to the Latin American Church, Ad ecclesiam Christi (June 24, 1955):

But since it will be a long time before vocations can answer the needs of each country, attentive concern should also be concentrated on the better means of utilizing to the service of the Church in Latin America the large number of clergy of other countries. These cannot be considered foreigners, for all Catholic priests who truly answer their vocations feel themselves native sons whenever they work in order that the Kingdom of God may flourish and develop.[82]

One indication of Pius' concern that missionaries consider themselves natives was his stipulation regarding lay medical missionaries working under missionary priests. In Evangelii praecones Pius XII wrote: "They should also voluntarily agree to

forsake their homeland to serve the missionaries."[83] Such forsaking would presumably include
citizenship. It could not, however, be assumed
that such was the case with missionaries. Benedict XV had recognized in Maximum illud that missionaries in the past had often not renounced primary loyalty to their native land:

> We have been deeply saddened by some recent
> accounts of missionary life, accounts that
> display more zeal for the profit of some par-
> ticular nation than for the growth of the
> Kingdom of God. We have been astonished at
> the indifference of their authors to the
> amount of hostility these works stir up in
> the minds of unbelievers.[84]

Though both Benedict XV and Pius XI referred
to the missionary's need to know the native language of the people to whom he ministers,[85] no real
account of how native culture was or should be
treated was given until Pius XII. By the time of
his pontificate independence movements were active
all over the world and the tension between European
and native culture had become a prominent issue.
Pius XII defended the Church against nativist attacks on her colonialist associations, it having
been noted that the Church was centered in Europe
and administered by Europeans in the colonies:

> Another matter, moreover, remains to be
> treated, and we are very anxious that it be
> understood as clearly as possible by all. The
> Church from the very beginning down to Our own
> day has followed this wise policy. When the
> Gospel is accepted by diverse races, it does
> not crush or repress anything good and honor-
> able and beautiful which they have achieved
> by their native genius and natural endowments.
> When the Church summons and guides a race to a

higher refinement and a more cultured way of
life, under the inspiration of the Chr cian
religion, she does not act like a woc sman
who cuts, fells, and dismembers a l xuriant
forest indiscriminately. Rather ue acts like
an orchardist, who grafts a cult vated shoot
on a wild tree so that later cu fruits of a
more tasty and richer quality may issue forth
and mature.[86]

.   .   .   .   .

Accordingly, the Catholic Church has not
scoffed at or rejected pagan learning, but
rather has freed it from all error and alloy,
and then sealed and perfected it by Christian
wisdom. The same holds true for the fine
arts and liberal studies which some pagans
had already advanced to lofty heights. The
Church received them in sympathy, cultivated
them assiduously, and lifted them to a peak
of beauty never, perhaps, previously ex-
celled.[87]

The above defense of the Church's missionary
methods and approach was a common topic in the
works of Pius XII.[88] It is clear here and elsewhere that in Pius XII's understanding, the Christian life involved more than the faith of the
apostles. In the last two thousand years the faith
had become, at least in the mind of Pius XII, in-
tertwined with the culture in which it spread and
which it helped to nourish.

John XXIII denied that the Church was an
alien institution imposed on the life of the people.[89] He quoted Pius XII on the Church's historic
respect for national culture,[90] but this was not a
common theme in his work.

Paul VI in _Populorum progressio_ did not refer
to the Church's past policy with regard to Third

World culture, but, reflecting the new conditions in the Third World, he referred rather to the effects of cultural contact between developed and underdeveloped nations:

> Rich or poor, each nation possesses a civilization handed down by their ancestors: institutions called for by life in this world and higher manifestations of an artistic, intellectual, and religious character. When the latter possess true human values, it would be a grave error to sacrifice them to the former. A people that would act in this way would thereby lose the best of its patrimony; in order to live, it would be sacrificing its reasons for living.[91]

Another aspect of the Church's attitude toward native culture is the training given native clergy. There was a trend, as we saw, in the direction of increasing respect for native culture between the time of Benedict XV (who demanded an end to political chauvinism and economic greed on the part of missionaries) and that of Paul VI (who urged the retention of native customs and institutions as integral to personality and existence). This trend is not so visible in the case of the training of native clergy. Leo XIII had urged that the more promising among the natives with vocations be sent to Rome for their education. In his July 2, 1894 encyclical, _Litteras a vobis_, he had instructed the bishops of Brazil to erect seminaries in each diocese, and to send the most promising and gifted students to Rome for seminary.[92] In his apostolic letter _Quae mari sinico_ of September 17, 1902, Leo had urged the bishops of the Philippines to foster native vocations, and send the qualified students on to Rome.[93] This training in Rome was no doubt meant to prepare some native priests to carry on the work of training and presiding over others by giving these few advanced education not available in the mission country. This practice seems to have continued until recently, if, indeed, it is ended. There was in Pius XI's <u>Rerum ecclesiae</u>, a reference (quoted above) to the numerous seminarians from the mission lands (from "the most remote areas of Asia and Africa") studying in schools in Rome.[94] Twenty-five years later, in <u>Evangelii praecones</u>, there was a reference not only to new institutes and chairs of missiology at Rome, but to the College of St. Peter, which Pius announced had been specially equipped to minister to the needs of seminarians from the mission lands.[95]

John and Paul did not address this particular aspect of the question of Third World culture and the training of native priests. But it is clear that this was not merely a practice of bygone days, for it is still inveighed against by liberation theologians. Hugo Assman quotes Joseph Comblin on this: "Any Latin American who has studied in Europe has to undergo detoxification before he can begin to act."[96] Enrique Dussel adds:

> If we want to train people, we send them to Europe. There they study liturgy, catechetics, theology, and a host of other subjects. When they come back, they are completely lost in Latin America. They are out of touch and never get their feet back on the ground. They are Frenchified, Germanized, or otherwise alienated. It is not simply a matter of reading the Gospel message. We must read it <u>within tradition</u>. And tradition has come down to <u>us</u>, not through Italy or Germany, but through a Spain that came to America and through a concrete Church in Latin America to which we belong.[97]

This question of the Church and culture is

perhaps the most prominent question in African and Asian liberation theology, and indeed, within non-liberation Third World theology as well. The Third World is much occupied with the question of what is the relationship between the Christian faith and the cultural context in non-Christian lands. In African and Asian Christianity, "contextualization" is a major, if not the dominating, theme everywhere.[98] Within a Christian context such as Latin America, a similar aspect of the faith-culture issue arises in the form of a question concerning the relationship between Christian faith and popular religion.[99] This popular religion Segundo describes as the result of a fusion between religious elements brought by the Catholic conquistadors and indigenous and African religious elements.[100]

Racism

It should be apparent that the issues of racism and of native culture and clergy are closely related in the papal teaching, and indeed, in the history of the Third World. Within the twentieth-century social teaching the explicit treatment of racism has not significantly altered. As we saw above, Pius XI and Pius XII condemned racial discrimination in the missions, in particular among the clergy.[101] Pius XI condemned Nazi racism in Mit brennender sorge.[102] Gaudium et Spes added its authority to the long list of Church condemnations of racism,[103] building on John XXIII's affirmation that "Hence, racial discrimination can in no way be justified at least doctrinally or in theory."[104] Paul VI's Populorum progressio also condemned racism as contrary to the inviolable rights of the human person.[105] The popes unanimously condemned racism as contrary to and irreconcilable with the brotherhood of the human race, with our status as redeemed by Christ, and with God's love for all of

139

us. But, as we shall see, there are reasons for continuing concern about the existence of racism in papal teaching.

The background to the papal treatment of racism is the papal treatment of slavery. Many, many popes and theologians have credited the Church with ending slavery through her preaching and practice of the brotherhood/sisterhood of human beings. Of the modern popes, Leo XIII gave the most exhaustive account of how the Church ended slavery in his encyclical In plurimis, May 5, 1888.[106] Benedict XV referred to some of this history in his encyclical on slavery and the South American Indians, Lacrimabili statu, June 7, 1912.[107]

Exhibiting the same assumption, Pius XII wrote C'est bien volontiers, March 9, 1956, in which he described how the Church ended ancient slavery:

> Then, too, the Church has, since the time of its inception, instilled in humanity definite principles which, little by little, silently and unobtrusively, but in all the more permanent manner, influenced cultural life and modified it profoundly from within. . . . It is thus, let us add in passing, that the ancient practice of slavery was cut down at its roots long before it was possible to suppress it as an economic institution. Read the brief letter of the Apostle Paul to Philemon. Considered from this point of view, it is a cultural document of primary importance.[108]

There are two points in this passage which require attention. Pius was only speaking of the "ancient practice of slavery" being destroyed by the Church, and did not imply that the Church was responsible

140

for the end of slavery in the nineteenth and twentieth centuries. What Pius meant by the phrase
"long before it was possible to suppress it as an
economic institution" is not clear. Whatever he
meant, the relevant question for Pius at this
point was why the Church was less effective with
the modern slave trade which not only began at a
time when the West was securely Catholic (1441 is
the date of the first African slaves in Europe),
but which was conducted almost entirely by the
Catholic countries of Europe for the first century.
The Spanish and Portugese slave traders had no competition from other nations until the sixteenth
century, for Britain and France were interested
neither in buying nor in selling slaves until the
New World was opened and economic exploitation began. Even then, the bulk of the New World slave-
holders (whether the slaves were Indian or Negro)
were Catholic, and all were Christian.

The historic claim of the Church to be responsible for the end of the slave trade in earlier
times (and some statements imply in modern times
also) has not been based on any specific anti-
slavery stance the Church has advocated, but solely
on her preaching of the love of the Gospel. This
is an evangelical idealist approach to ethics, a
belief both that ideas are direct causes of events
and that if one converts souls, then justice will
prevail among the saved.

The claim that the Church destroyed slavery
and opposes racial discrimination, and the twentieth-century policy of the Church in, for example,
South Africa, are not necessarily contradictory.
Until recently, the Catholic Church in South Africa
had complied with all the regulations of the apartheid policy. A book published by the Archdiocese
of Capetown in South Africa in 1951 to commemorate
the founding of the hierarchy in that country by

141

Pius XII revealed the changes made in the Catholic
schools there upon the establishment of the Union
of South Africa in 1909:

> Before the Union, in the Cape, there was
> no rigid distinction between the white and
> the coloured. Schools were founded for the
> poorer sections and to these coloured as well
> as white children came equally.
> With the advent of the Union and the
> numerical growth of the coloured people, sep-
> arate schools and institutions had to be pro-
> vided. . . .[109]

William Eric Brown quoted a 1952 statement of the
South African hierarchy in his book, The Catholic
Church in South Africa:

> Were the attitude of the Europeans the
> sole reason for South Africa's racial pro-
> blem, it would be simple enough to condemn
> it as unjust and unChristian, and, by a de-
> termined process of education, endeavor to
> modify it. However, the problem is far more
> complex than that. Its complexity arises
> out of the fact that the great majority of
> non-Europeans, and particularly the Africans,
> have not reached a state of development that
> would justify their integration into a homo-
> geneous society with Europeans. A sudden and
> violent attempt to force them into the mold
> of European manners and customs would be dis-
> astrous. There must be gradual development,
> and prudent adaptation.[110]

These statements are not papal ones, but episcopal ones. And yet one can assume that this is
also the view of the pope, for on April 29, 1951
Pius XII addressed the newly created South African
hierarchy and, in keeping with past policy toward

the racial situation in South Africa, did not mention race at all.[111] His address, In the liturgical office, applauded the schools, hospitals and orphanages run by the Church, without reference to their compliance with the apartheid policy. He did devote one sentence to urging more native vocations, but did not relate this to the political situation.

Both books referred to above on the Church in South Africa acknowledged that the Church has largely seen her function in South Africa as ministering to the South Africans of European descent who brought the faith to South Africa.[112] The Church regarded the evangelization of the natives as secondary, which effectively meant that because of the shortage of priests, other missionaries had a significant head start of 50-100 years on the Catholic effort. Brown maintains that this late start meant that the Catholic effort was just getting under full steam when the election of 1954 ended public support for religious schools and therefore crippled the Church's missionary work among the Bantu.[113] The result of all this is that the total Catholic population in South Africa is less than 7%, and the Catholic European population has never been over 5% of the population.

The anti-Catholicism which persisted in South Africa,[114] combined with the minority status of Catholics and with the self-interest of the European sector, pressured the Catholic Church in that country to accept apartheid. That the pressure was successful is clear from this quote from the Capetown diocese's book on the race issue:

> The Church does not preach absolute equality between black and white, for there are some natural distinctions in the world which have to be recognized and some artificial

distincitions have been made which have to be observed.

There is unanimity of conviction as to the duty of the white inhabitants of South Africa to protect and to preserve their own civilization, and no sane man will argue this point. In our contact with a primitive race on a low cultural level and far away from the centers of western culture we feel rightly obliged to be jealous of our precious heritage passed down to us through ages and generations and to try by all means to preserve our civilization with all its cultural traditions.[115]

It is difficult to miss the similarity between this statement of the Capetown diocese and Pius XII's views on the superiority of Christian cultures. Pius had written: "When the Church summons and guides a race to a higher refinement and a more cultured way of life under the inspiration of the Christian religion . . ."[116] Here we see again that the issues of race and culture are interwoven. It is the presence of that same general cultural view in the South African episcopacy which we saw in Pius XII that leads to and justifies apartheid racial views. If the culture of Europe is to be considered the norm and standard of culture for the world, and that of the Third World considered inferior, such superiority and inferiority will be the appropriate statuses for representatives of those cultures when they meet. For Pius XII, European culture was the apex, and so we do not hear papal objections to the South African defense of its racial policies in terms of the need to preserve superior European culture. Pius XII, of course, is not, nor are any of the popes, responsible for the racism of South African whites. But it is clear that the South African Church does not stand in opposition to the historic

Church policy in such cases. That policy was to
look for a gradual change toward justice as the
result of the workings of the Gospel in the hearts
of individual Christians. The ties between views
on culture and views on race are historically so
strong that the effectiveness of the teaching on
racism seems to hinge upon the appreciation of
Third World cultures vis-a-vis European culture.

Colonialism and Neo-Colonialism

The papal attitude toward colonialism is not
systematically developed in any of the papal documents. Pius XI did not deal with the topic at
all, nor had Benedict XV before him. The insight
that native clergy are more accepted and less resented than foreign clergy did not lead to any
statements on colonialism, its justification, advantages or problems. Pius XII similarly ignored
the grievances of the natives towards the West
when discussing native resentment and reaction
toward western missionaries. In Evangelii praecones he remarked of the expulsion from Korea and
China of Christian missionaries:

> We may hope, too, that these people may come
> to appreciate the loving Christian goodness
> of the foreign missionaries and indigenous
> priests, who, by their toil and the surrender
> of their lives when necessary, aim solely at
> their genuine and sincere welfare.[117]

But Pius XII revealed even more of his attitude toward colonialism in his encyclical Fidei
donum, April 21, 1957, on the Church in Africa:

> The Church which has seen so many nations
> born and grow during the past centuries,
> cannot but give particular heed today to the
> accession of new peoples to the responsibili-

ties of political freedom. Several times
already We have invited the nations concerned
to proceed along this road in a spirit of
peace and mutual understanding.

'Would that a just and progressive political freedom be not denied to these people
and that no obstacle be set in the way,' We
said to some. We warned others 'to credit
Europe with their progress, without whose influence, extended to all domains, they could
have been dragged by a blind nationalism to
hurl themselves into chaos and slavery.'[118]

In this passage Pius seemed to be of the opinion
that colonialism had benefited the colonies and
that gratitude was in order. John XXIII was also
of this opinion; he made a similar observation in
his address to the Congo, June 30, 1960 when he
spoke of "generous Belgium."[119]

John most often spoke of colonialism as an
outdated aspect of history, now obstructive. In
Mater et Magistra he said:

Moreover, economically developed countries
should take particular care lest, in giving
aid to poorer countries, they endeavor to turn
the prevailing political situation to their
own advantage, and seek to dominate them.
Should perchance such attempts be made,
this clearly would be but another form of
colonialism, which, although disguised in
name, merely reflects their earlier but outdated dominion, now abandoned by many countries. When international relations are thus
obstructed, the orderly progress of all peoples is endangered.[120]

In Pacem in terris John expressed a similar disapproval of colonialism as a part of a more primitive,

146

less civilized era:

> Finally, the modern world, as compared with the recent past, has taken on an entirely new appearance in the field of social and political life. For since all peoples have either achieved, or are on the way to achieving, independence, there will soon no longer exist a world divided into peoples who rule others and peoples who are subject to others.
>
> Men all over the world today have--or soon will have--the rank of citizens in independent nations. No one wants to feel subject to political power located outside his own country or ethnic group. Thus, in our day, in very many human beings the inferiority complex which endured for hundreds and thousands of years is disappearing, while in others there is an attenuation and gradual fading of the corresponding superiority complex which had its roots in socio-economic privileges, sex, or political standing.[121]

Paul VI was more critical of colonialism than his predecessors, in that he connected colonialism with the present need for development. He did, in _Populorum progressio_, find that there were positive aspects to the colonial experience, even for the colonies themselves, but his overall assessment was critical:

> Though insufficient for the immensity and urgency of the task, the means inherited from the past are not lacking. It must certainly be recognized that colonizing powers have often furthered their own interests, power, and glory, and that their departure has sometimes left a precarious economy, bound up, for instance, with the production of one kind of crop whose market prices are subject to sudden

and considerable variation. Yet while recognizing the damage done by a certain type of colonialism and its consequences, one must at the same time acknowledge the qualities and achievements of the colonizers who brought their science and technical knowledge and left beneficial results of their presence in so many underprivileged regions. The structures established by them persist, however incomplete they may be; they diminished ignorance and sickness, brought the benefits of communications and improved living conditions.

Yet once this is admitted it remains only too true that the resultant situation is manifestly inadequate for facing the hard reality of modern economics. Left to itself, it tends to widen the differences in the world's level of life, not to diminish them: rich peoples enjoy rapid growth whereas the poor develop slowly.[122]

With this statement the papal view moved from an approval of colonialism as a beneficial, though outmoded, service to the colonies and the Third World in general, to a recognition that colonialism has operated both to the detriment and to the benefit of these nations. This new attitude toward colonialism is important, even fundamental, for the papal stance on economic development taken by John XXIII and Paul VI. The basis of papal development policy was expressed by John XXIII in Mater et Magistra:

In this matter We consider it Our duty to offer some warnings.

First of all, it seems only prudent for nations which have thus far made little or no progress, to weigh well the principal factor in the advance of nations that enjoy abundance.

148

Prudent foresight and common need demand
that not only more goods be produced, but
that this be done more efficiently. Likewise
necessity and justice require that wealth
produced be distributed equitably among all
the citizens of the commonwealth. Accordingly, efforts should be made to ensure that improved social conditions accompany economic
advancement. And it is very important that
such advances occur simultaneously in the
agricultural, industrial, and various service
sectors.[123]

Almost twenty years have elapsed since John XXIII
wrote these lines. The suggestion that underdeveloped nations copy the efficiency of the developed nations seems much more naive now, when
even orthodox economists recognize how the developed nations have created the conditions preventing
efficiency in the production of underdeveloped
countries. (Paul later mentioned some of these
ways.[124]) John assumed that the underdeveloped
nations were merely late starters, that they, too,
were on the road to being developed. The dependency concept accepted by the liberation theologians
who criticize development[125] played no part in
John's understanding. The prosperity of his day
encouraged him to think that development was almost
inevitable:

However, the underlying causes of poverty
and hunger will not be removed in a number of
countries by these means alone. For the most
part, the causes are to be found in the primitive state of the economy.[126]

John urged the cooperation of the First World
in developing the Third World, and restricted the
legitimate actions of developed states with regard
to underdeveloped ones, in Mater et Magistra:

149

Now when economically developed countries assist the poorer ones, they not only should have regard for these [cultural] characteristics and respect them, but also should take special care lest, in aiding these nations, they seek to impose their own way of life upon them.[127]

Genuine necessity, as well as justice, requires that whenever countries give attention to the fostering of skills or commerce, they should aid the less developed nations without thought of domination, so that these latter will be in a position to progress economically and socially on their own initiative.[128]

In _Pacem in terris_ John XXIII's central thesis was that tied to each right of the individual or group is an obligation which must be fulfilled. Each individual or nation possessing some superiority over others must, said John, make a greater contribution to the development of other individuals or nations rather than subjecting others to their control.[129] The implications for the development of the Third World are apparent. Specifically, John wrote:

Since nations have a right to exist, to develop themselves, to acquire a supply of the resources necessary for their development, to defend their good name and the honor due them, it follows that they are all likewise bound by the obligation of effectively guarding each of their rights and of avoiding those actions by which these rights can be jeopardized. As men in their private enterprises cannot pursue their own interests to the detriment of others, so too states cannot lawfully seek that development of their own resources which brings harm to other states and unjustly

150

oppress them.[130]

Paul VI differed from John on this subject
not so much in his prescriptions and teaching concerning what development should mean, but in his
analysis of what development policy was actually
doing as implemented. He had the benefit of a
later period of observation than John, and was
able to be more technically critical. In Populorum progressio Paul began by admitting that modern
economics as exemplified in international economic
relations operated to enrich the already rich at
the expense of the ever more impoverished poor.[131]
Inequality was not limited to possessions but extended to the exercise of power.[132] The cultural
institutions which provided stability were, in the
Third World, giving way to the foreign civiliza-
tions which accompanied development.[133] Paul's
disapproval of this invasion of civilization from
the First World set him apart from his predecessors.

Paul condemned societies which held profit as
the key motive for economic progress, competition
as the supreme law of economics, and private ownership of the means of production as an absolute
right, carrying no corresponding social obligation.
He called for a defense of the family as an important aspect of the milieu in which persons achieve
identity. Paul demanded a rectification of trade
relations between rich nations and poor nations.
He urged individuals:

> Let each one examine his conscience, a con-
> science that conveys a new message for our
> times. Is he prepared to support out of his
> own pocket works and undertakings organized
> in favor of the most destitute? Is he ready
> to pay higher taxes so that public authorities
> can intensify their efforts in favor of de-

velopment? Is he ready to pay a higher price
for imported goods so that producers may be
more justly rewarded? Or to leave this country, if necessary and if he is young, in order
to assist in the development of the young
nations?[134]

When Paul shifted his demands from individuals to
the developed nations, he wrote:

Although it is normal that a nation
should be the first to benefit from the gifts
that Providence has bestowed on it as the
fruit of the labors of its people, still no
country can claim on that account to keep its
wealth for itself alone. . . . Given the increasing needs of the underdeveloped countries, it should be considered quite normal
for an advanced country to devote a part of
its production to meet their needs, and to
train teachers, technicians, and scholars
prepared to put their knowledge and their
skill at the disposal of less fortunate people.[135]

Paul called for careful planning to put such a
plan into effect. He also suggested again, as he
had done in Bombay, that a proportion of the sums
spent in the developed world for arms be donated to
the World Fund for development. He suggested that
such funding and collaboration could prevent the
current situation of developing nations being over-
whelmed by debts whose repayment eats up all their
income,[136] and he provided some general suggestions
for changing this situation.

Whereas John had stipulated that development
should be done to benefit the Third World, and not
the First, Paul's emphasis was on the actual situation in which the benefit from development policy

152

was at least ambiguous, if not definitely accruing
to the developed world. Paul noticed that the ex-
ports of developed nations were largely manufac-
tured goods, whose prices were steadily rising.
Developing countries, for the most part, exported
raw material whose prices were subject to sudden,
wide fluctuation. The situation, Paul said, required action.

Paul VI's conclusion was that liberal economics does not make for justice, a conclusion which
all the other popes since Leo had recognized.
Paul further observed that the free market system
must be held within the bounds of justice on an
international scale just as the developed nations
attempt to do domestically.[137] The free market
system will otherwise strangle the Third World.
In Octogesima adveniens Paul returned to this
point:

> But, as we have often noted, the most impor-
> tant duty in the realm of justice is to allow
> each country to promote its own development,
> within the framework of a co-operation free
> from any spirit of domination, whether econom-
> ic or political. The complexity of the pro-
> blems raised is certainly great, in the pre-
> sent intertwining of mutual dependencies.
> Thus it is necessary to have the courage to
> undertake a revision of the relationships be-
> tween nations, whether it is a question of the
> international division of production, the
> structure of exchanges, the control of profits,
> the monetary system--without forgetting the
> actions of human solidarity--to question the
> models of growth of the rich nations and
> change people's outlooks, so that they may
> realize the prior call of international duty,
> and to renew the international organizations
> so that they may increase in effectiveness.[138]

In these passages from _Populorum progressio_ and _Octogesima adveniens_ Paul noted many aspects of "development" policy which instead fostered dependency. He did speak of economic systems, institutions and models, and acknowledged that modern economics works to the disadvantage of the poor. But Paul offered no political or economic alternative to the capitalist economics he criticized. The absence of any alternative, and the papal tradition of relying on evangelization to gradually correct injustice, did not allow Paul to abandon the dominant development model and begin afresh with the dependency model of liberation theologians.

NOTES

[1]Personal conversation, November 1977.

[2]A Theology of Liberation, pp. 287-302; History and the Theology of Liberation, pp. 123-126; Allan Boesak, Chapter One in Farewell to Innocence (New York: Orbis, 1977) and "Coming IN Out of the Wilderness," in The Emergent Gospel, pp. 89-90.

[3]ASS 23:641-642, para. 1 and 2.

[4]Ibid., p. 641.

[5]See Quadragesimo anno, para. 59ff on poverty, and para. 55, 111ff on false solutions to the problem, AAS 23 (1931):197-198 and 212-218; Mater et Magistra on poverty, para. 68, 123, 150, AAS 53 (1961):418, 431-432, 438 and on erroneous philosophies, para. 212ff, AAS 53 (1961):451-453; Populorum progressio's entire theme is poverty, but especially see para. 1, 3, AAS 59 (1967):257-258; Octogesima adveniens, on poverty, para. 2, AAS 63 (1971):402, on less perfect solutions, para. 30-31, AAS 63 (1971):421-425.

[6]Rerum novarum, ASS 23:647, para. 12.

[7]AAS 23 (1931):191, para. 44.

[8]Ibid.

[9]AAS 33 (1941):199 (Italian), 221 (English).

[10]Evangelii praecones, June 2, 1951, AAS 43 (1951):517, para. 68.

[11]AAS 53 (1961):427, para. 109: "Siquidem jus privati dominii . . . per omne tempus valet. . . ."

[12]Church and Social Justice, pp. 194-197.

[13]La doctrine sociale de l'Eglise, pp. 39-41.

[14]Leo XIII established Thomism as the basis of all Catholic philosophy and theology in his encyclical, Aeterni patris, August 4, 1879. (ASS 12: 97-115) This establishment was reiterated by Pius XI in Officiorum omnium, August 1, 1922 (AAS 14 (1922):449-458) and by Pius XII in Nous nous souhaitons, September 14, 1955 (AAS 47 (1955):683-91).

[15]Summa Theologiae la2ae 94:4,5 and 2a2ae 66: 1,2.

[16]Ibid., 2a2ae 66:2 and la2ae 94:6 (3).

[17]Ibid., la 98:1.

[18]Ibid., 2a2ae, 66:2.

[19]Supra, p. 156, #14.

[20]Etienne Gilson, The Social Teachings of Leo XIII (Garden City: Doubleday, 1954), pp. 1-3.

[21]Rerum novarum, ASS 23:644, 645, 647; Quod apostolici muneris, ASS 11:370: "jus proprietis naturale lege sanctitum impugnant."

[22]Rerum novarum, ASS 23:651-652, para. 19.

[23]Quadragesimo anno, AAS 23 (1931):193-194, para. 49.

[24]Ibid.

[25]Church and Social Justice, pp. 205-206.

[26]Ibid., p. 205; La doctrine sociale de l' Eglise, pp. 236-283, especially p. 239.

[27]Church and Social Justice, p. 205.

[28]Summa, la2ae 94:5.

[29]Rerum novarum, ASS 23:643-644, 647; Quod apostolici muneris, AAS 11:370.

[30]Quadragesimo anno, AAS 23 (1931):193; Divini Redemptoris, AAS 29 (1937):78; La solennita, AAS 33 (1941):221; Mater et Magistra, AAS 53 (1961): 427, para. 109.

[31]Leo wrote: "The law, therefore, should favor ownership, and its policy should induce as many as possible to become owners." Rerum novarum, ASS 23:662-663, para. 35. Also Rerum novarum, ASS 23:643, para. 4; Quadragesimo anno, AAS 23 (1931): 198, para. 61; Oggi, al compiers, AAS 36 (1944): 254; Con sempre nuova, AAS 35 (1943):17. John XXIII made this point in Mater et Magistra, AAS 53 (1961):420-421, 423, 428, 429, para. 77, 91, 112, 113, 115 and Paul VI in Populorum progressio, AAS 59 (1967):267, para. 21.

[32]Leo is most explicit about this in para 9 and 10 of Rerum novarum, ASS 23:645-646.

[33]Divini Redemptoris, AAS 29 (1937):81, 88-89; Rerum novarum, ASS 23:648; Sertum laetitiae, AAS 31 (1939):642.

[34]Rerum novarum, ASS 23:643, para. 5.

[35]Ibid., p. 662, para. 35.

[36]Ibid.

[37]La solennita, AAS 33 (1941):202-204; Papal Ideology, p. 102.

[38]Quadragesimo anno, AAS 23 (1931):193, 214, para. 49, 114. However, in some other writings this is seemingly denied, as we saw in the treatment Pius gave to the principle of subsidarity.

[39]Quadragesimo anno, AAS 23 (1931):196, para. 57.

[40]La solennita, AAS 33 (1941):221; Sertum laetitiae, AAS 31 (1939):654; Evangelii praecones, AAS 43 (1951):518-519; Con sempre nuova, AAS 35 (1943): 17.

[41]October 28, 1956 address, AAS 48 (1956):823.

[42]La solennita, AAS 33 (1941):221.

[43]Papal Ideology, p. 298; Church and Social Justice, pp. 286-287; Nous nous addressons, AAS 42 (1950):487.

[44]Papal Ideology, p. 133; Nous nous addressons, AAS 42 (1950):487; January 31, 1952 address on labor, Osservatore Romano, February 1, 1952, p. 1.

[45]AAS 42 (1950):486-487.

[46]Que hermoso espectaculo, AAS 43 (1951):213-216.

[47]Papal Ideology, pp. 150-152; La solennita, AAS 33 (1941):223.

[48]AAS 38 (1946):315-318.

[49] *AAS* 33 (1941):221.

[50] *Pacem in terris*, *AAS* 55 (1963):262, para. 21.

[51] *Mater et Magistra*, *AAS* 53 (1961):406.

[52] Ibid., pp. 421-422, para. 82.

[53] Ibid., p. 429, para. 116.

[54] Ibid., p. 430, para. 118.

[55] Ibid., p. 429, para. 117.

[56] Ibid., pp. 420-421, 423, 428-429, para. 77, 91, 112-113, 115.

[57] *Pacem in terris*, *AAS* 55 (1963):268, para. 42-43.

[58] Ibid., p. 267, para. 40; *Mater et Magistra*, *AAS* 53 (1961):441, para. 163.

[59] *Pacem in terris*, *AAS* 55 (1961):267-268, para. 41.

[60] *Papal Ideology*, p. 160.

[61] *Mater et Magistra*, *AAS* 53 (1961):427, 428, 424-425, 425, 423, 434-435, para. 109, 111, 93, 98, 91, 97, and 136.

[62] *Gaudium et Spes*, *AAS* 58 (1966):1090-91, para. 69; translation: *Renewing the Earth*, p. 249.

[63] Ibid., p. 1092, para. 71.

[64] Pius XII's emphasis on corporative units and their necessity was a similar (though more

159

timid) action in this vein, done without reference to the principle of subsidiarity.

[65]Populorum progressio, AAS 59 (1967):268, para. 22; translation: Renewing the Earth, p. 320.

[66]Ibid., p. 280, para. 47.

[67]Ibid., pp. 267-268, para. 21; translation: Renewing the Earth, pp. 319-320.

[68]De Justitia in Mundo, AAS 63 (1971):926, para. 15; translation: Renewing the Earth, p. 393.

[69]Fidei donum, AAS 49 (1957):227, 229.

[70]Populorum progressio, AAS 59 (1967):264, para. 14. Also see Mater et Magistra, AAS 53 (1961):443, para. 175-177 and Populorum progressio, AAS 59 (1967):265-267, para. 15-21.

[71]Carlos A. Lewis, Catholic Negro Bishops (Bay St. Louis: Divine Word Publications, 1958), p. 6.

[72]Ibid., p. 7.   [73]ASS 25:718-719.

[74]AAS 11 (1919):445, para. 14.

[75]February 28, 1926, AAS 18 (1926):73, para. 22.

[76]Ibid., p. 74, para. 24.

[77]Ibid., pp. 74-75, para. 25.

[78]Rerum ecclesiae, AAS 18 (1926):77, para. 30.

[79]October 20, 1939, AAS 31 (1939):430.

[80]Evangelii praecones, June 2, 1951, AAS 43

(1951):449, para. 6.

81Catholic Negro Bishops, p. 34.

82AAS 47 (1955):542; translation: The Pope Speaks, Vol. 2, pp. 253-254.

83AAS 43 (1951):517, para. 66.

84AAS 11 (1919):447, para. 20.

85Maximum illud, AAS 11 (1919):448-449, para. 24; Rerum ecclesiae, AAS 18 (1926):74-75, para. 25.

86Evangelii praecones, AAS 43 (1951):521-522, para. 87.

87Ibid., para. 89.

88Summi Pontificatus, AAS 31 (1939):429; 1944 address to Mission Aid Society, AAS 35 (1944):210 (quoted in Evangelii praecones, AAS 43 (1951):523). Also Sie Haben, The Pope Speaks, Vol. 2, No. 2, pp. 227-228.

89Mater et Magistra, AAS 53 (1961):444, para. 180.

90Ibid., para. 181.

91AAS 59 (1967):277, para. 40 and 41; translation: Renewing the Earth, p. 327.

92ASS 27:3-7.

93Not in ASS; from Catholic Negro Bishops, p. 7.

94Rerum ecclesiae, AAS 18 (1926):77, para. 30.

[95]Evangelii praecones, AAS 43 (1951):500, para. 7.

[96]Theology for a Nomad Church, p. 56.

[97]History and the Theology of Liberation, p. 18, emphasis mine.

[98]Another term which is sometimes synonymous with contextualization is indigenization (though more often indigenization refers to returning to the native conditions or culture as they were prior to colonization, and not as they are now, affected by the European presence and the last four hundred years). In examining a work such as Torres' and Fabella's account of the August 1976 meeting of Third World Theologians in Dar es Salaam, The Emergent Gospel, one finds that the following authors constructed their chapters around contextualization/indigenization: Patrick Masanja (Tanzania), P. A. Kalilombe (Malawi), Charles Nyamiti (Tanzania), Kwesi Dickson (Ghana), Ngindu Mushete (Zaire), Manas Buthelezi (South Africa), Orlando P. Carvajal (Philippines), Allan Boesak (South Africa), Carlos H. Abisamis (Philippines), Peter K. H. Lee (Hong Kong), D. S. Amalor Pavadass (India), and J. R. Chandran (India). Other sources attesting to the dominance of this theme: Sebastian Kappan, Jesus and Freedom (New York: Orbis, 1977); What Asian Christians Are Thinking, edited by Douglas J. Elwood (Quezon City, Philippine: New Day Publishers, 1976); and The Challenge of Black Theology in South Africa, edited by Basil Moore (Atlanta: John Knox Press, 1975).

[99]History and the Theology of Liberation, pp. 162-164; The Liberation of Theology, pp. 183-208; and the theme of the October 1978 Bishops Conference for the Latin American Catholic Church is popular religion in Latin American culture.

162

[100] The Liberation of Theology, p. 185.

[101] Supra, pp. 132-134.

[102] March 15, 1937, AAS 29 (1937):145-168.

[103] AAS 58 (1966):1048-1049, para. 29.

[104] Pacem in terris, AAS 55 (1963):268, para. 44.

[105] AAS 59 (1967):287-289, para. 62-64.

[106] ASS 20:545-549.

[107] AAS 4:521-525.

[108] AAS 48 (1956):216; translation: The Pope Speaks, Vol. 3, No. 2, p. 162.

[109] The Catholic Church in Southern Africa (Capetown: Galvin and Sales, for the Diocese of Capetown, 1951), p. 111.

[110] London: Burns and Oates, 1960, p. 343.

[111] AAS 43 (1951):381-382.

[112] Catholic Church in South Africa, pp. 194-197; Catholic Church in Southern Africa, pp. 109-113.

[113] Catholic Church in South Africa, pp. 194-197.

[114] Ibid., p. 344.

[115] "The Church and the African," Catholic Church in Southern Africa, p. 158.

[116]Evangelii praecones, AAS 43 (1951):521-522, para. 87; page 136.

[117]Evangelii praecones, AAS 43 (1951):509, para. 39.

[118]AAS 49 (1957):229, para. 20-21.

[119]Accueillant avec, AAS 53 (1960):568.

[120]Mater et Magistra, AAS 53 (1961):442-443, para. 171-172; translation: Seven Great Encyclicals, p. 255.

[121]Pacem in terris, AAS 55 (1963):268, para. 42-43; translation: Seven Great Encyclicals, pp. 297-298.

[122]Populorum progressio, AAS 59 (1967):261-262, para. 7-8; translation: Renewing the Earth, p. 315.

[123]Mater et Magistra, AAS 53 (1961):442, para. 166-168; translation: Seven Great Encyclicals, pp. 254-255.

[124]Populorum progressio, AAS 59 (1967):282-283, 284, 285, 291, para. 52, 54, 57, 70.

[125]History and the Theology of Liberation, pp. 115-116; Ethics and the Theology of Liberation, pp. 2-13; A Theology of Liberation, pp. 88-92; Theology for a Nomad Church, pp. 37-38, 45-50.

[126]Mater et Magistra, AAS 53 (1961):441, para. 163; translation: Seven Great Encyclicals, p. 255.

[127]Ibid., p. 442, para. 170.

[128]Ibid., p. 443, para. 173.

[129]AAS 55 (1963):281, para. 87-88.

[130]Ibid., p. 282, para. 92.

[131]Populorum progressio, AAS 59 (1967):261, para. 8.

[132]Ibid., pp. 261-262, para. 9.

[133]Ibid., p. 262, para. 10.

[134]Ibid., pp. 280-281, para. 47; translation: Renewing the Earth, p. 330.

[135]Ibid., p. 281, para. 48; translation: Renewing the Earth, p. 330.

[136]Populorum progressio, AAS 59 (1967):283-284, para. 54.

[137]Ibid., p. 287, para. 61.

[138]Octogesima adveniens, AAS 63 (1971):431-432, para. 43; translation: Renewing the Earth, p. 376.

CHAPTER IV

PAPAL TEACHING ON MARXISM

Within the current debate in the Catholic
Church over liberation theology, the Vatican has
taken a position that is somewhat ambiguous.
Though Paul did not, as we have seen, adopt the
method of liberation theology, he did endorse the
goals and some of the language and concepts of liberation theology. Not only did his <u>Populorum pro-
gressio</u> and <u>Octogesima adveniens</u> attest to this,
but his acceptance of the 1968 CELAM documents from
the Medellin conference and the failure of his
theological commission to condemn liberation theology[1] were evidence of some degree of approval.

But in the ten years since the Latin American
bishops took a strong stand for the liberation of
the oppressed at the CELAM conference at Medellin,
the conservative hierarchy in both Latin America
and the First World have reorganized. Paul VI was,
in his last years, considered to be ranged on the
side of the conservative hierarchy in the current
struggle over the position to be taken at the upcoming CELAM conference in Puebla, Mexico, in January 1979.[2] Preparations for the conference made
clear[3] that the surge of conservative strength
since Medellin[4] had been given support by the Vatican, and that the conservatives saw themselves as
representing the official Vatican position. Attributed to Paul were fears concerning the politiciza-
tion of the Church and the almost certain repression it would encounter as a result.[5] Probably the
issue most central to these fears was the use of
and importance of Marxism in liberation theology.[6]

167

The longstanding Vatican position on Marxism
in the twentieth century has been unambiguous condemnation. Though this position is more ambiguous
recently, with Paul's _Octogesima adveniens_, the
last papal teaching on Marxism, we were given extensive warnings about the use of Marxism,[7] of its
ideological as well as the political dangers in
its historical results. Similarly, Marxism was
identified as the fundamental reservation and problem for the International Commission on Theology
which studied liberation theology.[8] Just as liberation theologians concentrate on the deficiencies
of traditional theological method, their opposition,
including the Vatican under Paul, has had as its
fundamental objection the use of Marxism in liberation theology. Thus the _New York Times_ recently
reported:

> The region's [Latin America's] Catholic
> Church has moved sharply to the left in the
> last decade, with bishops and priests not
> only speaking out against military dictator-
> ships but also identifying increasingly with
> the struggle for social and economic changes.
> But conservative Catholic leaders, who
> believe that the Church is now too deeply em-
> broiled in politics and is even flirting dan-
> gerously with Marxism, has launched a strong
> counteroffensive, hoping to slow down, if not
> reverse, this leftist swing towards 'Christian
> socialism.'[9]

Given the historical position of the Church
vis-a-vis Marxism, the centrality of Marxism to the
debate over liberation theology was to be expected.
But there is another aspect of the disagreement
over Marxism which complicates the discussion and
necessitates careful examination. For it has been
claimed that Paul himself, and other twentieth century popes as well, have used aspects of Marxism in

their social teaching. One of the liberation theologians, Jose Porfirio Miranda, writes:

It is well known that many European and
North American evaluations of Populorum progressio referred to it as 'the complete re-
sume of Marxist and pro-Marxist cliches.'
But this judgement is not only the resentful
position of conservatives. Already in 1951,
years before the publication of the encyclical and even before Mater et Magistra, Oswald
von Nell-Breuning, S.J., a recognized spokes-
man for Catholic social doctrine in Germany,
had this to say in his commentary to no. 100
of Quadragesimo anno: 'This analysis of
economic society and--for what it says concerning the industrialized countries--of
society as a whole is the imperishable
achievement of Marx. All subsequent critiques of capitalism are based, to one degree
or another, upon it.'
And in 1967 the same author in his article
on 'The Catholic Church and the Marxist Critique of Capitalism' spells out how 'we are all
riding on Marx's shoulders.' There is no
doubt that the encyclicals take their diagnosis of society from Marx, a society divided
into classes, in which some are owners of the
means of production and others, the proletari-
at, are able to contribute only their own labor and are forced to submit to the capitalists. The inevitability of the confrontation
between the two classes, affirmed by Quadragesimo anno, is also a thesis taken from Marx;
the only difference is that Pius XI calls
'confrontation' what Marx calls 'struggle.'
The necessity of building a classless society
--with the difference that Marx calls it such
while the pontifical doctrine terms it a
'society free from classes'--is another note-

169

worthy loan. The need to conceive and seek a transformation of structures and institutions and not only a reform of attitudes and persons, as Catholics taught before Marx, is another outstanding and most important example. With the transformability of institutions we also learn from Marx to think with a historical mentality about the social problem; this is perhaps still more important.'
    To this analysis of Nell-Breuning we could easily add a whole list of passages from Populorum progressio which directly or indirectly are derived from Marx. The list would include paragraphs of the greatest human profundity, those dedicated to the search for 'a new humanism which will enable modern man to find himself anew' (Populorum progressio, no. 20). The encyclical affirms 'The development of which we speak cannot be limited to mere economic growth. . . . We do not believe in separating the economic from the human' (no. 14).[10]

Miranda thus finds it disconcerting to find attacks on Marxism even in recent papal teaching. This claim is equally upsetting for conservatives, for it moves the debate to the issue of what aspects of Marxism are acceptable. If the popes utilize aspects of Marxism, the conservatives can no longer maintain that Marxism must be entirely rejected, or that Marxist analysis is inseparable from Marxist ideology.[11]

Marxism and Liberation Theology

    Liberation theologians object to the condemnations of Marxism by past popes and the rejection of it today by the Church.[12] They assert that commitment to the liberation of the poor and oppressed of Latin America necessitates rejecting the dependency

170

which characterizes their countries vis-a-vis the
First World because of their participation in the
international capitalist system. That capitalist
system is unmasked and attacked by Marxism, which
is, therefore valuable in opposing the dependency
of their region.[13]

There are differences among the Latin American liberation theologians with regard to Marxism
and its appropriation by Christians; these differences are by no means insignificant.[14] But there
is general agreement on the relevance of the Marxist critique of and attack on capitalism and on,
in particular, the Latin American dependency which
results from the dynamics of advanced capitalist
political relations. There is also general agreement that it is inappropriate for the Church to
reject the possibility of a socialist political
option for Catholics, even among those who are not
ideologically committed to a Marxist alternative.
This consensus is at least partly due to a common
assessment of tercerismo (a third way, between
capitalism and socialism): that it finally ends up
supporting the capitalist status quo.

Various particular tenets of Marxism are incorporated in Latin American liberation theology in
addition to the analysis of the dynamics of economic dependence. The dialectical relationship between theology and praxis is very influenced by the
Marxist concept of theory and praxis. Reflection
on praxis (itself an interplay between reflection
and action) yields new theory, which when implemented is continually the object of reflection. As we
saw in Chapter Two, theology is critical reflection
on praxis in the light of faith. That is, Christians reflect on their engagement in the liberation
struggle in the light of their faith. That reflection is theology, which informs ongoing praxis.
Continuing reflection on this new praxis, which is

171

theology, constantly inspires adaptations in the praxis. The process is a spiral one in which both theology and praxis are constantly changing, and each informing the other.

Historical materialism underlies much of the sociological critique in liberation theology, as does Marxist class analysis. These aspects of Marxism reflect the extent to which liberation theology is initially secondary to engagement in the political liberation movements, which in Latin America utilize Marxism. Because commitment is the first step in doing liberation theology, and because commitment to liberation in a given society may entail joining or cooperating with certain groups, reflection on the praxis of that commitment will be dependent upon the options open to one in that political engagement.

The debate between the conservatives and the liberation theologians on the use of Marxism revolves around the claim of many Latin American liberation theologians that ideology is inescapable, and that no theology can be non-ideological in dealing with the world.[15] This point can be somewhat confusing to readers, however, since some other liberation theologians, especially the Christians for Socialism group in Chile, assert that Marxism can be used as a "tool," without adopting the Marxist ideology.[16] The eighty priests who began the Christians for Socialism group in Chile wrote that they saw Marxism as "an instrument for analysing and transforming society." The Coordinating Committee of the Christians for Socialism groups wrote a letter to Cardinal Silva in which they maintained: 1) that the scientific analysis proposed by Marxism is partial and incomplete, 2) that the temptation exists to turn any of the sciences into a philosophy and ultimately a religion, and that this temptation must be resisted, 3) that

the scientific validity of Marxism as a sociological methodology is not universally clear and self-
evident, but that it more than any other methodology clearly spotlights the all embracing and in-
terrelated character of the different phenomena
blocking their liberation, 4) that Marxism is not
a cure-all, and is part of the ongoing historical
process, 5) that the Marxist valuation of the pro-
letariat is not identical with the gospel's blessing on the poor, yet one cannot deny any dovetail-
ing between them, and 6) that authentic religion
is not the opiate of the people, but a liberating
stimulus to revivify and renew the world constantly. "In short, one cannot simply take over this
doctrine [Marxism]; one must create it anew."[17]

It is important to note that these Chilean
theologians are utilizing a _papal_ formulation. As
we shall see, John differentiated a historical
movement from the ideology with which it began.
Paul went further, maintaining that there are different levels of expression of Marxism ranging
from the total ideology to the use of Marxism as a
tool for understanding reality. There seems to be
a contradiction between this use of Marxism as a
tool, without adopting its ideology, and the use
of some of the ideological aspects. However, both
positions are nevertheless true of these liberation
theologians and of Paul's position in _Octogesima_
adveniens. The clue to understanding this apparent
contradiction lies in the meaning of "ideology."
What this group of liberation theologians and Paul
seem to indicate by the term "ideology" is the complex of anthropological and ontological underpin-
nings of the movement. The liberation theologians
who claim to use Marxism as a tool are defending
the use of and participation in Marxist movements
without an adoption of the atheistic materialism of
traditional Marxist ideology.

Even those liberation theologians who refer
to Marxism as a tool of social analysis agree that
since there are two competing economic systems in
the world, capitalism and socialism, and no other
possibilities, to totally refuse Marxist ideology
is to embrace, necessarily, capitalist ideology.
What they seem to mean by their adoption of Marxism as a tool, not an ideology, is that they see
no necessity for embracing Marxist ideology in its
entirety, uncritically; aspects not useful for
Christians (such as atheism) need not be appropri-
ated. Aspects of the ideology need to be rethought,
critically, for a new age and new situations. They
believe that Christians should be free to examine
Marxism, and to decide as to the utility of various
dimensions of the Marxist perspective in their engagement in the struggle for liberation.

Background and Early Papal Teaching
on Marxism

In examining papal documents dealing with
Marxism it becomes clear that the popes have often
used "socialist," "communist," and "Marxist" as
synonymous terms. Their use of the term "socialists" refers to Marxian socialism, as is clear because they link "socialist" to condemnations of
specifically Marxian doctrines, such as class struggle. The same is true of the term "communist."
For this reason, and because it is the use of Marxist ideology by liberation theology which is today
contested by the popes, we will use the term "Marxist" within the following discussion of papal
teaching. The single exception to this will be
papal discussion of the ideological split between
socialism and communism, in which those two terms
will be retained for clarity.

The history of papal teaching on Marxism might
be said to begin with the pontificate of Pius IX,

174

who, in the first year of his reign (1846) issued
a broad condemnation of "that infamous doctine of
so-called communism which is absolutely contrary
to the natural law itself, and if once adopted
would utterly destroy the rights, property and
possessions of all men and even society itself."[18]
In 1864 Pius IX again condemned all communism and
socialism when he included them with freemasonry,
biblical societies, liberal clerical societies, and
other "scourges" for which the Protestant Reforma-
tion was responsible.[19] These references were not
specifically to Marxist communism or socialism,
which was not distinct from that of other socialist
groups until after 1848, when the Manifesto was
published. Pius referred to all such groups in
these documents, and not to any specific group or
type of communism or socialism.

Leo XIII referred to socialism in his first
encyclical, Inscrutabili, February 10, 1878, on the
evils in society.[20] Later in 1878 Leo issued his
encyclical Quod apostolici muneris against the socialists. The charges made by Leo in Quod apostolici muneris form the basis of the papal attacks on
Marxism in the twentieth century. Leo listed four
objections to false teachings promulgated by the
Marxists: (1) their rejection of God, the Church,
and religion, (2) their refusal of obedience to the
State, based on their false proclamation of the absolute equality of all, (3) their debasement of
marriage, and (4) their attack on private property.

This teaching, Leo argued, denied the theological truth that the foundation of all power and order
is in God, who gave the duty of safeguarding humanity to the Church. The power of God, he declared,
is delegated to the civil powers; to rebel against
these powers is to rebel against God. The order
created by God is a graded order, in which some are
subject to others. Within the family, which was for

Leo the cornerstone of all society and government, God ordained the indissoluble union of man and woman in which the man is the head of the woman and the master of the children. For Leo, the right of private property was indispensable for the ordering of society and for the health of the family. It was also derived from the natural inequalities which exist among human beings.

In addition to these explicit objections to Marxist teaching, there is, in Quod apostolici muneris (and other writings of Leo as well) another implicit charge against the Marxists. Though not integrated into the overall critique or formulated as a specific part of the papal objections, this charge, like the others, originates a major strand of later papal teaching against Marxism. This is the objection that Marxism advocates the use of violence and aims at the creation of conflict. Leo saw the goal of Marxism as "the overthrow of all civil society whatsoever."[21] The opening paragraph of Quod apostolici muneris charged that the Marxists used false propaganda to inflame the masses, causing violent uprisings.[22]

At the base of the Leonine objection to violence and conflict is a different model of how society should work. The Marxists advocated a conflict model; Leo assumed a hierarchical harmony model for society and history. This difference is important in the consideration of the papal teaching on class struggle. Because the popes assumed that society was an organic whole, with each part as necessary as the organs of a body, conflict was unthinkable. It signified death to the whole. The cooperation of all parts was necessary for survival.

Use of this model of society which assumes harmony is closely related to the papal tradition on violence. Violence is unacceptable within a

176

society against the prevailing order because it spells death to the whole. But just as bodies can fight each other, so can societies. The popes accepted the use of violence between societies, under certain well defined conditions. This acceptance of violence between societies within certain limits is known as the just war theory, a traditional part of Church teaching.[23] Within the just war theory, violence can only be acceptable (just) within the following conditions:

(1) there must be grave injury or grave violation of rights by a state, continued in spite of diplomatic representations made to it;

(2) only states can legitimately wage war;

(3) the war must be conducted for a limited end and by legitimate means;

(4) the foreseeable evil consequences of the war must not be greater than the actual injury sustained.[24]

These conditions do not prohibit physical aggression, or even first use of violence. They allow the initial injury to be of various kinds, only insisting that it be serious, and that diplomatic representations have been futile. These conditions rule out as morally legitimate wars of annihilation, wanton conquest, aggrandizement, ideological war, and preventive first strike.

Because all the popes between Leo XIII and Paul VI relied on the just war theory, violence within a society was never found legitimate.[25] In effect, papal use of the just war theory made approval of any revolution impossible, since a revolution is, by definition, conflict between the members of a society. On the other hand, violence to

177

reestablish a previous order between societies has been considered legitimate. The tolerant attitude of Pius XI toward German rearmament and expansion contrary to treaty is an example of papal approval of this, though rearmament and expansion merely set the stage for war, and were not violent in themselves. That Pius XII begged the western democracies to aid the Hungarians fighting the USSR in 1956 is a much clearer example of use of just war theory to justify the use of violence.

The relationship between the papal reliance on harmony in society and the distinction the popes draw between war and revolution exemplifies the papal view of order and its static character. In the papal model, not only is the ideal of society a harmony based on a (hierarchical) order, but disorder is a sinful breach of that order. A disorder such as slavery (and a major objection of Leo XIII to slavery was that it produced unrest) was not to be corrected by force. Rather, action was to aim at ending the sin which caused the disorder. Thus in his encyclical on the abolition of certain kinds of slavery in Brazil, In plurimis, of May 5, 1888, Leo credited the Church with so successfully spreading the Gospel that manumission had come to these slaves. He went on:

> And this [the credit due the Church on the slavery issue] becomes still more apparent when we consider carefully how tenderly and with what prudence the Church has cut out and destroyed the dreadful curse of slavery. She has deprecated any precipitate action in securing the manumission of the slaves, because that would have entailed tumults and wrought injury, as well to the slaves themselves as to the commonwealth, but with singular wisdom she has seen that the minds of the slaves should be instructed through her discipline

178

in the Christian faith, and with baptism
should acquire habits suitable to the Christian life. Therefore, when among the slave
multitude whom she has numbered among her
children, some, led astray by the hope of
liberty, have recourse to violence and sedition, the Church has always condemned these
unlawful efforts and opposed them and through
her ministries has applied the remedy of patience. She taught the slaves to feel that,
by virtue of the light of the holy faith, and
the character they received from Christ, they
enjoyed a dignity which placed them above
their heathen lords; but that they were bound
all the more strictly by the author and found-
er of their faith never to set themselves up
against these lords, or even to be wanting in
the reverence and obedience due them.[26]

Thus Leo XIII not only condemned the use of violence by slaves desirous of freedom, but insisted
that the faith obliged them to respect and obey
their masters. This attitude on the part of Leo
is somewhat different from his injunctions to laborers. Both groups were forbidden the use of violence,
even against property.[27] But the slaves were forbidden any show of assertiveness which might con-
ceivably lead to violence, while laborers were, on
the contrary, allowed the right to strike.[28] In
Leo's day strike was almost synonymous with violence. In the eyes of many of Leo's audience the
parts of _Rerum novarum_ which forbid workers the use
of violence were severely undermined by the implicit permission to strike. The levels of assertiveness allowed to the two groups is thus very different, though in both instances assertiveness was
likely to lead to violence.

As we examine the teachings of the individual
twentieth century popes on Marxism and violence it

179

will become more apparent that <u>both</u> aspects of the papal tradition on violence are utilized. The popes condemn Marxism for its advocacy of class struggle and revolution because these cannot be legitimated by the just war theory. Yet in the very situations in which the popes of the twentieth century have explicitly or implicitly approved of violence using the just war theory (in Mexico, Hungary, Spain and against the USSR in World War II), the proposed violence was invariably aimed against Marxist forces.

Pius XI on Marxism

The five points we found in Leo's description of Marxism (atheism, refusal of obedience to authority based on equality, debasement of marriage, rejection of private property, and use of conflict and violence) are all present in the teaching of Pius XI on Marxism. Pius' objections to these points are not radically different from those of Leo. Nevertheless, there had been by this time some change in the papal perception of what these Marxist points entail. These shifts reflect two major changes between Leo's time and the situation in which Pius wrote: (1) the fact of the Russian revolution, which had provided a base for Marxist penetration of other countries, and (2) a substantial knowledge and experience of a particular kind of Marxism--Stalinism. The Russian revolution was a major event for the papacy in that it not only began wholesale persecution of the Church in Russia, but it provided a national base from which Marxism progressively spread to Catholic lands such as Spain and Mexico. The spread of Marxism during the twenties and the thirties was, moreover, the extension of one kind of Marxism--Stalinism. The kind of Marxism that became influential in Russia even before Lenin's death, during his illness of 1923, and dominated not only Russian policy but

180

international Marxist theory for decades thereafter
was Stalinist. When Pius XI wrote about Marxism he
wrote about Stalinist Marxism; he spoke out of total ignorance of at least some of the major Marxist
writings, for the writings of the young Marx were
unknown and unpublished until after Quadragesimo
anno. Even after 1931 the corpus of Marxist human-
ist writings was largely unknown until after World
War II except to a handful of European Marxist
scholars. During these decades Marxist meant Russian Marxist, and the Russian version was not only
Stalinist, but it claimed to be universally authoritative and applicable. It is therefore understandable that the conflictual and violent aspects
of Marxism assumed greater prominence for Pius XI
than for Leo XIII.

The very efforts of the Russians to foment revolution in Europe contributed to the increased
knowledge of Marxist principles by the people of
Europe. Pius XI clearly knew a great deal more of
Marxist writings and principles, even if largely
Stalinist, than had Leo XIII. In contrast to Leo,
Pius XI understood that violence and conflict were
not merely the result of the dangerous teachings of
the Marxists, but were actually viewed as the key
to history and the vehicle of progress. Pius XI
was able to connect (in a very rudimentary way) materialism, class struggle, and atheism, as he did
in the opening of Divini Redemptoris.

Even so, Pius XI's knowledge of Marxism was
not extensive for understandable reasons. Clearly
he did not comprehend some subtle Marxist points
such as the distinction between productive and non-
productive property. Neither was he clear about
the nature of Marxist materialism, as we shall see.
This apparent failure to comprehend Marxism is not
so surprising if one considers that idealism as an
emphasis upon ideas to the neglect of reality was

181

relatively unchallenged in papal thought until recently, and that the sheltered lives of the popes were not conducive to calling into question the conclusions of the traditional approach. This becomes more evident if we consider specific papal teaching.

Though all five of the Leonine objections to Marxism reappear in the teaching of Pius XI, the latter gave them differing emphases than did Leo. On one occasion he defined Marxism in terms of only two of the five points:

> Now communism teaches and pursues a twofold aim: class warfare and the complete abolition of private property.[29]

This apparent change in Pius' position over against Leo's is more a result of a change in the general political situation in which Pius wrote than of a change in papal perceptions of Marxism. Atheism, the debasement of marriage, and the egalitarian attack on obedience to all civil authority were no longer exclusively Marxist positions; these positions were well represented among the left of center parties and governments of the west. Since the general acceptance of egalitarianism and representative democracy in the West, suspicion of authority unsupported by the express consent of those from whom obedience was demanded had increased so as to become common. Also common to such democratic governments were guarantees of freedom of religion which protected atheism and severed marriage from religious control, thus allowing civil marriage and divorce.

In Ubi arcano[30] and Casti connubi[31] Pius XI repeated, in the main, Leo's condemnations of atheism, attacks on Christian marriage, and the doctrine of human equality. These aspects of the papal position

were still intact; the papal opponents had merely
been diversified by the addition of many non-Marx-
ists. Pius XI recognized this fact. The coming
of democratic forms to the West had involved the
eventual acceptance of what are commonly called
democratic freedoms: religious liberty, civil marriage and divorce, political and social rights for
women, and elective governments, all of which Pius
opposed to some degree.

Pius did write concerning his objections to
the Marxist view of marriage, reaffirming the sacramental nature of marriage which Marxists denied.
He insisted that marriage was indissoluble, contrary to the Marxist position, and objected in particular to civil marriage, divorce, and the emancipation of women, all of which were advocated by
Marxism. In Divini Redemptoris he characterized
the Marxist stance on marriage and woman thus:

> [in communism] There exists no matrimonial
> bond of a juridico-moral nature that is not
> subject to the whim of the individual or of
> the collectivity. Naturally, therefore, the
> notion of an indissoluble marriage-tie is
> scouted. Communism is particularly character-
> ized by the rejection of any link that binds
> woman to the family and the home, and her
> emancipation is proclaimed as a basic prin-
> ciple. She is withdrawn from the family and
> the care of her children, to be thrust instead
> into public life and collective production
> under the same conditions as man. The care
> of the home and children then devolves upon
> the collectivity.[32]

Pius XI felt that the state should treat marriage as
did the Church, adopting the Church regulations on
marriage.[33] One aspect of the Marxist treatment of
the family and marriage which seems to have greatly

concerned Pius XI was the emancipation of woman.
This was a position which was peculiarly Marxist
during his time, and Pius saw it as an attack on
the family and therefore on society, of which the
family was the basic unit. This topic will be
treated more fully in Chapter Five.

Perhaps the most basic flaw of Marxism for
Pius was its atheism, a more dogmatic atheism under
Stalin than under Lenin or even Marx. He maintained the "absolute necessity of God for human life."
The impossibility of either meaningful existence or
the solution of temporal disorder without belief in
God was fundamental for Pius. And for him theistic
affirmation was identified with acknowledgement of
and obedience to the Church as the representative
of Christ on earth:

> In the Holy Scripture we read: 'They that
> have forsaken the Lord shall be consumed.'
> (Isaias 1,28) No less well known are the
> words of the divine Teacher, Jesus Christ,
> who said: 'Without me you can do nothing.'
> (John xv,5) and again, 'He that gathereth not
> with me, scattereth.' (Luke xi,23)
>   These words of the Holy Bible have been
> fulfilled and are at this very moment being
> fulfilled before our very eyes. Because men
> have forsaken God and Jesus Christ, they have
> sunk to the very depths of evil. They waste
> their energies and consume their time and
> efforts in vain attempts to find a remedy for
> these ills, but without even being successful
> in saving what little remains from the exist-
> ing ruin. It was a quite general desire that
> both our laws and our governments should exist
> without recognizing God or Jesus Christ, on
> the theory that all authority comes from men
> and not from God. Because of such an assump-
> tion, these theorists fell very short of being

able to bestow upon law not only those sanc-
tions which it must possess but also that secure basis for the supreme criterion of justice that even the pagan philosopher, Cicero,
saw clearly could not be derived except from
the divine law. Authority itself lost its
hold upon mankind, for it had lost that sound
and unquestionable justification for its right
to command on the one hand and to be obeyed on
the other hand. Society, quite logically and
inevitably, was shaken to its very depths and
even threatened with destruction, since there
was left to it no stable foundation, everything having been reduced to a series of conflicts, to the domination of the majority, or
to the supremacy of special interests.[34]

.   .   .   .   .

It is apparent from these considerations
that true peace, the peace of Christ, is impossible unless we are willing and ready to
accept the fundamental principles of Christianity, unless we are willing to observe the
teachings and obey the law of Christ, both in
public and in private life. If this were done,
then society being placed at last on a sound
foundation, the Church would be able, in the
exercise of its divinely given ministry and by
means of the teaching authority which results
therefrom, to protect all the rights of God
over men and nations.[35]

Atheism was responsible for a great loss of souls,
and for a lack of efficacy in human efforts to reform the world. But for Pius XI, an equally serious aspect was the lack of respect atheism engen-
dered for all authority, not only divine, but civil
and ecclesiastical as well. This lack of respect
for authority he viewed as the root of disorder in
society, the cause for further loss of souls, and
an obstacle to the spread of the Gospel.

In _Divini Redemptoris_, which concerns the
Russian context, Pius XI considered atheism and
Marxism as synonymous. In this encyclical on com-
munism he wrote:

> During Our Pontificate We, too, have fre-
> quently and with urgent insistence denounced
> the current trend to atheism which is alarm-
> ingly on the increase. In 1924 when Our re-
> lief mission returned from the Soviet Union
> We condemned communism in a special allocu-
> tion which We addressed to the whole world.
> In Our encyclicals, _Miserentissimus Redemptor_,
> _Quadragesimo anno_, _Caritate Christi_, _Acerba_
> _animi_, _Dilectissimo Nobis_ We raised a solemn
> protest against the persecutions unleashed in
> Russia, in Mexico, and now in Spain. Our two
> allocutions of last year, the first on the
> occasion of the opening of the International
> Catholic Press Exposition, and the second dur-
> ing Our audience to the Spanish refugees, a-
> long with Our message of last Christmas, have
> evoked a world wide echo which is not yet
> spent. In fact, the most persistent enemies
> of the Church, who from Moscow are directing
> the struggle against Christian civilization,
> themselves bear witness, by their increasing
> attacks in word and act, that even to this
> hour the Papacy has continued faithfully to
> uphold the sanctuary of the Christian reli-
> gion, and that it has called public attention
> to the perils of communism more frequently and
> more effectively than any other public author-
> ity on earth.[36]

Here as elsewhere, Pius XI not only equated atheism
and Marxism, but he assumed an interconnection between atheism and attacks on the Church and Christian civilization.

Pius seemed unable to attribute any other

motive to the persecution of the Church than atheistic materialism. Though in other contexts he
did refer to the charge of the Marxists that the
Church was ranged against the cause of the poor
and workers (a charge he then refuted by reference
to the social teaching of the Church[37]), he never
appeared to grasp the functionalist critique of
religion used by the Marxists. That the Church
operated on the basis of a political ideology was
incomprehensible to Pius XI; his response was always to refer to the importance of the poor to
Christ, and to the Church's urging of charity and
justice. That the effect of limiting Church activity to such teaching was to leave the political and
economic structures intact, and in essence to support them, simply did not occur to him.

In the above passage cited from <u>Divini</u> <u>Redemp-</u>
<u>toris</u> Pius also mentioned the Marxist persecutions
against the Church in Mexico, Spain and Russia.[38]
During his pontificate Pius wrote two apostolic
letters and two encyclicals concerning the situation in Mexico. The encyclicals were <u>Iniquis</u> <u>af-</u>
<u>flictisque</u> (November 18, 1926) and <u>Acerba</u> <u>animo</u>
(September 29, 1932). The apostolic letters were
<u>Paterna</u> <u>sane</u> <u>solicitudo</u> (February 2, 1926) and
<u>Firmissimam</u> <u>constantiam</u> (March 28, 1937). These
accounts of the situation in Mexico, though they
make little overt reference to Marxism,[39] clearly
implied (as did <u>Divini</u> <u>Redemptoris</u>) that the events
and upheavals there were the result of the presence
of Marxism.

In the apostolic letter <u>Firmissimam</u> <u>constanti-</u>
<u>am</u>, which was addressed to the Catholic Action
hierarchy in Mexico, Pius XI set out the conditions
for the use of violence in this controversy.

Pius reminded the hierarchy that the Church
has protected peace and order, condemning "unjust
insurrection or violence against constituted

powers." But he noted the bishops had remarked that "whenever these powers arise against justice and the truth" citizens can legitimately unite to defend themselves and the nation. Pius insisted that in so acting resistence must be a means not an end, that the means must not be intrinsically evil, and must not cause greater damage to the common good. He stipulated that clergy and leadership of Catholic Action not exercise political rights in their fullness ("embracing also problems of order purely material and technical, or of violent response") since they are consecrated to uniting all, and must contribute to the prosperity of all.[40]

This passage appears to have reversed the previous papal refusal to approve any use of violence by one group in a society against the constituted order. But though this passage and other papal writings on the Mexican situation afford us papal teaching which approaches such a reversal, Pius did not view his position as outside the papal tradition. That he did not is doubtless due in some part to the papal dislike of innovation, and abhorrence of reversals in papal teaching. But more than that, the situation within Mexico was not one which the assumptions of the just war theory presupposed. At least in Pius' view, there had been no legitimate government in Mexico since the 1911 revolution. From that time until 1924, occupation of the office of president depended upon the success of the army at one's back, and even after that time control of the army was the surest means of being elected. Calles, who was president from 1924-28, continued to control Mexico until 1934 through his ability to put his puppets into the presidency. These years were dominated by continuing revolution and bloodshed, suppressed civil liberties, open graft and profiteering in the government.[41]

The chief reason for Pius' dissatisfaction with the state of affairs in Mexico was the savage

anticlerical campaign which began with the 1911 revolution and intensified after 1917.[42] For Pius,
the continuation and intensification of anticlericalism were due to the continuation of the revolution which had given birth to Mexican anticlericalism. Since from his viewpoint the revolution as a
revolution was illegitimate in the first place,
continuing revolutionary governments were also illegitimate. This illegitimacy, coupled with the
fact that Pius viewed the Marxist element in Mexico
as the result of foreign intervention (by Moscow),
made it seem to Pius XI that approving the right of
Catholics to take a stand for order amidst the
chaos that existed within Mexico surely stood within the traditional teaching. The similarity of the
limitations put on the use of violence in <u>Firmissi-</u>
<u>mam constantiam</u> and in the just war theory cannot
be co-incidental. Pius XI may neither have intended to break nor recognize that he broke new ground
in approving violence internal to a nation in the
Mexican situation. Yet this action of his was a
transition on the way to the stand later taken by
Paul VI in <u>Populorum progressio</u>. Paul's step assumes much more importance because Paul's implicit
approval of violence in some limited situations was
given not only within the national context, but on
the side of <u>leftist</u> movements. The Mexican situation was such that here papal approval of limited
violence was given to a rightist, anti-revolutionary movement, and was, as such, not a shift from
the anti-revolutionary tradition.

     The role of violence, especially in the form
of class struggle, was commonly linked to atheism
in Pius XI's teaching. In <u>Divini Redemptoris</u> he
discussed atheism (in terms of materialism) and
class struggle as follows:

     The doctrine of modern communism, which is
     often concealed under the most seductive
     trappings, is in substance based on the prin-

189

ciples of dialectical and historical material-
sm previously advocated by Marx, of which the
theoreticians of Bolshevism claim to possess
the only genuine interpretation. . . . In
such a doctrine, as is evident, there is no
room for the idea of God; there is no difference between matter and spirit, between soul
and body; there is neither survival of the
soul after death, nor any hope in a future
life. Insisting on the dialectical nature of
their materialism the communists claim that
the conflict which carries the world toward
its final synthesis can be accelerated by
man. Hence they endeavor to sharpen the an-
tagonisms which arise between the various
classes of society. Thus class struggle with
its consequent violent hate and destruction
takes on the aspect of a crusade for the progress of humanity. On the other hand, all
other forces whatsoever, as long as they resist such systemic violence, must be annihi-
lated as hostile to the human race.[43]

Pius here ignored the distinction that Marxist
theory makes between persons and other material
entities, and ignored as well Marx's insistence
that the earth should be ordered to the fulfillment of human life. Though Pius recognized that
the Marxists claimed that human effort could successfully accelerate the conflict and its resolution, he nevertheless saw Marxism as completely
determinist. He failed to recognize that the professed goal of Marxian conflict was a society in
which freely chosen activity became the way to the
self-creation of truly human persons. It is possible that the use of a new terminology, and re-
vulsion for the proposed vehicle of change (conflict) obscured for Pius whatever degree of agreement might have been reached with Marxist theory
concerning the direction in which human society

190

should develop. But it is even more likely that, given the Church persecution and terrorism in communist Russia, Pius was not open to finding any utility in Marxist theory.

Pius XI's description of class struggle implies that conflict and violence are synonymous, and that class struggle inevitably leads to "violent hate and destruction." Underlying this discussion is the implication that atheism is the root of the violence; later in Divini Redemptoris (paragraphs 20 and 21) this relation is claimed more explicitly:

Even where the scourge of communism has not yet had time enough to exercise to the full its logical effect, as witness our beloved Spain, it has, alas, found compensation in the fiercer violence of its attack. Not only this or that Church or isolated monastery was sacked, but as far as possible every Church and every monastery was destroyed. Every vestige of the Christian religion was eradicated, even though intimately linked with the rarest monuments of art and science! The fury of communism has not confined itself to the indiscriminate slaughter of bishops, of thousands of priests and religious of both sexes; it searches out above all those who have been devoting their lives to the welfare of the working classes and the poor. But the majority of its victims have been laymen of all classes and conditions. Even up to the present moment, masses of them are slain almost daily for no other offense than that they are good Christians or at least opposed to Atheistic Communism. And this fearful destruction has been carried out with a hatred and a savage barbarity one would not have believed possible in our day. No man of good sense, nor any statesman conscious of his responsibility can

191

fail to shudder at the thought of what is happening today in Spain may perhaps be repeated tomorrow in other civilized countries.

Nor can it be said that these atrocities are a transitory phenomenon, the usual accompaniment of all great revolutions, the isolated excesses common to every war. No, they are the natural fruit of a system which lacks all inner restraint. Some restraint is necessary for man considered either as an individual or in society. Even the barbaric peoples had this inner check in the natural law written by God in the heart of every man. And where this natural law was held in higher esteem, ancient nations rose to a grandeur that still fascinates--more than it should--certain artificial students of human history. But tear away the very idea of God from the hearts of men, and they are necessarily urged by their passions to the most atrocious barbarity.[44]

The use of such violence will be, Pius declared, the downfall of Marxism, for no social or economic order can be based on conflict:

But the law of nature and its Author cannot be flouted with impunity. Communism has not been able, and will not be able, to achieve its objectives even in the merely economic sphere. . . . After all, even the sphere of economics needs some morality, some moral sense of responsibility, which can find no place in a system so thoroughly materialistic as Communism. Terrorism is the only possible substitute, and it is terrorism that reigns today in Russia, where former comrades in revolution are exterminating each other. Terrorism having failed despite all to stem the tide of moral corruption, cannot even prevent the dissolution of society itself.[45]

In this passage we see the reasoning behind Pius' rejection of a socialist option, even as distinguished from a communist one. For Pius the inevitable end of basing a social system on conflict will be total terrorism and the dissolution of society. But Pius' attack on the doctrine of class struggle did not end here. He even went so far as to attribute the Russian armament program to the doctrine of class struggle:

> Thus, aware of the universal desire for peace, the leaders of communism pretend to be the most zealous promoters and propagandists in the movement for world amity. Yet at the same time they stir up a class warfare that causes the rivers of blood to flow, and realizing that their system offers no internal guarantee of peace, they have recourse to unlimited armaments.[46]

There are two questionable assumptions here. The first is that the rest of the world was sincerely interested in peace, and that only the Russian communists were insincere about wishing for peace. The second is that the Russian armament program was intentionally offensive. Pius totally ignored the Russian claim that a strong defensive military capability was necessary in the light of the historic western hostility to the USSR as manifest in the Allied expeditionary force sent against the Bolsheviks at the end of the first World War, and in the more recent arming by those European fascist powers pledged to the elimination of communism.

Similarly, in the Mexican situation when Pius condemned the specific laws and actions he viewed as anti-Church it did not occur to him that Mexi-

cans might have any cause for hostility to the
Church. The natural hostility of Mexican nation-
alists for a Church dominated by foreign clergy,
controlled out of Europe, tied not only to colonialist powers but to the landed powers within Mexico itself--all of this was incomprehensible to
Pius XI. To reject or attack the Church in any
way was to reject or attack God; the notion of a
possible legitimate cause for such action was in-
conceivable to him. That the wealth of the Church
(the confiscation of which he condemned) might be
resented and contribute to the political agitation
against the Church did not, evidently, occur to
Pius. This was God's property.

The clearest example of this inability to understand the hostility of Marxists appears in
paragraph 36 of <u>Divini Redemptoris</u>:

> But the enemies of the Church, though forced
> to acknowledge the wisdom of her doctrine,
> accuse her of having failed to act in con-
> formity with her principles, and from this
> conclude the necessity of seeking other solu-
> tions. The utter falseness and injustice of
> this accusation is shown by the whole history
> of Christianity. To refer only to a single
> typical trait, it was Christianity which first
> affirmed the real and universal brotherhood of
> all men of whatever race and condition. This
> doctrine she proclaimed by a method, and with
> an amplitude and conviction, unknown to pre-
> ceding centuries; and with it she potently
> contributed to the abolition of slavery. Not
> bloody revolution, but the inner force of her
> teaching made the proud Roman matron see in
> her slave a sister in Christ.[47]

In this passage Pius used the same understanding

of the Church that we observed in Chapter Two:
the Church is a teacher, and her action is teaching. If her principles promote justice, equality
and dignity, then, for Pius XI, the Church was on
the side of justice, whatever her institutional
impact. He did not separate the doctrine of the
Church from her personnel or from their political
ties and loyalties with regard to nation or class.
For Pius these latter were not in question; the
Church, identified with Christianity itself, was
her verbal teaching.

Similarly, it was almost impossible for Pius
XI to look beyond the persecution of the Church to
the situation and perceptions of the Marxist groups
and nations. The work of the Church was the only
hope for the solution of the problems of the world
for Pius; hence, he was unable to consider any progress which did not begin with the Church, or to
recognize the validity of hostility to any aspect
of her work:

> At the same time the State must allow the
> Church full liberty to fulfill her divine and
> spiritual mission, and this in itself will be
> an effectual contribution to the rescue of
> the nations from the dread torment of the
> present hour. Everywhere today there is an
> anxious appeal to moral and spiritual forces;
> and rightly so, for the evil we must combat
> is at its origin primarily an evil of the
> spiritual order. From this polluted source
> the monstrous emanations of the Communist
> system flow with Satanic logic. Now the
> Catholic Church is undoubtedly pre-eminent
> among the moral and religious forces of to-
> day. Therefore the very good of humanity
> demands that her work be allowed to proceed
> unhindered.[48]

For Pius XI, the essentiality of the Church to any improvement in the world, caused him to consistently label Marxist (atheist) programs and promises as delusive propaganda:

> The Communism of today, more emphatically than similar movements in the past, conceals in itself a false messianic idea. A pseudo-ideal of justice, of equality, and of fraternity in labor impregnates all its doctrines and activity with a deceptive mysticism, which communicates a zealous and contagious enthusiasm to the multitudes entrapped by delusive promises. This is especially true in an age like ours, when unusual misery has resulted from the unequal distribution of the goods of the world. This pseudo-ideal is even advanced as if it were responsible for a certain progress. As a matter of fact, when such progress is at all real, its true causes are quite different, as for instance the intensification of industrialism in countries which were formerly without it, the exploitation of immense natural resources, and the use of the most brutal methods to insure the achievement of gigantic projects with a minimum of expense.[49]

One of the most complex charges Pius XI made against Marxism concerned its denial of human rights. This is an interesting charge to examine today:

> Communism, moreover, strips man of his liberty, robs human personality of all its dignity, and removes all the moral restrictions that check the eruptions of blind impulse. There is no recognition of any right of the individual in his relations to the collectivity; no natural right is accorded

to human personality, which is a mere cog-
wheel in the Communist system. In man's relations with other individuals, besides, Communists hold the principle of absolute equality, rejecting all hierarchy and divinely
constituted authority, including the authority of parents. What men call authority and
subordination is derived from the community
as its first and only font. Nor is the individual granted any property rights over material goods or the means of production, for
inasmuch as these are the source of further
wealth, their possession would give one man
power over another. Precisely on this score,
all forms of private property must be eradicated, for they are the origin of all economic enslavement.

Refusing to human life any sacred or
spiritual character, such a doctrine logically makes of marriage and the family a purely
artificial and civil institution, the outcome
of a specific economic system. There exists
no matrimonial bond of a juridico-moral nature that is not subject to the whim of the
individual or the collectivity. Naturally,
therefore, the notion of an indissoluble
marriage-tie is scouted. . . . Finally the
right of education is denied to parents, for
it is conceived as the exclusive prerogative
of the community, in whose name and by whose
mandate alone parents may exercise this
right.[50]

Here Pius XI not only denounced the denial of
rights he considered fundamental, but condemned as
perversions the rights asserted by Marxism: communal education of children, communal child care,
absolute equality of all, and communal use of material goods. Charges of human rights violations
were as common against the communists of Pius' day

as they are in our own. The most common charges--
the denial of freedom to worship, freedoms of
speech and the press, the right to participate in
government--are not mentioned by Pius. Although
these, too, characterized the regime he was criti-
cizing, Pius could not take an accusatory stance
with regard to them because he, too, opposed all
of these rights to some degree. Instead, he
criticized Marxism's denial of the right to control productive property, to control production,
and to determine the education of one's children.

There can be little surprise at the fact that
Pius XI's conclusion concerning Marxism in Quadragesimo anno was that it was completely opposed to
Christian principles, and therefore forbidden to
Catholics. In separately examining socialism and
communism and their relationship to Christian
principles, Pius wrote of socialism:

> If, like all errors, socialism contains a
> certain element of truth, (and this the Sov-
> ereign Pontiffs have never denied) it is
> nevertheless founded upon a doctrine of hu-
> man society peculiarly its own, which is
> opposed to true Christianity. 'Religious
> socialism,' 'Christian socialism,' are ex-
> pressions implying a contradiction in terms.
> No one can be at the same time a sincere
> Catholic and a true socialist.[51]

In a consideration of communism and its relation
to Christianity Pius left no doubt that communism
was even more anathema, if possible, than socialism.[52] This was the general message of every passage of Divini Redemptoris, six years later.

It is in this context--the argument that all
forms of Marxism are irreconcilable with Christi-
anity--that Pius discussed what would be important

198

themes in later papal teaching. He differentiated
different forms of Marxism, and he began a discussion as to the relationship between a movement and
its ideology. Of the split in the Marxist ranks
he said:

> No less profound than the change in the
> general economy has been the development oc-
> curing within socialism since the days when
> Leo XIII contended with the latter. At that
> time socialism could be termed a single sys-
> tem, generally speaking, and one which de-
> fended definite and coherent doctrines. To-
> day, indeed, it has, for the most part, split
> into two opposing and hostile camps. Neither
> of them, however, has abandoned socialism's
> fundamental principles, which do not accord
> with Christian belief.[53]

Quadragesimo anno then discussed the differences between socialism and communism. This discussion was preparatory to the papal answer to the
question whether it is ever legitimate to separately judge a historical movement in distinction
from the ideology which gave rise to it. The difference between movement and ideology had been
suggested, Pius said, as a rationale for approving
collaboration with the socialists.[54] In his examination of the differences between communism and
socialism Pius implied that the real difference
between the two was the degree of violence sanctioned by each. Communism, said Pius, does not
hesitate to use the most violent of methods to
promote merciless class warfare and the abolition
of private property, and shows itself cruel and
inhuman when in power. Socialism, he said, is
less radical in its views, condemning physical
force and moderating class warfare and abolition
of private property. Its programs often resemble
Christian social teaching, and "it may well come

about that gradually the tenets of mitigated socialism will no longer be different from those who
seek to reform human society according to Christian principles."[55]

In examining Pius' discussion of class warfare it is important to note that Pius did not
challenge the reality of different classes in society, nor did he deny that their interests were
opposed (at least in the short-term, material
sense).[56] Considering the world of 1931 in which
Pius wrote, we must acknowledge the affirmation
of class society in which class interests were
opposed as a significant move in itself. Class
divisions are still not universally recognized
today; in Pius' day such recognition was a radically leftist affirmation. It is, after all, over
fifty years since Quadragesimo anno, and quite
easy with hindsight to criticize Pius for not taking one step further, the affirmation of class
struggle.

In his consideration of class warfare Pius
made it clear that he shared the Leonine view of
a harmonious world in which justice and love both
preserved peace and required peace and order in
order to flourish. But Pius was forced by his
times to acknowledge that the existence of labor
unions had not rectified the injustice which characterized the worker's lot. The need for continued organization and political action was ongoing
because the material interests of workers and employers were directly opposed, and existing power
was vested in the employers.[57]

Though Pius acknowledged the existence of
classes and their opposing interests he did not
accept this situation readily:

Now this is a major and pressing duty of

200

the State and of all good citizens: to get
rid of the conflict between 'classes' with
divergent interests, and to foster and promote harmony between the various 'ranks' or
groupings of society.

.   .   .   .   .

Labor, indeed, as has been well said by
Our Predecessor in His Encyclical, is not a
mere chattel, and since the human dignity of
the workingman must be recognized in it, and
consequently it cannot be bought and sold
like any other piece of merchandise. None
the less the demand and supply of labor di-
vides men on the labor market into two classes, as into two camps, and the bargaining between these parties transforms this labor
market into an arena where the two armies are
arranged in combat. To this grave disorder
which is leading society to ruin a remedy
must evidently be applied as speedily as possible. But there cannot be a question of any
perfect cure, except this opposition be done
away with, and well ordered members of the
social body come into being: functional
'groups,' namely, binding men together not
according to the position they occupy in the
labor market, but according to the diverse
functions which they exercise in society.
For as nature induces those who dwell in
close proximity to unite into municipalities,
so those who practice the same profession or
trade, economic or otherwise, constitute, as
it were, fellowships or bodies.[58]

This passage illustrates Pius XI's continuing reluctance to accept the fact that conflict is a
fundamental aspect of societies with inequality of
wealth, status, and opportunity. It did not seem
to occur to Pius that even without workers' resentment of owners making profit on their labor,

if these workers joined forces within each industry, there would still be conflict between these
groups and others because capitalist society is
built upon competition for profit.

Pius' text continued with the subject of order in society, and his next assertions are even
more revealing as to his underlying presuppositions:

> Order, as the Angelic Doctor well defines,
> is unity arising from the apt arrangement of
> a plurality of objects; hence, true and genu-
> ine social order demands various members of
> society, joined together in a common bond.
> Such a bond of union is provided on the one
> hand by the common effort of employers and
> employees of one and the same 'group' joining
> forces to produce goods or give service, and
> on the other hand, by the common good which
> all 'groups' should unite to promote, each in
> its own sphere, with friendly harmony. Now
> this union will become powerful and efficaci-
> ous in proportion to the fidelity with which
> the individuals and the 'groups' strive to
> discharge their professional duties and to
> excel in them.[59]

Underlying Pius' argument here there appears to be
an assumption that what makes Marxism blameworthy
is not that it recognizes class conflict but that
it exaccerbates this conflict as the key to progress in history rather than seeking to minimize
it.[60] Pius could not find such a view acceptable
because he defined order in a static manner and
assumed that order was the normal state of human
society, as had Thomas Aquinas. Pius supposed
that the "apt arrangement" of any given moment was
permanent. He maintained that the conflict should
be lessened as much as possible by an acceptance

of "the perfect order which the Church preaches"[61]
and by the use of charity.[62]

The most conclusive statements of Pius XI
concerning Marxism and its possible relation to
members of the Church appear at the end of the
section of Quadragesimo anno, where he is discussing the widening gulf between the socialist and
the communist camp:

> For it is rightly demanded that certain forms
> of property must be reserved to the state,
> since they carry with them an opportunity of
> domination too great to be left to private
> individuals without injury to the community
> at large.
>   Just demands of this kind contain nothing
> opposed to Christian truth, nor are they in
> any sense peculiar to socialism. Those there-
> fore who look for nothing else, have no reason
> for becoming socialists.[63]

Yet this decision concerning the present suffici-
ency of Christian social principles and consequent
superfluity of Marxism was not Pius' last word on
the subject. While he admitted that socialism
seemed to be becoming innocuous, he both maintained
that it would never be completely innocuous because
of its origin, and that even were some socialist
platforms to take up Christian principles, there
was no reason to split the unity of the Catholic
bloc to support socialism.

> Now, when false principles are thus mitigated
> and in some sense waived, the question arises,
> or is it unwarrantedly proposed in certain
> quarters, whether the principles of Christian
> truth also could not be somewhat moderated
> and attenuated, as it were, so as to meet
> socialism halfway upon common ground. Some

are engaged by the empty hope of gaining in
this way the socialists to our cause. But
such hopes are vain. Those who wish to be
apostles among the socialists should preach
the Christian truth whole and entire, openly
and sincerely, without any connivance with
error. If they wish in truth to be heralds
of the gospel, let their endeavor be to con-
vince socialists that their demands, in so
far as they are just, are defended much more
cogently by the principles of the Christian
faith, and are promoted more efficaciously
by the power of Christian charity.

But what if, in questions of class war
and private ownership, socialism were to become so mitigated and amended, that nothing
reprehensible could any longer be found in
it? Would it by that very fact have laid
aside its character of hostility to the
Christian religion? This is a question which
holds many minds in suspense; and many are
the Catholics, who, realizing clearly that
Christian principles can never be either
sacrificed or minimized, seem to be raising
their eyes toward the Holy See, and earnestly
beseeching Us to decide whether or not this
form of socialism has retracted so far its
false doctrines that it can now be accepted
without the loss of Christian principle, and
be baptized into the Church. In Our fatherly
solicitude We desire to satisfy these peti-
tions and We pronounce as follows: whether
socialism be considered as a doctrine, or as
a historical fact, or as a 'movement,' if it
really remains socialism, it cannot be brought
into harmony with the dogmas of the Catholic
Church, even after it has yielded to truth
and justice in the points We have mentioned;
the reason being that it conceives human society in a way utterly alien to Christian

truth.[64]

Pius XI, then, said that no separation shall be
made between a movement and the ideology which
gave it birth. If the ideology is unacceptable,
so must the movement be, no matter how far it
stands temporally and in terms of program from its
origins. This was an important pronouncement, not
only for its effect at this point in European politics, but also because it set up the argument for
John's later reconsideration.

Pius XII

We recall that Pius XII did not articulate
any major social teaching in general; neither did
he write any major teaching documents on Marxism.
However, he did often incorporate either warnings
about or condemnations of Marxism in many of his
addresses and letters. Since the Church's opposition to all forms of Marxism had been fully publi-
cized by his predecessor, Catholics knew that any
collaboration with, much less membership in, Marxist groups was forbidden. For the most part Pius
XII limited himself to the issuance of reminders
of the irreconcilable differences at stake, of
Marxist cruelty and deception, and of Marxism's
insidious propaganda techniques. Nor was his discussion of Marxism in any sense systematic. His
comments related more to the political events of
the day than to any consideration of Marxist
theory.

A major concern of Pius XII's was materialism.
In addressing this subject, Pius spoke of two aspects. First, he identified the source of materialism as Marxism.[65] In a passage on Marxism in
Les paroles si élevées Pius even used the term
"militant materialism" as a synonym for Russian
Marxism:

The bitter experiences of the past century
should be enough to explain this. Were not
promises of a technically and economically
perfect world made then as they are now?
Did they not lead to cruel disillusion? The
social upheavals brought about by the application of science in a spirit that was too
often materialistic ruined the existing order
without replacing it with a better or stronger one.

. . . . .

Slogans like 'national unity' and 'social
progress' should not deceive us. For militant materialism, 'peacetime' means only a
truce, a precarious truce during which it
awaits the social and economic collapse of
other peoples.[66]

Similarly, in Pius XII's letter to Cardinals
Mindzenty, Stepinac, and Wynszynski, Dum maerenti
animo, June 29, 1956, he attributed the persecution of the Church in Eastern Europe to the ascen-
dency of "atheistic materialism."[67]

The second aspect of materialism which Pius
addressed was the danger that materialism posed
in the West. Pius indicated that excessive attachment to goods of this world distracted one
from what was truly valuable (God) and thus tended
to produce atheism.[68] He especially warned those
who support programs for more equal distribution
of worldly goods:

Individuals and whole nations have allowed themselves to be led astray by God's enemies, because the latter have promised a better distribution of material goods and proclaimed that they desired to preserve liberty
and protect the family. They assure their
dupes that eventually the people will seize

206

power, the workmen will own the factories, and the peasants will own land.

But on the contrary, when they come to power after sowing hatred, subversion, and fomenting discord, they actually impoverish the people and initiate a reign of terror. What is happening these days to the sorely tried Hungarian people is bloody evidence of the extremes to which those who hate God are prepared to go.[68]

Pius proposed that the danger materialism posed to the West was directly linked to the materialism of the Russian communists, and that western materialism could be viewed as an advance guard of Marxism. In this discussion of materialism, Pius apparently failed to distinguish capitalist materialism from the doctrine of Marxist materialism. This is not to deny that excessive attachment to human products (capitalist materialism) was operative in Russian society. But the doctrine of Marxist materialism, to which Pius often referred, was directly opposed to the granting of power over human persons to products (material goods). Pius seems to have equated Marxist concern for conditions of human life with just such an elevation of products over human beings, and therefore he did not take seriously the purported goals of the Marxist program--to free human beings from the control of human products.

Pius XII also took up the theme of totalitarianism in many speeches. He lost few opportunities to condemn the over-planned economy in which no personal or family freedoms were allowed.[70] Like Pius XI, who had condemned the Russian system for its overplanning and consequent denial of freedom, Pius XII insisted that such totalitarian determinism would never prove successful even in the economic realm, because it was contrary to both God and human nature.

In Pius XII's first encyclical he wrote of the errors and terrors afflicting society. He warned against "the error contained in those ideas which do not hesitate to divorce civil authority from every kind of dependence upon the Supreme Being. . . ."[71] In this connection he attacked the idea that the state is ultimate, and that to it all else should be subordinated. He added that the state direction of private enterprise may be to the detriment of the common good.[72] But Pius' strongest objection to Marxism was that one of its consequences was damage to the family, especially to the family's right to oversee and control the education of children.[73]

In an address to Christian workers on May 1, 1955, Pius XII substantially repeated the conclusion of Pius XI concerning the Marxist attack on the Church's attitudes toward workers:

> How many times have we declared and explained the love of the Church for the working classes? Yet the malicious calumny that 'the Church is aligned with capitalism against the workingman' is widespread. The Church, Mother and Teacher of all men, has always been especially solicitous of those of her children who are in less fortunate circumstances. She has, in fact, contributed greatly to the genuine progress already made by various groups of workers. We Ourselves, in Our Christmas message of 1942, declared that 'the Church, impelled always by religious motives, has condemned the various systems of Marxist Socialism and continues to condemn them today, because it is both her duty and her enduring right to protect mankind from every trend and every influence

which jeopardizes its eternal salvation.'[74]

The progress of communism among the working classes of Italy after the Second World War prompted many of Pius XII's references to Marxism. In his address _E'ancora vivo_ Pius referred to the May Day address above. He implied that Marxism consciously manipulates the hopes and desires of workers for rights and dignity in order to destroy their faith and gain their support. The presupposition that the attacks on the Marxists on the Church are attacks on the faith underlies this entire passage, in the style of Pius XI:

> On the first day of May of this year . . . the thought came to Us that surely something new was in the air, something clear and palpable for all that group [of workers]. Indeed, something had happened. The world of those who more than any others needed defense --both juridically and socially--until they gained greater awareness of their dignity as men and saw many of their rights gradually come to be recognized, was none the less the victim of a cunning and divisive activity on the part of men eager to deceive the workers with false promises and pledged to draw them away from the practice of their faith and even to destroy that faith.[75]

This address, however, went on to reject materialism and to imply a rejection of class struggle and support for a program of gradualism, "not based on hatred or that which, caring only for the material life, ignores or denies what is more excellent, the life of the soul."[76]

It is interesting that it did not occur to Pius that souls might be going to their ruin because of the "social problem" in that it was human beings who were responsible for it, as well as human beings with souls who were deformed by the consequent injustice. Instead, Pius poses the possible loss of souls which he feels would result from an immediate attack on social injustice as the reason for advocating gradualism. In this same connection, he went on to deny that there was any just cause for the opposition of Marxists to the Church:

> Deceived by a malicious propaganda--and how mistaken they [workers] are--that the Church which loves them so tenderly wishes to obstruct them in their progress toward a just improvement of their lot. They fear to approach her and they fear to leave that, which, on the contrary, cannot truly wish their good if it destroys in them peace with God, if it turns love into hatred, and action, appropriate and just for the defense of one's own rights, into a bitter struggle.[77]

Pius maintained that the Church does act in the world to end the injustice against the worker:

> For this reason the Church does not limit itself to appeals for a more just social order, but points out clearly the fundamental principles upon which it might be based. The Church urges the rulers of the nations, their legislators, employers and management to put these principles into practice.[78]

This approach is, we note, the traditional interpretation of the Church's task. This response was a further indication of papal inability to distinguish the Church's doctrine and teaching from both her personnel and the social praxis of the institution which results from the ideological and political leanings of that personnel. Christian

210

doctrine for Pius XII <u>was</u> the Church.

On the other side, however, it should be noted that the Church's enemy, Marxism, did not challenge this understanding of the nature of the Church. Because the Church had, in the view of Marxists, allied herself with the ruling classes and taught the workers to passively wait for the rewards of the next life, the Marxists totally dismissed not only the institution but the entirety of Christianity as well. For Marxism until recent days, there has been <u>no</u> truth or worth to Christianity.

Pius XII did not concentrate on the issue of class struggle to the extent that Pius XI had, or at least not in the same way. The gradual improvement in the lot of many workers had ameliorated some former injustices, so the danger of violent uprising through the preaching of class struggle was considered to have abated.[79] Pius spoke more often of the division between employers and employees, the privileged and the needy.[80] However, this present division of society into economically opposed groups was considered neither natural nor normative by Pius XII. His position was a complex one. He insisted that great discrepancies in wealth between classes produced enmity, but also maintained that inequality was both natural and inevitable.[81] Evidently he assumed that the existence of classes did not indicate necessary social unrest and that neither the wage system nor the organizational structure produced such unrest. The unrest and disruptions were rather the result of the hatred and agitation preached by the Marxists in response to world injustice:[82]

An erroneous doctrine affirms that you, the representatives of labor, and you, the

211

owners of capital, are compelled, by what
might be called a natural law, to fight each
other, cruelly and implacably, and that only
by this means and at this price can industrial peace be obtained. . . .[83]

Pius XII rejected not only the violence which
he believed was fomented by the Marxist interpretation of class struggle, but the conflictual
model of society itself:

How could these organizations [trade unions]
dare to claim that they serve the cause of
peace within a country, when, to defend the
interests of their members, they do not seek
the application of the rules of law and the
common good, but lean instead on the organized force of members?[84]

In a similar context he said:

justice and recovery are to be found, not in
revolution (which proceeds by way of injustice and civil uproar) but in change in a
spirit of harmony.[85]

Pius XII believed that the overall social objective was the union of classes. This union, he
insisted, would be accomplished not through the
elimination of any class or classes, but by preserving the various class distinctions and unify-
ing the diverse social elements: "The Church has
not for an instant renounced its struggle to see
that the apparent opposition between capital and
labor, employers and employees, is merged into a
higher unity, an organic collaboration such as
nature itself commends."[86] The union of classes
was to be built upon the reinstitution of justice
into social and economic relationships. Pius XII
recognized that this justice was lacking, and that

its absence was a major initial cause of present
conflict between classes. The restoration of justice, he assumed, would minimize the differences
in wealth between classes and pave the way for
unity. Either Pius did not consider, or was not
persuaded, that class divisions were not merely
marks of cultural diversity but also divisions of
power which prevented those deprived of justice
from achieving it. When Pius used the term "justice" in this context he employed the traditional
sense of equity proportional to social status, an
idea of justice radically different from the
Marxist notion. Christian charity was to accompany this proportional equity in sufficient degree
to bring about the union of classes.

This idea of a union of classes is an obvious
illustration of the papal harmony model of society.
Pius XII, like Pius XI before him, recognized the
need for workers to organize. He also perceived
that the restoration of justice would be a struggle, though his reliance on evangelizing the world
as the way to restore that justice tended to mini-
mize/eliminate the conflictual aspects. There is
no sense in which he visualized both the enormity
of the struggle for justice and the ongoing (permanent) aspect of that struggle. He constantly
spoke of the need to "restore" justice. This is
the source of his discomfort with Marxism's idea
of working for a system of social justice through
ever present conflict in history. Despite all
Pius' pessimism concerning the sinfulness of human nature, he could not accept struggle as integral to capitalist society:

The world must be brought back to the
original harmony that was the plan of its
Creator from the very first moment in which
He gave his creatures a share in His perfec-
tions.[87]

Similarly, the documents of Pius XII which specifically deal with the use of violence must be understood in the light of the traditional just war theory. Pius formally rejected violence which did not fall within the boundaries of the conditions for just war, and the instances of violence which he approved, or at least condoned, did fall within those limits, or could at least be construed to do so. He was partial to the Axis powers, and uncomfortable with the inclusion of the USSR in the Allied pact. This attitude stemmed from his view that only the fascist powers would preserve the West and rid it of the communist menace from the East--a task of which he strongly approved.

But the clearest instance of Pius XII's approval of the use of violence within the just war context is the 1956 Hungarian revolt and the documents he wrote concerning it. In these documents he applauded those in Hungary who had taken up arms, implied that the West should support the uprising, and deplored the force used against these freedom fighters of the revolt. The first document to take this stance was his encyclical letter Luctuoissimi eventus of October 28, 1956, issued when the revolt was just underway.[88] Pius acknowledged that the revolt was violent; he referred more than once to "bloodstained Hungary." But overall he was hopeful, anxious for the success of the revolt, which he thought could return freedom to Hungary and her people. On the diplomatic side, he spent this time urging and expecting western intervention on the side of the revolt.[89] The letters and encyclicals he wrote were designed to achieve this goal, for it was not usual to address the entire Church in an encyclical concerning a matter confined to a single country. Pius' aim in sending this letter to bishops in all corners of the world to be read in each diocese was to mobilize support for western intervention.

When the Soviet reaction to events in Hungary
came and the heavy-handed Soviet army crushed the
revolt, Pius XII issued <u>Datis</u> <u>nuperrine</u>, November
5, 1956, in which he said:

> In the encyclical letter which We recent-
> ly wrote to you, Consecrated Shepherds of the
> Catholic world, We expressed Our hope that a
> new day of peace based on justice and liberty
> might be dawning on the noble people of Hun-
> gary. For conditions in that country seemed
> to be improving.
> But tidings have reached Us lately which
> fill Our heart with pain and sorrow. There
> is being shed again in the cities, towns and
> villages of Hungary the blood of citizens who
> long with all their hearts for their rightful
> freedom. National institutions which had
> just been restored have been overthrown again
> and violently destroyed. A blood drenched
> people have been reduced to slavery by the
> armed might of foreigners.[90]

The last sentences of this passage make clear that
for the purposes of determining who it was who
waged the war, Pius did not consider the Communist
government of Hungary as the Hungarian state.
Clearly the revolt was, in his eyes, a war fought
by the Hungarians against the trespassing Russians,
with the objective of restoring national institutions.

On two other occasions connected with the
Hungarian situation Pius XII gave explicit approval to the use of violence. His address of November 10, 1956, <u>Allo</u> <u>strazio</u>, deplored the failure
of the Hungarian revolt, and urged support for the
freedom of the Hungarian people.[91] In the context

215

of that period, this statement should surely be read as a more or less explicit demand for western intervention. In his subsequent address of December 23, 1956, _Inesaurabile mistero_, Pius was explicit that Christians were justified in using force under certain (unspecified) conditions in opposing such evil, because of its opposition, not only to God, but to the legitimate rights of human beings.[92]

Pius XII did not connect his position on the Hungarian revolt with the just war theory explicitly. But the just war tradition provides the most useful context for understanding the positions taken by Pius XII on the use of violence. The criteria for just war, especially the restriction of the right to wage war to states, can explain why he found the use of violence, while always regretable, acceptable in World War II and in Hungary in 1956, at the same time he generally claimed that violence was unacceptable, as he did in his first encyclical:

> It is not from outward pressure, Worshipful Brethren, it is not from the sword that deliverance comes to nations; the sword cannot breed peace, it can only impose the terms of peace. The forces, the influences, that are to renew the earth must spring from men's hearts. . . .[93]

Pius' use of the just war theory also explained his prohibition on the use of violence in labor situations:

> But let the unions in question draw their vital force from principles of wholesome liberty, let them take their form from the lofty rules of justice and honesty and conforming themselves to these norms let them

act in such a manner that in their care for
the interests of their class they violate no
one's rights; let them continue to strive
for harmony and respect the common weal of
civil society.[94]

Like his predecessor, Pius XII could not countenance the use of violence as an appropriate method for bringing about social change, except where the redressing of injuries was at issue, as stipulated in just war theory. Change in the direction of social justice was to be achieved through evangelization of the world; "the forces, the influences, that are to renew the face of the earth must spring from men's hearts. . . ."

Finally, we need to examine Pius XII's teaching on the possibility of Catholics either working with or becoming members of Marxist organizations. The attacks on the Church in Eastern Europe, and Pius XII's definite stance with the West in the Cold War of the post-war years prevented this question from ever becoming a serious one for him. For him, Catholics who became Marxists had "deserted" the Church for Marxism; no matter how naively they took up Marxism. With divergent values and language, nothing can be gained from meetings. Even more strongly he quoted Corinthians 10:20 to the effect that no one should wish to sit down both at the table of God and at that of his enemies.[95] Pius XII made clear that even collaboration was banned; joint membership in the Church and Marxist groups was, in the words of Pius XI, "a contradiction in terms."[96]

JOHN XXIII

In John's first public address he deplored the "persecution" of the Church in the East under Marxism.[97] In his first encyclical, Ad petri

217

cathedram, he wrote that it is only our hope in
immortal life that can prevent "lusts, dissentions
and disputes." We need to turn our attention away
from those things that degrade and separate, and
collaborate on our true goals.[98]

John agreed with his predecessors that there
were classes, that inequality between classes was
natural, that the inequalities should be reduced
because great inequalities cause hostility.[99] He
also spoke, as had his predecessors, of the natural harmony in the world[100] and of the harmonious
unity of the Christian family.[101] In John's opinion, conflict was unnecessary, and violence unjus-
tifiable: "The just prosperity of citizens can be
achieved without violence and without oppressing
minds and hearts."[102] John's oft repeated belief
that the situation of the workers was improving
and would continue to do so was clearly influential
in forming these conclusions.

In Ad petri cathedram John addressed the
"false" attraction of the Marxist doctrine and the
relationship between Marxism and Christianity:

> With respect to social matters: it is
> Our paternal desire that relations with the
> various classes come under the guidance, con-
> trol and direction of the Christian virtue of
> justice. We are especially concerned here
> because the Church's enemies can easily take
> advantage of any unjust treatment of the
> lower classes to draw them to their side by
> false promises and deceptive lies.
> We ask these dear children of Ours to
> realize that the Church is not hostile to
> them or to their rights. On the contrary,
> she cares for them as would a loving mother.
> She preaches and inculcates a social doctrine
> and social norms which would eliminate every

sort of injustice and produce a better and
more equitable distribution of goods, if they
were put into practice as they should be. At
the same time she encourages friendly cooperation and mutual assistance among the various
classes, so that all men may become in name
and in fact not only free citizens of the
same society but also brothers within the
same family.

.   .   .   .   .

There is never any need, therefore, to
turn to proponents of doctrines condemned by
the Church; for they only draw men on with
false promises and when they obtain control
of the state, try boldly and unscrupulously
to deprive men of their supreme spiritual
goods--the Christian commandments, Christian
hope, and Christian faith. Those who adhere
to the doctrines these men propose, minimize
or eliminate all that our present age and our
modern civilization hold dearest: true liberty, and the authentic dignity of the human
person. Thus they attempt to destroy the
bases of Christianity and civilization.

All therefore, who wish to remain Christians must be aware of their serious obligations to avoid these false principles, which
Our predecessors--especially Pius XI and Pius
XII--have condemned in the past, and which We
condemn again.[103]

In making clear his opposition to Marxism in
Mater et Magistra, John devoted many paragraphs to
the themes of materialism and atheism. He also
discussed ideology, condemning especially ideologies which ignore religion or "imagine that man's
natural sense of religion is nothing more than the
outcome of feelings or fantasy, to be eradicated
from his soul as an anachronism and an obstacle to
human progress."[104]

The importance of God, of the spiritual dimension, and of a hierarchy of values were also themes of John's in _Pacem_ _in_ _terris_.[105] Even so, _Pacem_ _in_ _terris_ was more conciliatory toward Marxism than John's other documents. And overall, the documents of John are much less hostile to Marxism than those of his predecessor. As is obvious in the phrasing of the above passage from _Ad_ _petri_ _cathedram_, he began his pontificate with much the same attitude as his predecessor.[106] This soon changed, however. John deliberately set out to cool the antagonism between the Vatican and Eastern Europe in an effort to improve the conditions of the Church in those nations. As his diplomatic stance toward the nations of Eastern Europe changed, his references to Marxism became less frequent and less hostile.

The most significant result of this detente was John's discussion in _Pacem_ _in_ _terris_ of collaboration between Catholics and Marxists, and his distinction between the philosophy or ideology of a movement and the movement itself. While Pius XI had found the two inseparable, John did not:

> It is, therefore, especially to the point to make a clear distinction between false philosophical teachings regarding the nature, origin and destiny of the universe and of man, and movements which have a direct bearing either on economic and social questions, or cultural matters or on the organization of the state, even if these movements owe their origin and inspiration to these false tenets. While the teaching once it has been set clearly forth is no longer subject to change, the movements, precisely because they take place in the midst of changing conditions, are readily susceptible of change. Besides, who can deny that those movements, in so far as they

conform to the dictates of right reason and
are interpreters of the lawful aspirations of
the human person, contain elements that are
positive and deserving of approval?[107]

John illustrated criteria for determining that a
movement was sufficiently divorced from its false
ideological beginnings to warrant Catholic involvement, while at the same time reiterating the
Church's authority to decide when these criteria
were fulfilled. Prudence, he said, should be the
guiding light which regulates our actions. The
decisions should be made by those who live and
work in the sectors in which the problems arise.
Always, however, in accordance with natural law,
Christian social principles, and the direction of
ecclesiastical authority. For the Church has the
duty of safeguarding Christian teaching and of intervening authoritatively with her children in
applying this teaching.[108]

As we can see, John was not unreservedly approving collaboration with Marxism. His new will-
ingness to differentiate a movement and its ideology, and his resultant conclusion that collaboration with certain movements might be a possibility,
did not involve any lessening of the papacy's opposition to the tenets of Marxism. In fact, the
subsequent paragraph of Pacem in terris referred
immediately to what was, for John, a chief objection to Marxism: its espousal of violence and
conflict.

There are some souls, particularly endowed with generosity, who, on finding situations where the requirements of justice are
not satisfied or not satisfied in full, feel
enkindled with the desire to change the state
of things, as if they wished to have recourse
to something like a revolution.

221

It must be borne in mind that to proceed
gradually is the law of life in all its expressions; therefore in human institutions,
too, it is not possible to renovate for the
better except by working from within them
gradually. As Pius XII proclaimed: 'Salvation and justice are not to be found in revolution, but in evolution through concord.'
Violence has always achieved only destruction, not construction; the kindling of passions, not their pacification; the accumula-
tion of hate and ruin, not the reconciliation
of the contending parties. And it has reduced men and parties to the difficult task
of rebuilding, after sad experience, on the
ruins of discord.[109]

It is clear that here in <u>Pacem</u> <u>in</u> <u>terris</u> John
took the same attitude toward violence that he had
advanced earlier. In his first encyclical, <u>Ad</u>
<u>petri</u> <u>cathedram</u>, he had written:

The various classes of society, as well
as groups of individuals, may certainly protect their rights, provided this is done by
legal means, not violence, and provided that
they do no injustice to the inviolable rights
of others. All men are brothers. Their differences, therefore, must be settled by
friendly agreement, with brotherly love for
one another.[110]

On June 3, 1962 John demonstrated the same
evaluation of violence in an address on the bloodshed current in Northern Africa:

Do not kill! Neither by the sword or by
the spoken word or the press, neither by ac-
quiescence or by an aggravating nationalism.
The earth and all it contains belong to

222

God. _Domini_ _est_ _terra_ _et_ _plenitudo_ _ejus_.
God is the master, and we the inhabitants of
earth. It is our duty on this earth to favor
that peaceful evolution of peoples which recognizes the rights of one's neighbors, even
when this involves personal limitations or
renunciation.

. . . . .

With the abandonment of all obstinacy and
all violence, may the dominion of law and
mutual charity prevail and may the authors
and builders of peace be blessed on the blood
drenched soil of Africa.[111]

John XXIII was consistent in his opposition to the
use of violence. He did not refer to the just war
tradition, but those instances of violence of
which he disapproved were those illegitimate under
the conditions for just war, since the violence
was not between states, but within a state.

Despite John's overall consistent position on
the illegitimacy of violence in solving social
problems, he did sound one note concerning violence which became the starting point for a new
perspective within the social teaching. In _Pacem_
_in_ _terris_ John quoted St. Thomas on human law:

In so far as it falls short of right reason,
a law is said to be a wicked law; and so,
lacking the true nature of law, is rather a
kind of violence.[112]

This brief, unelaborated statement is a reference
to a sort of violence not directed by the masses
against authority. This recognition of a kind of
violence, called structural or institutionalized,
was a milestone in the social teaching. Although
John did no more than present this single line
from a theological work on which the Church had

223

long based much of his philosophy and theology, it
was sufficient to open up the subject for his successor. This recognition of another kind of violence shifted much of the burden of responsibility
for violence from the masses (and their Marxist
agitators) to the powerful who control and maintain
the social, political, and economic system. Paul's
Populorum progressio is dependent upon this particular perspective on violence.

Paul VI

In the pastoral constitution of Vatican II,
Gaudium et Spes, which bore Paul's signature, there
was a further elaboration of the opening toward
Marxism that was observable in John's Pacem in terris, and moreover, a discernible change from the
traditional papal position on Marxism.[113] No longer was Marxism discussed in terms of its false
promises, of its attempts to delude the masses
about the possibilities of equality and liberation
from suffering. Instead, the sincerity of Marxism's efforts to relieve suffering in the world
was recognized as a fact,[114] regardless of whether
the Marxist approach in a given situation was considered to be the appropriate one. More than this,
it was recognized that the atheism which characterizes Marxism was not unrelated to the behavior of
the Christians of the world, whose irresponsibility
had often led others to reject God and religion:

> Moreover, atheism results not rarely from
> a violent protest against the evil in the
> world, or from the dissolute character with
> which certain human values are unduly invest-
> ed, and which thereby already accords them
> the stature of God.
>
> .   .   .   .   .
>
> Yet believers themselves frequently bear
> some responsibility for this situation. For,

taken as a whole, atheism is not a spontane-
ous development but stems from a variety of
causes, including a critical reaction against
religious beliefs, and in some places against
the Christian religion in particular. Hence
believers can have more than a little to do
with the birth of atheism. To the extent
that they neglect their own training in the
faith, or teach erroneous doctrine, or are
deficient in their religious, moral or social
life, they must be said to conceal rather
than to reveal the authentic face of God and
religion.

.   .   .   .   .

Not to be overlooked among the forms of
modern atheism is that which anticipates the
liberation of man especially through his
economic and social emancipation. This form
argues that by its nature religion thwarts
such liberation by arousing man's hope for a
deceptive future life, thereby diverting him
from the constructing of the earthly city.
Consequently, when the proponents of this
doctrine gain governmental power they vigor-
ously fight against religion. They promote
atheism by using those means of pressure which
public power has at its disposal. Such is
especially the case in the work of educating
the young.[115]

The response of Paul and the bishops to this
last mentioned form of atheism which utilizes the
Marxist functionalist critique of religion was
that: "while rejecting atheism, root and branch,
the Church sincerely professes that all men, believers and unbelievers alike, ought to work for
the rightful betterment of this world in which all
alike live."[116] They assert also that: "The remedy which must be applied to atheism, however, is
to be sought in a proper presentation of the

225

Church's teaching as well as in the integral life of the Church and her members."[117]

In an address on the meaning of the pastoral updating called for by Vatican II, Paul felt called upon to clarify his position concerning Marxism and its atheism:

> Let no one believe that this pastoral solicitude which the Church underlines in its program today, which absorbs its attention and requires its care--let no one believe that this signifies a change of judgement regarding the errors spread in our society and already condemned by the Church, such as atheistic Marxism, for example.[118]

Nevertheless, the recognition that Marxists are concerned for the true welfare of human beings, and are not merely using the desire of the masses for liberation in order to achieve power, together with the recognition that the Marxists' rejection of religion is related to the false views of religion and the Church spread by Church members-- these signaled a new era in the Christian-Marxist encounter. Opposition had not ceased, but the ground for the disagreement shifted.

This shift was clear in Paul's Populorum progressio:

> All social action involves a doctrine. The Christian cannot admit that which is based on a materialistic and atheistic philosophy, which respects neither the religious orientation of life to its final end, nor human freedom and dignity. But, provided that these values are safeguarded, a pluralism of professional organizations and trade unions is admissible, and from certain points of

226

view useful, if thereby liberty is protected and emulation stimulated. And We most willingly pay homage to all those who labour in them to give unselfish service to their brothers.[119]

Paul did not endorse indiscriminate collaboration with Marxist movements and continued to stipulate that certain philosophical aspects of Marxism are unacceptable to Christians. But he did go one step further than John. John had argued that movements could diverge from their unacceptable philosophical beginnings to such an extent as to make them, in the future, acceptable. Paul accepted this distinction of John's with explicit reference to Marxism in Octogesima adveniens[120] and implied that collaboration under certain conditions was a present possibility.

Paul reiterated the traditional position that Christians cannot accept the Marxist ideology:

Therefore the Christian who wishes to live his faith in a political activity which he thinks of as service cannot without contradicting himself adhere to ideological systems which radically or substantially go against his faith and his concept of man. He cannot adhere to the Marxist ideology, to its atheistic materialism, to its dialectic of violence and to the way it absorbs individual freedom in the collectivity, at the same time denying all transcendence to man and his personal and collective history; nor can he adhere to the liberal ideology which believes it exalts individual freedom by withdrawing it from every limitation, by stimulating it through exclusive seeking of interest and power, and by considering social solidarities as more or less automatic consequences of in-

227

dividual initiatives, not as an aim and a
major criterion of the value of the social
organization.[121]

Paul went on to insist that it was fatuous to ignore the extent to which historical socialist
movements are conditioned by the ideologies from
which they sprang. He also warned against disre-
garding the connections between the various levels
of expression of Marxism:

> Some Christians today are attracted by
> socialist currents and their various develop-
> ments. They try to recognize therein a cer-
> tain number of aspirations which they carry
> within themselves in the name of faith. They
> feel that they are a part of that historical
> current and wish to play a part within it.
> Now this historical current takes on, under
> the same name, different forms according to
> different continents and cultures, even if it
> drew its inspiration, and still does in many
> cases, from ideologies incompatible with
> faith. Careful judgement is called for. Too
> often Christians attracted by socialism tend
> to idealize it in terms which, apart from
> everything else, are very general: a will
> for justice, solidarity, and equality. They
> refuse to recognize the limitations of the
> historical socialist movements, which remain
> conditioned by the ideologies from which
> they originated. Distinctions must be made
> to guide concrete choices between the vari-
> ous levels of expression of socialism: a
> generous aspiration and a seeking for a more
> just society, historical movements with a
> political organization and aim, and an ide-
> ology which claims to give a complete and
> self-sufficient picture of man. Neverthe-
> less, these distinctions must not lead one

to consider such levels as completely separate and independent. The concrete link which, according to circumstances, exists between them must be clearly marked out. This insight will enable Christians to see the degree of committment possible along these lines, while safeguarding the values, especially those of liberty, responsibility, and openness to the spiritual, which guarantee the integral development of man.[122]

Thus we see that Paul took a major step in accepting Christian involvement with Marxists in certain projects, while preserving, in the form of warnings, the traditional objections to Marxist ideology. In another section of Octogesima adveniens Paul discussed the possibilities for a rapprochement which, some had suggested to him, might result from the present split in the Marxist movement. In this discussion, he reflected on four proposed levels of Marxist expression:

> For some, Marxism remains essentially the active practice of class struggle. Experiencing the ever present and continually renewed force of the relationships of domination and exploitation among men, they reduce Marxism to no more than a struggle--at times with no other purpose--to be pursued and stirred up in permanent fashion. For others it is first and foremost the collective exercise of political and economic power under the direction of a single party, which would be the whole expression and guarantee of the welfare of all, and would deprive individuals and other groups of any possibility of initiative and choice. At a third level, Marxism, whether in power or not, is viewed as a socialist ideology based on historical materialism and the denial of everything transcendent. At

229

other times, finally, it presents itself in a more attentuated form, one also more attractive to the modern mind: as a scientific activity, as a rigorous method of examining social and political reality, and as the rational link, tested by history, between theoretical knowledge and the practice of revolutionary transformation. Although this kind of analysis gives a privileged position to certain aspects of reality to the detriment of the rest, and interprets them in the light of its ideology, it nevertheless furnishes some people not only with a working tool but also a certitude preliminary to action: the claim to decipher in a scientific manner the mainsprings of the evolution of society.[123]

Here Paul did not discuss the relative merits and demerits of the four levels of Marxist expression. It is nonetheless apparent that the fourth level of expression, the "attenuated form" which furnishes some people with "a working tool" for "examining social and political reality," contains almost none of the terms used to condemn Marxism within the papal tradition. Though he noted that this level does give a "privileged position to certain aspects of reality to the detriment of the rest," Paul revealed a preference for this level over the others by affirming its usefulness in the task of transforming the world.

Because Paul considered that even this fourth level of Marxism interprets data "in the light of its ideology" he concluded that Marxism was really more than a working tool, in that it provides a certitude as to its ability to explain the world. This determination led him to warn, in concluding his discussion of Marxism:

230

While, in this Marxian doctrine one can
distinguish these various aspects and the
questions they pose for the reflection and
activity of Christians, it would be illusory
and dangerous to reach a point of forgetting
the intimate link which radically binds them
together, to accept the elements of Marxist
analysis without recognizing their relationships to ideology, and to enter into the process of class struggle and Marxist interpretation, while failing to note the kind of
totalitarian and violent society to which
this process leads.[124]

Despite the papal reservations regarding
Marxism because of its violence and class struggle, there was, in Paul's documents, the first
significant shift from the papal tradition on
violence. The setting for this pronouncement is
important to the message, in that the encyclical
Populorum progressio dealt with the situation of
the Third World and the injustice which characterizes that situation--and not with the traditional social problem of labor. Paul cited his
trips to Latin America, Africa, India, and the
Holy Land as significant for his education in the
problems of development.[125] The course of world
events since the death of John had made less
plausible John's optimistic view of economic progress; development policies were under attack in
other areas, especially in the Third World itself.
The increasingly widespread criticism of development policies combined with Paul's exposure to
some of the problems of the Third World resulted
in a shift in the social teaching on social violence. This shift was not by any means a total
reversal of the traditional position. It was rather an adaptation of traditional conditions on
the use of violence to new situations where, within explicit criteria, violence might be determined

231

to be the best available means of redress of injury:

> There are certainly situations whose in-
> justice cries out to the heavens. When whole
> populations destitute of necessities live in
> a state of dependence barring them from all
> initiative and responsibility, and all oppor-
> tunity to advance culturally and share in
> social and political life, recourse to vio-
> lence, as a means to right these wrongs to
> human dignity, is a grave temptation. We
> know, however, that a revolutionary uprising
> --save where there is manifest longstanding
> tyranny which would do great damage to funda-
> mental personal rights and dangerous harm to
> the common good of the society--produces new
> injustices, throws more elements out of bal-
> ance, and brings on new disasters. A real
> evil should not be fought against at the cost
> of greater misery.[126]

It is important to note that in making this
pronouncement Paul also modified the criteria of
the just war theory so that they applied to domestic situations. Now individuals and groups had
the basic right to defense of their life and dignity that the traditional interpretation of just
war extended only to states.

The shift in the papal approach to violence
is not unconnected to the more gradual changes in
the papal attitude we have just examined toward
Marxism. The increasing recognition that Marxist
commitment to justice in the world was often sincere could not help but call forth an examination
and reconsideration of other tenets of Marxism,
including the Marxist interpretation of class
struggle. But Paul's approach to Marxism as a
whole was hesitant. Octogesima adveniens made

232

clear his explicit rejection of the inevitability
of class struggle. But his shift on violence remains significant. The most that can be said is
that the subject of Marxism in papal teaching remains unsettled, open to discussion and dispute,
at the end of the pontificate of Paul.[127]

Conclusion

Though there is hardly an area of the social
teaching which has undergone more change in the
last century, even the last quarter century, the
situation of Marxism vis-a-vis the Catholic Church
is still unsettled. Within the social teaching
the attitude toward Marxism has now become a kind
of cautious green light to various kinds of collaboration for the achievement of shared goals. The
Latin American liberation theologians have indicated they will not accept Church rejection of
class struggle. And yet we see in the current
struggle over Marxism in Latin American episcopal
circles that the Vatican is not so acquiescent to
applications of class struggle and of the present
social teaching on Marxism. The possibility looms
that instead of continuing the trend toward the
left, the Vatican may impede the implementation
of present social teaching on Marxism to the point
of retracting it.

The treatment the Church has received from
Marxists in Europe over the last century has some
bearing on the Vatican attitude, and many political commentators believe that if the Vatican should
come to some working agreement with the Italian
communist party, Church policy throughout the world
would be affected. Such an agreement would almost
undoubtedly provide some assurance to the Vatican
that Marxism and communism need not be her sworn
enemies. The proliferation of independent Marxist
and communist governments and groups throughout the

world might also remove the fear that all Marxist movements lead to governments of the Russian type. In short, the Church's moves towards Marxism in part depend upon the political events in the world in the next few years. Should the Church, despite the Vatican, be drawn into the struggle against repression in Latin America, the Vatican might begin to rally around her martyrs under the only political flag available--the red one. As far as papal teaching is concerned, the groundwork to allow this move is already done. Its implementation remains to be seen.

[1]Declaration Sur Le Promotion Humaine et Le Salut Chretien, La Documentation Catholique, 4-8 Septembre, 1977, No. 1726.

[2]"CELAM Draft Drops Latin Input," by Peter Hebblethwaite, National Catholic Reporter, April 21, 1978, Vol. 14, no. 26, p. 20; "Catholic Bishops in Latin America Wage Bitter Struggle Over Church's Leftist Trend," by Alan Riding, New York Times, April 6, 1978, p. A3; "Taking on the Vatican," Time, May 8, 1978, p. 80; "Liberation Theology Under Attack," by Peter Hebblethwaite, National Catholic Reporter, March 24, 1978, Vol. 14, no. 22, p. 15. (The meeting was postponed from October 1978 by John Paul I's death.)

[3]Up to the time of this writing, October 1978; the reportage of the conference will undoubtedly increase as the date draws near.

[4]"Catholic Bishops in Latin America Wage Bitter Struggle Over Church's Leftist Trend," New York Times, April 6, 1978, p. A3.

[5]"Will the Latin American People Be Heard at CELAM III?" by Gary MacEoin, Latin American Press, Vol. 10, no. 1, March 9, 1978, p. 7; "Taking on the Vatican," Time, May 8, 1978, p. 80.

[6]"CELAM III Will Test the Reality of Medellin," by Gary MacEoin, Latin America Press, January 5, 1978, Vol. 10, no. 1, p. 1; "Liberation Theology Under Attack," National Catholic Report-

er; "CELAM Draft Drops Latin Input," National Catholic Reporter; "Taking on the Vatican," Time: "He [Paul] wants the Church to help correct social injustice without prescribing any single political approach for Catholics to follow." The attacks on liberation theology from the right center on the use of Marxism, as is clear in the book by Bishop Alfonso Lopez Trujillo (secretary of CELAM), Liberation or Revolution? (Huntington, Indiana: Our Sunday Visitor Press, 1977). It is also true in the German response to the conservative attack on liberation theology signed by Karl Rahner and J.B. Metz, Memorandum from Theologians in the Federal Republic of Germany Concerning the Campaign Against the Theology of Liberation.

[7]AAS 63 (1971):421-425, para. 26-34.

[8]Declaration Sur Le Promotion Humaine et Le Salut Chretien, pp. 763, 767.

[9]"Catholic Bishops in Latin America Wage Bitter Struggle," New York Times, April 6, 1978, A3.

[10]Jose Porfirio Miranda, Marx and the Bible (New York: Orbis, 1971), pp. xiii-xiv.

[11]For example, see the preparatory documents for the Puebla Conference referred to in Peter Hebblethwaite's article, "CELAM Draft Drops Latin Input," National Catholic Reporter.

[12]Except for the Argentinian right-wing of liberation theology, best known through the writings of Lucio Gera and Juan Carlos Scanonne: this group is "populist" rather than Marxist. Consideration of Latin American liberation theologians henceforth will exclude this group.

[13]Javier Iguiniz, "Statement of Javier Iguin-

iz," Theology in the Americas, edited by Sergio
Torres and John Eagleson (New York: Orbis, 1976),
pp. 284-285; Jose Porfirio Miranda, "Statement of
Jose Porfirio Miranda," Theology in the Americas,
p. 292; Leonardo Boff, "Statement of Leonardo
Boff," Theology in the Americas, p. 298; Hugo
Assman, Theology for a Nomad Church, pp. 129-130
and "Statement of Hugo Assman," Theology in the
Americas, pp. 202-203; Gustavo Gutierrez, A Theology of Liberation, pp. 88-92 and "Statement of
Gustavo Gutierrez," Theology in the Americas, p.
312; Juan Luis Segundo, The Liberation of Theology,
p. 132; Declaration of the 80, Christians for Socialism, edited by John Eagleson (New York: Orbis,
1975), pp. 3-4; Beltran Villegas, Letter to 80
Friends, Christians for Socialism, p. 7; Co-ordinating Committee to Cardinal Silva, Christians for
Socialism, p. 52.

[14]For example, see Dussel's discussion of
disagreements over the Christian appropriations
of Marxism in History and the Theology of Liberation, pp. 133-134.

[15]The Liberation of Theology, Chapter 4:
"Ideologies and Faith," pp. 97-122; "Statement of
Hugo Assman," Theology in the Americas, p. 300;
Jose Maria Diez-Alegria, "Forward," Marx and the
Bible, p. ix; and A Theology of Liberation, pp.
232-239. In Gutierrez one finds a different use
of terms. He uses the Marxist understanding of
ideology (the function of ideology being the preservation of the status quo) rather than the common definition (Webster's) of ideology as 'the
body of doctrine, myth, etc. with reference to a
political or cultural plan.' His definition of
utopia fits this latter definition of ideology,
and since he urges commitment to utopia as the
message of the Gospel, and presents ideology as

the alternative to utopia, he seems to agree that we have a choice of ideologies (in the common sense) and cannot opt, as Christians, for a non-ideological stance.

[16]Within the Christians for Socialism papers, see the Declaration of the 80, p. 4, The Response of the Co-ordinating Committee to Cardinal Silva, pp. 52-55. Also see Dussel's discussion in History and the Theology of Liberation, pp. 133-135.

[17]Ibid.

[18]Qui pluribus, November 9, 1846, Acta Pii PP IX (Romae: Typis Rev. Camarae Apostolicae, 1865), p. 13.

[19]Syllabus of Errors, December 8, 1864, Acta Pii PP IX, p. xiii. The common element in all of these was opposition to the authority of the Church.

[20]Inscrutabili, April 21, 1878, ASS 10:585, para. 2.

[21]ASS 11:369.

[22]ASS 11:370.

[23]The New Catholic Encyclopedia, Vol. 13, p. 653 (New York: McGraw-Hill, 1967).

[24]Ibid. This is a very general description of the conditions on waging a just war. There have been elaborations on the issues of what constitutes legitimate means and limited ends, whether or not possibility of success is necessary, and many other issues.

[25]Papal approval of violent resistence in

Hungary and Mexico did not violate just war theory.
The 1956 Hungarian revolt was considered by Pius
XII to be a national controversy between the Hungarians and the Russians (to which most historians
agree), and the Mexican troubles of the 20's and
30's were said to be caused by (1) foreign (communist) troublemakers, and (2) an illegitimate
"government." Pius implied, with some justification, that there had not been any civil order in
Mexico since the 1911 revolution.

[26]In plurimis, ASS 20:550-551; translation:
Social Wellsprings, ed. Joseph Husslein, S.J.
(Milwaukee: Bruce, 1940), p. 101.

[27]Ibid.; Rerum novarum, ASS 23:659, para. 30.

[28]Ibid., para. 31.

[29]Quadragesimo anno, AAS 23 (1931):213.
These two points also constitute the basis for his
consideration of socialism in the same section of
the encyclical. (AAS 23 (1931):213.)

[30]AAS 14 (1922):683-685.

[31]AAS 22 (1930):567-573.

[32]Divini Redemptoris, para. 11, AAS 29 (1937):
71; translation: Seven Great Encyclicals, p. 181.

[33]The Lateran Treaty, between the Vatican and
Mussolini's Italy, made Church legislation on marriage that of the Italian state. This was Pius'
price for recognition of the Mussolini government.

[34]Ubi arcano, AAS 14 (1922):683; translation
by James H. Ryan, The Encyclicals of Pius XI (St.
Louis, Mo.: Herder and Herder, 1927), pp. 20-21.

[35]Ubi arcano, AAS 14 (1922):690; translation: Encyclicals of Pius XI, pp. 31-32.

[36]Divini Redemptoris, AAS 29 (1937):67-68, para. 5; translation: Seven Great Encyclicals, pp. 178-179.

[37]Ibid., AAS 29 (1937):84, para. 36.

[38]In paragraphs 19 and 20 he referred to them in more detail.

[39]Iniquis only mentioned socialism once: to condemn mandatory participation by educators in a socialist parade.

[40]Firmissimam constantiam, AAS 29 (1937):196-197; translated by National Catholic Welfare Conference, Sixteen Encyclicals of His Holiness, Pope Pius XI (Washington, 1937), pp. 17-18.

[41]Encyclopedia Americana (New York: Americana Corp., 1953), Vol. 18, pp. 796-797.

[42]Divini Redemptoris, AAS 29 (1937):67-68, para. 5.

[43]Divini Redemptoris, AAS 29 (1937):69-70, para. 9; translation: Seven Great Encyclicals, p. 180.

[44]Ibid., AAS 29 (1937):75-76, para. 20 and 21; translation from Seven Great Encyclicals, pp. 184-185.

[45]Divini Redemptoris, para. 23, AAS 29 (1937): 76-77; translation from Seven Great Encyclicals, p. 185.

[46]Ibid., para. 57, AAS 29 (1937):94-95; trans-

lation from *Seven Great Encyclicals*, p. 198.

[47]*Divini Redemptoris*, para. 36, *AAS* 29 (1937):
84; translation: *Seven Great Encyclicals*, p. 190.

[48]*Divini Redemptoris*, para. 77, *AAS* 29 (1937):
104-105; translation: *Seven Great Encyclicals*, p.
205.

[49]Ibid., para. 8, *AAS* 29 (1937):69; translation: *Seven Great Encyclicals*, p. 180.

[50]*Divini Redemptoris*, *AAS* 29 (1937):70-71,
para. 10-11; translation: *Seven Great Encyclicals*,
p. 181.

[51]*Quadragesimo anno*, *AAS* 23 (1931):216, para.
120; translation: *Seven Great Encyclicals*, p. 158.

[52]Ibid., *AAS* 23 (1931):212, para. 112; *Seven
Great Encyclicals*, p. 155.

[53]Ibid., para. 111.

[54]*Quadragesimo anno*, *AAS* 23 (1931):215, para.
117.

[55]Ibid., *AAS* 23 (1931):213-214, para. 112-
114.

[56]Ibid., p. 204, para. 81-83. (This had also
been true of Leo: *ASS* 23:662, and *Church and
Social Justice*, pp. 344-345.)

[57]Ibid., pp. 186-187, para. 29-32.

[58]Ibid., *AAS* 23 (1931):204-205, para. 84-85;
translation: *Seven Great Encyclicals*, pp. 148-149.

[59]Ibid., *AAS* 23 (1931):204, para. 84; trans-

lation: _Seven Great Encyclicals_, p. 148.

[60]This had been true of Leo XII, also: Joseph Husslein, ed., _Social Wellsprings_ (Milwaukee: Bruce, 1940), p. 177.

[61]_Quadragesimo Anno_, AAS 23 (1931):222, para. 136.

[62]Ibid., AAS 23 (1931):223-224, para. 137.

[63]Ibid., AAS 23 (1931):213-214, para. 114, 115; translation: _Seven Great Encyclicals_, p. 156.

[64]Ibid., AAS 23 (1931):214-215, para. 116-117; translation: _Seven Great Encyclicals_, pp. 156-157.

[65]_Fulgens corona_, September 8, 1953, AAS 45 (1953):585-586: _We are deeply touched_, AAS 46 (1954):56-59; _Chers fils et cheres filles_, AAS 46 (1954):324-325; _Ecce ego declinabo_, AAS 47 (1955): 15-28.

[66]No original available; taken from _The Pope Speaks_, Vol. 3, No. 1, pp. 80-81.

[67]No original available; taken from _The Pope Speaks_, Vol. 3, No. 1, p. 227.

[68]February 17, 1956 letter to Italian Federation of Commerce, _The Pope Speaks_, Vol. 3, No. 1, p. 48; May 1, 1956 letter to Catholic labor rally, _The Pope Speaks_, Vol. 3, No. 1, p. 179; _A l'occasion_, September 9, 1956, _The Pope Speaks_, Vol. 3, No. 1, pp. 241-245; _Nel vedere il cielo_, September 12, 1948, AAS 40 (1948):409-414.

[69]_La Nostra Casa_, December 28, 1956, AAS 48 (1956):829; translation: _The Pope Speaks_, Vol. 3, p. 420.

70A l'occasion, September 9, 1956, AAS 48 (1956):672-673; translation: The Pope Speaks, Vol. 3, p. 243.

71Summi Pontificatus, AAS 31 (1939):550.

72Ibid., p. 551.

73Ibid., pp. 551-553.

74Poco Piu di dieci anni, May 1, 1955, Osservatore Romano, May 23, 1955; translation: The Pope Speaks, Vol. 2, No. 1, p. 149.

75June 26, 1955, AAS 47 (1955):512-513; translation: The Pope Speaks, Vol. 2, No. 1, p. 166.

76E'ancora vivo, AAS 47 (1955):516.

77Ibid.

78Poco Piu di dieci anni, Osservatore Romano, May 23, 1955; translation: The Pope Speaks, Vol. 11, No. 1, p. 150.

79Church and Social Justice, p. 345.

80Christmas message, December 24, 1943, AAS 36 (1944):14; July 19, 1947 letter, AAS 39 (1947): 445; Sertum laetitiae, AAS 31 (1939):642.

81Sertum laetitiae, AAS 31 (1939):642; Amadissimo hijos, March 11, 1951, AAS 43 (1951):214-215.

82Church and Social Justice, pp. 358-361.

83January 25, 1946 allocution, La Documentation Catholique, 46; 381; translation from Church and Social Justice, p. 373.

[84] August 15, 1945 address to wives of the Italian Society of Christian Workers, AAS 37 (1945):215; translation: Church and Social Justice, p. 373.

[85] June 13, 1943 address to Italian diocesan committees, AAS 35 (1943):175; translation: Church and Social Justice, p. 375.

[86] Radio address of September 4, 1949, AAS 41 (1949):460.

[87] Leva Jerusalem, December 22, 1957, AAS 50 (1958):11; translation: The Pope Speaks, Vol. 4, No. 1, p. 244.

[88] AAS 48 (1956):741-744.

[89] Popes in the Twentieth Century, pp. 267-268; Papacy in the Modern World, p. 217.

[90] AAS 48 (1956):748.

[91] Radio address, AAS 48 (1956):788-789; translation: The Pope Speaks, Vol. 3, No. 1, pp. 356-357.

[92] AAS 49 (1957):19; translation: The Pope Speaks, Vol. 3, No. 1, p. 343.

[93] Summi Pontificatus, AAS 31 (1939):440.

[94] Sertum laetitiae, AAS 31 (1939):665.

[95] AAS 49 (1957):17-18.

[96] Quadragesimo anno, AAS 23 (1931):216, para. 120.

[97] Hac trepida hora, October 29, 1958, AAS 50

(1958):839.

[98]AAS 51 (1959):503-504.

[99]Ibid., pp. 505-507.

[100]Ibid., p. 505.

[101]Ibid., p. 509.

[102]Ibid., p. 528.

[103]Ad petri cathedram, AAS 51 (1959):525-526.

[104]Mater et Magistra, AAS 53 (1961):452, para. 214.

[105]Pacem in terris, AAS 65 (1963):273, para. 57-59.

[106]Though the phrasing of John's treatment of Marxism in his first encyclical is very similar to Pius XII's style, John's detente movements were not completely unpredictable. While not being pro-Marxist in any way, he had not relished the anti-communist crusade of Pius XII, and had only reluctantly adopted the papal stance as Patriarch of Venice. John's reasoning in this matter was that Church hostility to Marxism only provoked worse conditions for the Church in Eastern Europe. (Paul Johnson, Pope John XXIII. Boston: Little, Brown, 1974, pp. 84-85.)

[107]Pacem in terris, AAS 55 (1963):300, para. 159.

[108]Ibid., pp. 300-301, para. 160.

[109]Ibid., p. 301, para. 161-162.

[110]AAS 51 (1959):506.

[111]Votre joyeuse presence, AAS 54 (1962):448;
translation: The Encyclicals and Other Messages
of Pope John XXIII (Washington: The Pope Speaks
Press, 1964), p. 220.

[112]Pacem in terris, AAS 55 (1963):271, para.
51.

[113]Pacem in terris, AAS 55 (1963):300, para.
151.

[114]Gaudium et Spes, AAS 58 (1966):1040-1048,
1061-1064, 1112, 1113-1114, 1114-1115, para. 21,
43, 90, 92, 93.

[115]Ibid., pp. 1039-1040, para. 19-20; translation: Renewing the Earth, pp. 193-195.

[116]Ibid., p. 1041, para. 21; translation:
Renewing the Earth, p. 196.

[117]Ibid.

[118]Voi avete participato, September 6, 1963,
AAS 55 (1963):752.

[119]Populorum progressio, AAS 59 (1967):276-
277, para. 39; translation: Renewing the Earth,
p. 326.

[120]Octogesima adveniens, AAS 63 (1971):421-
422, para. 30.

[121]Ibid., p. 420, para. 26.

[122]Ibid., p. 422, para. 31; translation: Renewing the Earth, pp. 368-369.

123Ibid., pp. 423-424, para. 33; translation: Renewing the Earth, pp. 369-370.

124Ibid., pp. 424-425, para. 34; translation: Renewing the Earth, p. 370.

125Populorum progressio, AAS 59 (1967):259, para. 4.

126Ibid., AAS 59 (1967):272-273, para. 30-31; translation: Renewing the Earth, p. 323. Emphasis mine.

127The report of Paul's International Theological Commission sheds no new light on this subject, warning only of uncritical approaches to politics. (Le Promotion Humaine et Le Salut Chretien, in La Documentation Catholique, 4-8 Septembre, 1977, No. 1726.)

CHAPTER V

PAPAL TEACHING ON WOMAN

The twentieth-century women's liberation movement has developed a large body of literature devoted to theology. This feminist theology takes
the form of a critique of the teaching, laws, and
structure of the Christian Church with regard to
woman. Though the women's liberation movement is
not in any way a "Catholic movement," as <u>could</u> be
claimed in the case of the Latin American liberation theology, there is a definite Catholic presence within it, as evidenced by the numerous
books, articles, and pamphlets which specifically
criticize the Catholic Church for its sexism. Two
of the earliest and best known feminist theologians
come from the Catholic tradition and clearly refer
to the Catholic Church in much of their writing--
Mary Daly and Rosemary Radford Ruether.[1]

It is not necessary, however, to look to the
theologians within the women's liberation movement
to perceive the challenge of that movement to the
Church and to papal teaching.[2] The papal teaching
on woman is essentially the traditional view of the
nature and role of woman, which is totally rejected
by the women's liberation movement. Feminist theologians refute the theology and the application in
the Church of this traditional view of woman found
in papal teaching. But it is not primarily feminist theologians who have made necessary papal de-
fenses of this view in the last decades, but rather the women's movement as a whole.[3] This is
contrary to the case of Latin American liberation

theology. Papal response to Latin American liberation theology has been directed at the theological position and its supporters within the Church, and not primarily to the political movement which gave rise to the theology. The case of women is much more similar to that of blacks in papal teaching. The papal stress accorded the subject of racism grew primarily with the political and social movements of blacks toward independence and self-rule, and not from the direct impact of black theology.

There are many different aspects of feminist critique of the Church, some of which has moved from an examination of the Church's treatment of women to an examination of the traditional Church views on Christian love, authority, the nature of human beings, and the relationship of soul and body as these are connected to the subject of woman within Church teaching. A cursory examination of the feminist literature on the Church suggests a parallel with the nineteenth-century feminist movement. That movement consolidated all of its critiques for social change (many maintain it abandoned all but one) into the movement for women's suffrage in the late nineteenth and early twentieth century, in the hope that votes for women would empower the movement to accomplish all the changes it espoused.

A survey of today's feminist literature on the Church might suggest to some that feminists are concentrating their energies into a single channel for change, that of ordination of women, in the hopes that this change would expose all the contradictions in the Church position on woman and lead to the satisfactory resolution of other feminist issues as well. But a more careful examination of the literature suggests that women have not studied the history of the first feminist movement in vain.

Many modern feminist writers seem aware that their
predecessors underestimated the ability of the
political system to meet the demand for women's
suffrage without significant change either in the
political system or the place of women in the society. Some women recognize that this is a danger, too, in the ordination question within the
Church context, in that the impetus for overall
change could be undermined by the acceptance of a
few celibate, token women priests (or possibly
even deacons) alienated from their sexuality and
from other women. These women are connecting
other aspects of the feminist critique with the
ordination question. Thus Clara Maria Henning in-
sists that feminists must oppose clerical celibacy as well as exclusively male clergy, for both
the origins and the maintenance of male clerical
celibacy involves misogyny.[4] And Sister Albertus
Magnus McGrath, O.P. wrote that: "The most appropriate and the most mutually helpful action to be
taken by the Church would be to go beyond tokenism
in admitting women to parish and diocesan decision-
making bodies."[5]

Another example of the fact that feminists
are not putting all their eggs in the ordination
basket is their insistence that feminist issues in
religion and theology are linked (and intimately
linked) to the issues of women in politics, the
family, and other spheres of life. That the sexism in all different spheres of life is interlocked
was the starting point for the analysis of Arlene
Swidler in her address to the Detroit Conference
on the Ordination of Women:

> The basic problem in the functioning of
> the present Church is that old patriarchal
> idea that one person has to have ultimate
> authority, and that person is the father or
> father substitute. I now believe that those

251

recurring Mass readings of "Wives, obey your husbands" are, as our poor embarrassed pastors try to tell us, not really aimed at women after all. What the Church is doing is safeguarding its own present structure. The idea that only one person makes a decision (though he ought to be benevolent--husbands, love your obedient wives) is essential to the operation of a Roman-style Church.

. . . . .

My point is that if our Church is to continue reflecting upon itself in familial terms--and I am sure it will--then it is essential that we direct more of our attention to the husband-wife relationship as the basic male-female relationship, and that we acknowledge and celebrate the partnership marriage as a model for ministry.[6]

This insistence that the women's ordination question is linked to the position of woman in the family is hardly surprising to anyone familiar with feminist writings. For the source of the unequal status attributed to women throughout the centuries is, in the general opinion of feminists, undeniably linked to their biology and the familial role which biological childbearing seemed to indicate for them. This has been the conclusion not only of feminists in such academic fields as anthropology, history, and other areas where the origins of human society are explored, but also of the feminists who are working to change the status and role of women in particular social situations today. These latter find that at the bottom of the troubles women have in unions, in banking, in business, in academia, and in politics is their biology. Women are trapped by the assumption that, because they can bear children, nature assigned childbearing and childcare as their proper role and function. Radical feminists like Shulamith Firestone

252

assume that "women throughout history before the advent of birth control were at the continual mercy of their biology--menstruation, menopause, and 'female ills', constant painful childbirth, wet-nursing and care of infants, all of which made them dependent upon males (whether brother, father, husband, lover, or clan, government, community at large) for physical survival."[7] Firestone argues that such dependence is no longer necessary, because of technology.

Dorothy Dinnerstein similarly begins with biology in her claim that a common unwarranted assumption (that because women bear children they should raise them) leads to societal misogyny.[8] She credits unresolved psychological conflicts with the mother during childhood with the origin and continuing mechanism of sexism.

Marxist feminists are generally uninterested in pursuing the origins of sexism. Thus Sheila Rowbotham writes that the origins of sexism are lost in history, and moves on to other approaches.[9] Juliet Mitchell[10] implies that women's inferior strength was a major cause for the beginning of sexism, but maintains that the situation of women today is determined by the forms of production, reproduction, sexuality and socialization of children in our society.[11] Consequently the liberation of women demands major changes in all four areas. This is explicitly accepted in the work of Eli Zaretsky,[12] Charnie Guettel,[13] Linda Jenness,[14] and (implicitly in) Sheila Rowbotham.[15]

These feminists begin with biology, too, but maintain that the original division of labor and its cause(s) are not the key to the solution of the problem because society has changed a great deal since then, and misogyny has permeated all the complex layers of social development. They

253

follow Marx, who observed that "With these [in-creases in productivity, needs and population] develops the division of labor, which was originally nothing but the division of labor in the sexual act, then the division of labor which develops spontaneously or 'naturally' by virtue of natural predisposition. . . ."[16] Engels similarly maintained in The Origins of the Family, Private Property and the State that the first division of labor was between man and woman, and that this was basic to society's development. What makes the Marxist-feminist stance different from the Marxist one is that Marx and Engels both asserted that the liberation of women would necessarily result from two events: (1) the entrance of all women into the productive sector of the society, and (2) the end of private ownership of the means of production. This latter step was necessary for the liberation of the working class in general; the former step would be responsible, said Marx, for the emancipation of women as women, in that it was a redress of the original division of labor by sex from which sexism flowed.

Marxist-feminists today observe that the entrance of women into production has done nothing but aggravate their exploitation; women who work carry not only the responsibilities of their work role, but the traditional responsibilities of the housewife and mother as well: childrearing, upkeep of the home, and the maintenance of the quality of family life. Women are viewed as naturally fitted for the role of homemaker and childrearer. Marxist-feminists see the pervasiveness of this assumption as the reason why women's liberation will not result solely from the advent of socialism and the entrance of women into production. The experience of women working in socialist countries has also informed this conviction. Hilda Scott, a confirmed socialist and a committed femin-

254

ist, concluded her study of women in Eastern Europe
with the observation that women can only be liber-
ated through a restructuring of the family in such
a way that the traditional woman's duties become
equally the responsibility of men and women.[17]

Feminist attack on the "biology is destiny"
understanding of woman constitutes a powerful challenge to the Church and her teaching. This is particularly true of the twentieth-century Church,
whose popes have been most vocal in stressing that
women's biology determines their role and function.
The great stress placed on this has been, of course,
a response to popular challenges of that understanding in the late nineteenth and the twentieth centuries. This papal "biology is destiny" attitude,
however, though more prominent in recent decades,
has constituted the core of the Church's understanding of women since the early Church. It is
significant that only recently has the subject of
woman in papal teaching been addressed outside the
family context. Furthermore, as the notes of this
chapter demonstrate, the largest portion of the
papal teaching on woman is not incorporated in the
major social teaching documents; most of it is not
even found in the Acta Apostolicae Sedis. The
great bulk of papal teaching on woman is in the
form of addresses to groups of women (especially
Italian women) visiting the Vatican. There are no
similar addresses to men on the nature of men, of
fatherhood, and of masculinity.

Addressing hundreds of visiting groups a year
is not a simple papal task. The common approach
is to seize upon the purpose of the group as the
theme of the address. Pius XII made the address
to visiting groups into an art, the greatest proof
of the breadth of his mind. But neither Pius XII
nor any of the other twentieth-century popes followed this approach for women's groups. The women

255

of Catholic Action, nurses, new brides, teachers, workers' wives, nuns--all were addressed on the same themes: motherhood, material or spiritual; feminine modesty; safeguarding the family; new dangers to marriage and the home; and respect and obedience to husbands. When the professional role was mentioned, it was viewed as secondary to, and an extension of, the primary domestic role.

But feminist attack on the Church teaching on woman has not limited itself to this issue of women's role. Feminists assert that there are many other misogynist aspects in Church teaching. Another aspect of the Church's preoccupation with biology in its view of women is the assumption of feminine uncleanness, though this is increasingly uncommon. Feminists see considerable evidence of menstrual taboo in the Church's laws and customs concerning women.[18] Another support for the Church's traditional view of women has been the universalizing of the Genesis account of the Fall. The image of Eve as temptress, luring a helpless Adam to his doom, is common.[19] Papal teaching has also been influenced by the assumptions of the age, and so we find a heavy stress in the papal teaching of this century regarding woman's moral superiority, as well as an attempt to place her on a pedestal to protect her moral virtue from the evils of the world.[20]

Earlier Papal Teaching on Woman

In the following section I will attempt to present the major themes in the papal teaching on woman during the fifty years prior to the beginning of the pontificate of Pius XI in 1922. In the teaching of the popes between Pius IX and Pius XI, especially Leo XIII and Benedict XV, one finds views on women similar to those prevailing in their age.

Leo XIII treated the subject of woman within
the context of marriage and the family. He defined the duties of husbands and wives in his February 10, 1880 encyclical, Arcanum:

> Secondly, the mutual duties of husbands
> and wives have been defined, and their sever-
> al rights accurately established. They are
> bound, namely, to have such feeling for one
> another as to cherish always very great mutu-
> al love, to be ever faithful to their marri-
> age vow, and to give to one another an un-
> failing and unselfish help. The husband is
> the chief of the family, and the head of the
> wife. The woman, because she is the flesh of
> his flesh and the bone of his bone, must be
> subject to her husband and obey him; not in-
> deed as a servant, but as a companion, so
> that of course her obedience shall be wanting
> in neither dignity nor honor. Since the hus-
> band represents Christ, and since the wife
> represents the Church, in him who governs and
> in him who obeys, may there always be love
> governing the duties of both.[21]

Leo XIII did not consider the Church's teaching on the proper obedience the wife owed the husband to be anti-female; he was among the first of
many Churchmen whose practical objections to divorce included the charge that it victimized women:

> Truly, it is hardly possible to describe
> how great are the evils which flow from di-
> vorce. Matrimonial contracts are by it made
> variable; mutual kindness is weakened; de-
> plorable inducements to unfaithfulness are
> supplied; harm is done to the education and
> training of children; occasion is afforded
> for the breaking up of domestic societies;
> the seeds of discord are sown among families;

the dignity of womanhood is lessened and lowered, and women face the danger of being deserted after having ministered to the pleasures of men.[22]

Leo was convinced that the hierarchical relationship within marriage was just and equitable, and afforded the best of all situations to all, as the following passage from the encyclical _Immortale Dei_, of November 1, 1885, demonstrated:

> Domestic society has its solid foundation in the sanctity of a marriage which is one and indivisible. The husband's and wife's rights and duties are regulated with the wisest justice and equity. [Proper honor is preserved to the wife and] the authority of the husband is based on that of God; the fatherly power is rightly tempered to the dignity of the wife and children: for the latter there must be provided maintenance, health and education.
> Augustine spoke admirably, as usual, in several of his works, of the value of these benefits, but especially so where he turns to the Catholic Church with these words: 'You guide children like children, youth with firmness, old age with solemn calmness, not so much according to the age of the body as the age of the soul. You subject wives to their husbands in chaste and faithful obedience not for the satisfaction of passion, but for the propagation of children and together raising a family. You set husbands over their wives, not to mock at the greater weakness of that sex [but under conditions of sincere love]. You unite children to parents without servitude, you set parents over children in gentle governance.'[23]

Leo made it clear that wifely subjection was not to be understood as a pronouncement of female inferiority, but as the result of the need for, and rightness of, hierarchy in the world's order. Leo followed the traditional understanding that there is, in every relationship, a dominant and a passive member. The dominant, that is, the active member of the relationship, is to love and care for the passive member, and the passive member is to obey. This is the relationship of Christ and the Church, God and humanity. Moreover, since all authority is from God, the authority of the dominant member links that person to God in a kind of kinship:

> Therefore, as the Apostle says (Eph. V), as Christ is the head of the Church, so is the man head of the woman; and as the Church is subject to Christ, who embraces her with a most chaste and undying love, so also should wives be subject to their husbands, and be loved by them in turn with a faithful and constant affection. In like manner does the Church temper the use of parental and domestic authority, that it may tend to hold children and servants to their duty, without going beyond bounds. For, according to Catholic teaching, the authority of our heavenly Father and Lord is imparted to parents and masters, whose authority, therefore, not only takes its origin and force from Him, but also borrows its nature and character.[24]

The prevailing picture of woman in Leo's writing is that of someone subject to another, secondary to him (quia caro est de carne illius et os de ossibus ejus as above in Arcanum),[25] and weaker than he. Leo's treatment of woman, was, therefore, that due a creature who needs to be supported,[26] sheltered, restricted and controlled through obedi-

ence to her natural master. He insisted that she
was to be respected and that her obedience to her
husband was linked to (possibly even conditioned
upon) his love for her.

A favorite point for Leo was that the Church
had rescued woman from the depths of depravity to
which paganism had assigned her by insisting on
the indissoluble, monogamous character of marriage
in which both partners were bound to the same laws
of love and faithfulness.[27] He maintained that in
pagan marriage woman's position was precarious and
her status lowly because she could be replaced
through divorce, polygamy, adultery and concubinage, all of which were accepted. In addition, said
Leo, she could be beaten, sold, and even killed by
father or husband.

The next pope to add to Leo's treatment of
woman was Benedict XV, who continued to treat the
subject of woman within the context of marriage
and the family. Benedict did not propose new understandings of woman so much as carry Leo's ideas
into the war and the postwar context. In his _motu
proprio_, _Bonum sane_, of July 25, 1920, Benedict
wrote:

> Let it be added, that the sanctity of
> conjugal faith and the respect for the pater-
> nal authority have not been lightly damaged
> for many peoples as a result of the war. One
> reason is that the absence of either husband
> or wife has diminished in the other party the
> bond of duty, or again that the absence of
> watchful care has accidentally led to indul-
> gence, or, especially among young women, in
> licentiousness. It is sad that public moral-
> ity is now more depraved and corrupt than be-
> fore and that the so-called 'social question'
> is aggravated to such a point as to threaten

irreparable ruin.[28]

In the statement that young women, especially, were living too freely, there is a hint of Eve, first and more easily tempted than Adam. But in his December 27, 1917 letter, <u>Natalis trecentesimi</u>, Benedict was much more explicit in portraying woman as the soul of society, the superior spiritual and moral force, which, when corrupted, doomed the entire society:

> It is, in fact, amazing what the woman can do for the good of the human race, or for its ruin; if she should leave the common road, both the civil and the domestic orders are easily upset.
>
> With the decline in religion, cultured women have lost with their piety also their sense of shame; many, in order to take up occupations ill-befitting their sex, took to imitating men, others abandoned the duties of the housewife, for which they were fashioned, to cast themselves recklessly into the current of life.
>
> And this is the deplorable perversion of morals, which the disorder bred of the war has multiplied and propagated beyond all belief.[29]

In an allocution to a group of Italian women concerning dress, Benedict spoke on October 21, 1919 regarding changes in the area of women's activities, insisting on the priority of the home:

> The changing conditions of our times have given to the woman functions and rights which preceding ages had not conceded her. But no change in man's attitude, no novelty of things, no diversity of circumstances will ever tear away from the family, her natural

261

setting, the woman conscious of her mission.
In the home she is queen; and even when she
is far away from home, like a wise governor
her maternal affection and all of her thoughts
must be centered therein, just as a king, away
from his realm, far from neglecting his subjects, places them always first in his cares
and preoccupations.

It is true that changes in the social
order have extended the field of activity
for women. The apostolate in the world outside has now been added to the more intimate
apostolate within the home. But this apostolate must be so exercised as to show that the
woman, whether inside or outside of the home,
is conscious that her first responsibility,
today as yesterday, is the family.[30]

More significantly, Benedict said at a later
point in this same document that women have power,
through their bodies, to induce evil in others,
often unconsciously:

. . . We know that certain modes of dress
which women are beginning to accept, are
harmful to society, for they are a cause of
evil. And on the other hand, We find to Our
amazement that those who spread this poison
seem to ignore its evil effects: those who
set the house on fire, as it were, seem not
to realize the destructive power of the
flames. And yet only such an ignorance can
explain the deplorable popularity of fashions
so contrary to the sense of modesty which
should be the most beautiful adornment of
the Christian woman. If she realized what
she was doing, woman would hardly go so far
as to enter the Church indecently clad, to
appear before those who are the natural and
authorized teachers in matters of Christian

262

morality.[31]

Benedict ended this allocution with a reference to the power of feminine virtue:

> It was said that the faithfulness of a woman brought back to the path of justice the husband who had gone astray: 'the unbelieving husband is sanctified by the believing wife.' May it soon be possible to repeat of the whole of society that it returned to the path of salvation through the example, the teaching, through the mission of the Catholic woman.[32]

Benedict drew a picture of woman as both more easily corrupted and more virtuous than man; as being in the public arena, but more intimately linked to the home; and as being powerful enough to take the world with her on the path that she chose. He did not deal with the relative position of man and woman in marriage, but can be assumed to agree with Leo's pronouncements. Though Benedict agreed with Leo on the nature and role of woman in general, his emphasis was very different. Rather than stressing the power relationship between men and women which is natural in this world, Benedict stressed the moral realm, and the moral aspects of woman's nature and role. The nature of the threat to the old order had changed in the years between Leo and Benedict. No longer was the primary threat from marching radicals, demanding changes in the legal and institutional treatment of women. Now the threat came from a change in the sexual and other social customs of the day, a change prompted by the war. Both the emphases of Leo and those of Benedict reappear in the teaching of the twentieth-century popes who followed them.

Pius XI: On Woman

In his first encyclical, Ubi arcano, of December 23, 1922, Pius XI repeated a theme of Benedict
XV's concerning the effect of the war on society:

> And it is truly sad to see how this poi-
> sonous evil has penetrated to the very root
> of human society, that is, into the family,
> the process of breaking up which, begun some
> time since, has since been accentuated by the
> terrible scourge of the war, with the taking
> away of fathers and sons from the homes and
> the corruptions of morals in many ways. The
> respect due paternal authority is often for-
> gotten, as is that due to blood relationships;
> masters and servants look on themselves as
> adversaries, and the conjugal bond is often
> violated. . . .[33]
> Jesus Christ reigns in the family when
> that family formed by the sacrament of Chris-
> tian matrimony, keeps inviolate its sacred
> character, where the authority of the parents
> is modelled on the Divine Fatherhood whence
> it gets its origin and name, where the chil-
> dren emulate the example of the Child Jesus
> and all life is filled with the holiness of
> the Family of Nazareth.[34]

The first paragraph of this passage states
that the absence of husbands and fathers has caused
a corruption of morals. The similarity of Benedict's statement to this effect is unmistakable.

Of the relation of women to the public sphere
and their proper role in it Pius XI wrote at some
length. On May 2, 1928 he sent a long letter to
the Cardinal Vicar of Rome protesting and condemning the upcoming national gymnastic and athletic
competition for women:

264

Such competitions always remain in vivid
contrast to the special and delicate needs of
womanly education. These needs become even
more delicate and venerable when that education is, as it ought to be, Christian.

It is impossible to conclude that such an
attitude ignores or underrates all that which
can give to the body, the noble instrument of
the soul, agility, grace, health, and strength.
But these means must be employed with due regard for the suitability of time and place;
they must not lessen the reserve and self-
possession which are both the ornament and
guarantee of virtue; they must never incite
vanity and violence.

This is Our hope and Our prayer: that the
hand of woman may never be raised except to
pray and to do good.[35]

Pius implied in this passage that a woman's
virtue particularly needs protection (since the
letter objects not to athletic competition, which
Pius approved for males, but to athletic competitions for females) and that a restricted public
role is necessary to the preservation of her vir-
tue--in fact, that such restriction not only guarantees that virtue, but is its best ornament.

In _Divini illius magistri_, December 31, 1929,
Pius XI condemned the practice of coeducation which
he said was founded

upon a deplorable confusion of ideas which
mistakes a levelling of promiscuity for the
legitimate association of the sexes. The
Creator has ordained and disposed perfect
union of the sexes only in matrimony, and,
with varying degrees of contact, in the family and in society. Besides, there is not
in nature itself, which fashions the two

265

quite different in organism, in temperament,
in abilities, anything to suggest that there
can be or ought to be promiscuity between
them, much less that they be fashioned one
and the same in education.[36]

This statement of Pius' utilizes what was a
common papal understanding of equality. For Pius
"equality" meant sameness, which was absurd for the
sexes, for they were not created to be the same,
but complementary. To educate them together, equally, was to educate them to the same role (presumably
the male role, for Pius) to the detriment of society, which required both. Pius instead urged a
return to a sound family-based society modelled on
the Holy Family, a common suggestion in papal
teaching.

In the encyclical _Lux veritatis_ of December
25, 1931 on the renewal of society through the restoration of family life, Pius XI quoted Leo XIII's
apostolic letter _Neminem fugit_, of January 14, 1892:

Indeed, Joseph is for Fathers of families
an excellent example of paternal and vigilant
protection; the Most Holy Mother of God is an
excellent example and pattern to mothers of
love, modesty, of the spirit of submission and
perfect faith; in the person of Jesus, who was
subject to them, children have a divine model
of obedience to be admired, venerated and imi-
tated.[37]

Pius XI dealt with the question of the emancipation of woman chiefly in two encyclicals, _Casti
connubi_, on Christian marriage, and _Divini Redemp-
toris_, on atheistic communism. The passage in
Divini Redemptoris is, by comparison with _Casti
connubi_, brief and general. It is nevertheless
important in that it identifies the source of the

266

demands for emancipation to which Pius responded:

> Communism is particularly characterized
> by the rejection of any link that binds woman
> to the family and the home and her emancipa-
> tion [from the tutorship of man] is proclaimed
> as a basic principle. She is withdrawn from
> the family and the care of her children, to be
> thrust, instead, into public life and collec-
> tive production under the same conditions as
> man. The care of the home and children then
> devolves upon the collectivity. Finally the
> right of education is denied to parents, for
> it is conceived as the exclusive prerogative
> of the community in whose name and by whose
> mandate alone parents exercise this right.[38]

Within his encyclical on marriage, Casti connubi, Pius XI dealt with the subject of woman's
emancipation at great length, opposing the popular
demands to the Church's traditional teaching.
There were three parts to Pius' description of the
wifely role in marriage. The wife is to be subject
to her husband; this is the primary aspect. But
Pius added secondarily that she is not subject unconditionally; only on the condition that reason,
freedom of conscience, and her own dignity are not
violated is she subject to her husband. As an example, Pius added that women are not to be considered unable to make decisions (like minors); they
are not incapable, only subject. Thirdly, Pius indicated that the response due to the husband is one
of respect for authority, and the response due to
the wife is one of love.

> Finally, the bond of charity having thus set
> its seal upon the home, there must reign in it
> what St. Augustine calls 'the order of love.'
> This implies the primacy of the husband over
> his wife and children, and the ready submis-

267

sion and willing obedience of the wife according to the commandment of the apostle: 'Let women be subject to their husbands as to the Lord, because the husband is the head of the wife as Christ is the head of the Church.'

The submission of the wife neither ignores nor suppresses the liberty to which her dignity as a human person and her noble functions as wife, mother, and companion give her the full right. It does not oblige her to yield indiscriminately to all the desires of her husband, which may be unreasonable or incompatible with her wifely dignity. Nor does it mean that she is on a level with persons who in the law are called minors, and who are ordinarily denied the unrestricted exercise of their rights on the ground of their immature judgment and inexperience. But it does forbid such abuse of freedom as would neglect the welfare of the family; it refuses, in this body which is the family, to allow the heart to be separated from the head, with great detriment to the body itself and even the risk of disaster. If the husband is the head of the domestic body, then the wife is its heart; and as the first holds the primacy of authority, so the second can and ought to claim the primacy of love.[39]

Pius' conclusion to this passage is that since men act and women feel, the response to the sexes should be conditioned to this. The response proper to give to a man is therefore respect and obedience for the decisions and commands he has made; the response properly returned to a woman, who is occupied with emotions and personal relationships, is love.

In another section of <u>Casti connubi</u> Pius XI went on to speak of the demands, current in his time, for the emancipation of women and how they were mistaken demands:

The same false teachers, who by the spoken and the written word seek to dim the luster of marital fidelity and chastity, attack also the loyal and honorable obedience of the wife to her husband, which some of them even describe as an ignominious servitude of one partner to the other. All rights between husband and wife, they say, are equal, and since the servitude of one partner is a violation of this equality, they blatantly proclaim the emancipation of woman. This, in their view, is threefold: social regarding the government of the home; economic, regarding the administration of property; and physiological, regarding the prevention or suppression of offspring. Physiological emancipation would free woman at will from the wifely and maternal responsibilities--and this, we have seen, is not emancipation but an abominable crime; economic emancipation would authorize the wife, without the knowledge of her husband and even against his will, to conduct and administer her own affairs without any regard to the welfare of children, husband or family; social emancipation, finally, would free the wife from the domestic cares of children and family, enabling her, to the neglect of these, to follow her own bent, and engage in business and even public affairs.

This is no true emancipation of woman, nor is it the reasonable and exalted liberty which is due to the high office of a Christian woman and wife. On the contrary it is a degradation of the spirit of woman and of the dignity of a mother; it is a total perversion of family life, depriving the husband of his wife, the children of their mother, and the home and the family of their ever-watchful guardian. The

wife herself cannot help but suffer from this
[false liberty and] unnatural equality with
her husband. If she abdicates the royal
throne upon which the gospel has set her in
the home, she will soon find herself reduced
(in reality, if not in appearance) to the
slavery of ancient days, and will become what
she was among the heathens, nothing more than
the tool of her husband.

Such demands for equality of rights between husband and wife are pretensions and
exaggerated. But there is a true equality
between them, which is to be recognized in
all that pertains to the dignity and person
of a human being, and in all that is implied
by the marriage contract and is inherent in
wedlock itself. Here, admittedly, each party
enjoys exactly the same rights and is bound
by the same obligations. In all else, however, there must be a certain inequality and
adjustment, demanded by the welfare of the
family and by the unity and ordered stability
which must reign in the home.

So far as the changed circumstances and
customs of human intercourse may render necessary some modification in the social and economic condition of the married woman, it rests
with the public authority to adapt the civil
rights of the wife to the needs and requirements of modern times, but with the stipulation that regard must always be had to the
needs of woman's special temperament, to moral
rectitude, and to the welfare of the family,
and provided also that the essential order of
the home remains inviolate. This order was
constituted by an authority higher than man's,
that is, by the authority of God Himself, and
neither the laws of the State nor the good
pleasure of individuals can ever change it.[40]

In this passage we find the beginning of a shift in the teaching on woman's role. Though Pius had often relied on the traditional interpretation of woman's nature to support her restriction to traditional domestic roles, here he did not use this argument. Instead, he proposed a three point defense of the traditional role. First, he threatened woman with the forfeiture of all rights and dignity if she steps outside the domestic role Christianity has dictated for her, predicting her eventual reduction to slavery to man. Second, Pius argued that the welfare of the whole community and the family and the stability of the society demand her inequality of rights. Third, Pius argued that women are truly equal to men in important matters, in matters of dignity and worth, as well as within the regulations concerning holy wedlock. This last point is a reference to two traditional points, the spiritual equality of man and woman before God, and the fact that indissolubility of and faithfulness in marriage were equally binding in the eyes of the Church on both men and women. This point is an important one. Beginning here the papal tradition began to shift from a total denial of equality between the sexes[41] to the distinction between true equality and false equality, and the subsequent condemnation of that labelled false equality.

This distinction between true and false equality was a kind of papal acknowledgement that it was no longer possible in the modern world to deny the equality of persons convincingly. Previously equality for the popes had meant sameness; the new papal distinction between true and false equality depended upon the idea of equality permitting differences. Thus Pius XI began a move from the view that woman occupied an unequal place in the world, despite her spiritual equality, to the view that men and women were completely equal and therefore deserving of equal rights, but were not the same

271

and therefore did not deserve the same rights. From the papal point of view, nothing was lost in this admission that woman was equal, for she still remained where and what she was; the major change was that she was no longer ordered quite so completely to be subject to man. The fact that the admission of woman's true equality produced no real change in the papal view of woman's nature or activities suggests that real change in the status quo depends upon a new understanding of woman's nature--complementarity of the sexes being to sexism what separate-but-equal was to racism.

Pius XII: On Woman

The documents and allocutions of Pius XII concerning woman are innumerable. No attempt will be made to present all of these, or even all of the major documents. Rather this section will attempt to present examples of the different approaches Pius XII made to the subject of woman, her nature, and her role in society.

In general, there was little change in the views of Pius XII towards woman from those of his predecessors. His view of her nature and talents was essentially the same as that of Pius XI. He also agreed with the implications of her role that Pius XI had drawn from his conception of her nature. Pius XII disapproved of working women, but seemed to recognize the larger public role of women in his day, both in the workplace and in society in general. The greatest shift between Pius XII and his predecessors was his view of how women should wield their limited power in the world. While earlier popes had proposed a "the hand that rocks the cradle rules the world" understanding of women's power in the world, Pius XII, while still using and promoting this view of women's power, also advocated women's taking a larger share of responsibility for

272

the entire society, especially politics. This shift, however, did not involve any new conception of the talents or role of women. Pius still thought that women's proper center was the home. But he also saw that the protection of the home was a task that now involved its defense in the arena of politics and public policy, so that woman's traditional role had, in a sense, expanded into the public sphere. She was now called upon to lobby and vote, to advise public officials and to protest legislation and policy which might have detrimental effects upon the home, the Church, the education of children, and public morality in general.

In examining the position of Pius XII on woman we will concentrate on five particular aspects of the question: (1) the nature of woman, (2) the relation of men and women, (3) the moral aspects of the woman question, (4) women and work, and (5) the Church and women.

The Nature of Woman

The key to Pius' conception of woman's nature is his conviction that woman is created for motherhood. This is her nature and her role for Pius, as we shall see. In an October 21, 1945 address to Italian women Pius said:

> Be she married or single, woman's function is seen clearly in the lineaments of her sex, in its propensities and special powers. She works side by side with man, but she works in her own special way and according to her natural bent. Now a woman's function, a woman's way, a woman's natural bent, is motherhood. Every woman is called to be a mother, a mother in the physical sense, or mother in a sense more spiritual and more exalted, yet real,

nonetheless.

To this end the Creator fashioned the whole of woman's nature; not only her organism, but also and still more her spirit, and most of all her exquisite sensibility. This is why it is only from the standpoint of the family that the woman, if she is a true woman, can see and fully understand every problem of human life. And this is why her delicate sense of her own dignity causes her a thrill of apprehension whenever the social or political order threatens danger to her vocation as a mother, or to the welfare of the family.[42]

Thus for Pius XII it was essential to involve women in social decisions since they (and only they) bring the home perspective which is so essential. But the fact that they see things only from the perspective of the family is also a great limitation, when less domestic matters are under discussion, as he later made clear.

Pius presented in the course of his documents on women the traditional view of women's gifts. He maintained that women "should strive to enrich their inborn gifts of intuition and tender feelings."[43] He often made the point that women are naturally opposed to war and violence of all kinds:

If indeed all women were to pass from that innate feeling, which makes them abhor war, to concrete action to impede war, it would be impossible that the total of such imposing efforts, which bring into play those forces best calculated to move the will, that is piety and love, it would be impossible, We say, that it should fail to achieve its end.

May the divine aid provoked in prayer

274

which, women, who are by nature pious, are
accustomed to offer with greater perseverance
to God, render still more fruitful these
efforts.[44]

Women, said Pius, have some other natural virtues. They have the ability "to make simple things
charming."[45] This virtue of women is a favorite of
Pius XII's. He often referred to the gift that
women have for making a "house into a home," a hum-
ble rented abode into a warm and welcoming family
hearth. Another natural virtue of woman for Pius
was her sense of modesty. In an address on the
occasion of the beatification of Maria Goretti,
who lost her life resisting the attempts of a rap-
ist, Pius XII spoke of the modern need for those
supernatural virtues which shone forth from Maria
Goretti: "the spirit of faith and modesty, and
this not only as an almost unconscious sense of
natural shame [sic], but as a conscious and carefully cultivated Christian virtue."[46] The phrase
"natural shame" is an unfortunate translation
which did not clearly convey Pius' meaning; modes-
tia does not usually mean shame in the way that
this word is used in English, but rather modesty,
or shyness. That women are given to a kind of
physical modesty was a conviction of Pius XII's,
and a constant theme of his was that this natural
modesty was being destroyed in the modern world.
Purity and modesty were especially ever-present
themes of Pius XII with regard to the behavior of
women, and fashion a frequent topic of his allocutions to women. In an October 6, 1940 allocution
to the girls of Catholic Action Pius said:

> Just as nature placed in every creature
> the instinct of self-preservation which con-
> cerns the life of the creature and the inte-
> grity of its members, thus conscience and
> grace, which do not destroy nature but per-

fect it, place in the soul, as it were, a
sense which renders it vigilant against the
dangers threatening purity. This is especially a characteristic of the young Christian
girl. We read in the 'Passio SS. Perpetuae
et Felicitatis'--rightly regarded as one of
the most precious gems of early Christian
literature--that in the amphitheatre of Car-
thage, when the martyr Vibia Perpetua, thrown
high into the air by a savage cow, fell to
the ground, her first thought and action was
to rearrange her dress to cover her thigh,
because she was more concerned for modesty
than for pain.[47]

One area in which Pius XII consistently pointed out the limitations of the feminine nature was
the susceptibility of woman to the lures of the
world because of her inability to penetrate past
the attraction of freedom and flattery. In a
September 28, 1948 allocution to the International
Association for the Protection of the Girl, Pius
XII declared:

Under the pretext that in the past the young
girl, brought up as it were in a hot-house,
surrounded by anxious cares, and jealously
preserved in her ingenuousness, ran the risk
of falling the victim of surprise on the first
contact with the world and with freedom, the
modern girl very often illudes herself that an
education and conduct which is direct opposite
will make her strong, inured, immune, ready
for defense or counterstroke. She takes as
personality and vigor what is, at bottom, only
impertinence, imprudence, and effrontery. She
cannot be persuaded that continual familiarity
with the other sex, the parity in occupation
and behavior, once contained within the limits
of a strict morality, lays her open to the

dangers of passing, sooner or later, these
limits.

Notwithstanding her unconstraint and sometimes even her masculine mentality, the young
girl qualified as 'modern,' willing or not,
retains the innate, indelible characteristics
of her sex: imagination, sensibility, the
tendency if not to a childish vanity, at
least, often enough, to most dangerous flirt-
ing; and so she allows herself to be caught
in the snare, if indeed she does not leap into
it herself head first.

.   .   .   .   .

The illusion of solidity and strength, the
illusion of experience and prudence; both of
them nourish a presumption to which her nature,
even if well trained, is only too prone. She
believes she can with impunity read everything,
see everything, taste everything.[48]

Here we have the other side of a creature
formed for motherhood. She is sensitive, emotional,
full of tender feelings. But her nature does not
equip her with strong discernment, with the ability
to distrust those who might attempt to seduce or
mislead her, or with the wisdom to escape being
victim and slave. She therefore needs to be protected from her own weakness.[49]

Relation of Men and Women

Pius XII was very clear that the first statement that needs to be made concerning the relationship of men and women is that they enjoy spiritual
equality. This is an oft repeated theme of his, of
which the following is one example:

As children of God, man and woman have a
dignity in which they are absolutely equal;
and they are equal, too, in regard to the

277

supreme end of human life, which is everlasting union with God in the happiness of Heaven.
    To have vindicated and proclaimed this
truth, and to have delivered woman from a
slavery as degrading as it was contrary to
nature, is one of the imperishable glories
of the Church. But man and woman cannot
maintain or perfect this equal dignity of
theirs unless they respect and make use of
the distinctive qualities which nature has
bestowed on each sex: physical and spiritual
qualities which are indestructable, and so
coordinated that their mutual relation cannot
be upset without nature itself intervening to
re-establish it. These peculiar characteristics which distinguish the sexes are so obvious to everybody that nothing short of will-
ful blindness, or a doctrinaire attitude as
disastrous as it is utopian, can ignore or
fail to see their importance in the structure
of society.[50]

This same theme appeared in a 1943 address to the
girls of Catholic Action:

    The present structure of society, based
on the almost absolute equality of man and
woman, rests on a false presumption. It is
true that as far as personality is concerned,
man and woman are equal in dignity, honor and
value. But they are not equal in every respect. Certain natural gifts, inclinations
and dispositions are proper only to the man,
or only to the woman, according to the distinct fields of activity assigned them by
nature. We are not speaking here of natural
dispositions or capacities of a secondary order, like an inclination or bias towards literature, the arts or sciences, but rather of
gifts of an essential efficacy in the life of

278

the family and of the nation. Everyone knows
that nature, even if suppressed by violence,
always reasserts itself. It remains to be
seen whether someday nature will impose a reform of the social structure of today.[51]

And again in his September 10, 1941 address to
newlyweds Pius XII said:

> In holiness, by means of grace, both
> spouses are equally and immediately united
> to Christ. In fact, St. Paul said that as
> many, as have been baptized in Christ and
> who have put on Christ, are all sons of God;
> there is neither male nor female, because all
> are one in Jesus Christ. Not so, however, in
> the Church and in the family, which are visi-
> ble societies: for this reason the Apostle
> warned: 'But I would have you know that the
> head of the woman is the man: and the head
> of Christ is God.' Just as Christ, as man,
> is subject to God, as every Christian is sub-
> ject to Christ, Whose member He is, so the
> woman is subject to man, who through matrimony
> has become with her 'one flesh.' The great
> apostle felt it necessary to remind the con-
> verts of Corinth of this truth. Many ideas
> and customs of the pagan world could have
> easily made them forget, or not understand,
> or overlook, this fundamental fact. Would be
> not perhaps feel the need of his warning just
> as necessary today for not a few Christians?
> Is it not true that in our age there is blow-
> ing the ill wind of a rebirth of paganism?[52]

This passage exemplified the second step of
the papal formulation of the place of woman in relation to man. She was equal to him in the eyes
of God, but unequal to him in "visible society."
Pius said this in another way in a 1957 address to

Catholic Women's Organizations when he declared
that women are not in any way inferior to men,
but they are nonetheless subject to them.[53]

One of the more interesting aspects of this
passage is the reference to the fundamental fact
overlooked by paganism. Considering the organization of the paragraph and the material immediately
preceding this statement, one is led to think that
the fact that the pagan world overlooked is that
woman is to be subject to man. The rebirth of
paganism seems to refer to the modern movement in
the direction of the equality of women. In fact
the following paragraph in Pius' address is:

> The conditions of life, which derive from
> the present economic and social fabric, direct
> both men and women to the professions, arts
> and trades, and bring them together in the
> workshop, in the office, in various occupa-
> tions. Thus they tend to generate and in
> practice to introduce a broad parity of the
> activity of women with that of men, so that
> husband and wife not rarely find themselves
> in a position of equality. Often they exer-
> cise professions of the same order, render to
> the family budget a contribution practically
> equal, while that same work leads them to live
> very independent one of the other. In the
> meantime, what of the children God sends them?
> How are these watched over, cared for, educa-
> ted and instructed?[54]

There are really two arguments in this paragraph.
The first is a continuation of the previous paragraph, a description of the pagan trend by which
women were, in Pius' view, achieving equality with
men in the workplace, and destroying natural hierarchy. The second is a question implying that another problem with equality is that the women are

not home to care for the children. As Pius continued with this train of thought, he asked the
questions: "Why wonder if in these circumstances
the sense of hierarchy in the family fades and begins to disappear? What wonder if the supervision
of the father and the care of the mother do not
suffice to render the family circle happy and lov-
able?"[55]

One of the more interesting conclusions of a
study of Pius XII's statements regarding the relationship of men and women is that, as we see above,
he lends support to the feminist thesis that domination (hierarchy) was and is patterned on the
relationship of the sexes. Equally interesting
from a feminist point of view is Pius' description
of the Church combatting paganism by urging the
subjection of women to men against the pagan view
which favored equality. We will see in our examination of Pius' statements on women and the Church
that he was by no means consistent in his opinion
that paganism tended to view woman as the equal of
man. It may well be that he meant that one of the
extremes to which paganism went was to allow some
women the sexual excesses often allowed to men--
such as divorce and serial marriages.[56] This will
be dealt with further within the topic of the
Church and women.

A major point in the consideration of the relation between men and women for Pius XII was the
concept of the headship of the man. This did not
only mean that women are subject to men; more
basically it involved an understanding of human
society in which hierarchy was essential. In every
relationship, the argument went, someone must dominate, and in the case of men and women that domin-
ator has been chosen by God, nature, and history--
man:

every family is a society; every well ordered
society needs a head; every power of headship
comes from God. And so, too, the family you
have founded has a head, invested with authority by God: authority over her who has been
given to him as a companion to constitute the
nucleus of this family, and over those who
with the Lord's blessing will come to swell
it and make it happy, like young shoots from
the bole of the olive.

Yes, the authority of the head of the
family comes from God, just as from God came
the dignity and authority of Adam as the
first head of the human race, endowed with
all the gifts which were to be passed on to
his offspring. Hence it is that he was the
first to be formed, and afterwards Eve. And
St. Paul said that it was not Adam who was
deceived, but the woman who allowed herself
to be seduced, and who transgressed God's law.
Oh, how much harm Eve's curiosity, in looking
at the beautiful fruit of the earthly paradise
and her conversation with the serpent, did to
the first man, to Eve herself, to all her
children, and to us! Besides multiplying her
sorrows and sufferings, to her God said that
she would be subject to her husband. Oh,
Christian wives and mothers, never be taken
off guard by the desire to wield the sceptre
in the family. Let your sceptre--the sceptre
of love--be that which the Apostle of the Gentiles places in your hands: to save yoursel-
ves through child-bearing, if you continue in
faith and love and sanctification with so-
briety.[57]

The overall position of Pius XII on women in
relation to men was a moderate one, well expressed
in his July 17, 1952 letter Der Katholische
Deutsche in which he called for a balance of

Gleichberechtigung und Unterordnung in the lives
of women:

> Withal, the duties assumed and the rights
> acquired [by women] must be transmitted, with
> their content conferred on them by Nature and
> Revelation, according to the Catholic faith--
> safeguarding, at the same time, the just bal-
> ance between freedom and responsibility, be-
> tween the duty to oneself and duty toward
> one's neighbor, between equality and subor-
> dination.[58]

Moral Considerations

Some elements of Pius' thought concerning
moral attributes of woman have already emerged in
the previous discussion. He characterized the
female as vain, not formed for making sound judg-
ments, of extreme sensibility, physically modest,
and imaginative. He referred to the Eve image of
the female as easily seduced, overly curious, and
as the temptress of man. It is not then surprising that in other addresses he held woman responsible for a serious portion of the evil in the
world as a whole:

> The world of today is very different.
> Those who study souls with greater attention
> and insight, to discover the causes and signs
> of the intellectual and moral crises which
> trouble mankind, are as one in pointing out
> the most dangerous forms of this unrest: the
> irreligion and lack of morality in a notable
> portion of the women. They explain that once
> she has banished from her heart every religi-
> ous thought and sentiment, the woman easily
> cleaves to the most tragic errors; and then
> under the impulse of passion, she does not
> hesitate to follow to their extremes however

283

unreasonable and repugnant, the doctrines which have seduced her; and thus, because she is so rich in sensibility, there is no longer any barrier which can restrain her either in the field of ideas or of morality.[59]

Probably a chief reason why so much of the evil in the world is blamed upon women in this passage is that Pius is of the opinion that women have power over not only their own actions, but those of men:

The woman has a great influence upon individual and social behavior, because she has a great influence upon her husband. Remember that Eve, deceived by the serpent, gave of the forbidden fruit to Adam, and he, too, ate of it.[60]

This image of woman as an "Eve," able to twist man around her little finger whether for good or for evil, runs throughout the writings of Pius. It is the reason that Pius could imply of woman that "when she was good, she was very, very good, but when she was bad she was horrid":

Beloved daughters, there are few things more saddening, more sorrowful, more reproachful, and even more horrifying than a young woman who becomes a scandal and an occasion of sin; just as there are few things more admirable, comforting, praiseworthy, and even more beautiful than a girl who is an apostle and an occasion of good.[61]

One of the specific ways in which women led men to sin in the opinion of Pius XII (as for his predecessors) was through immodest dress. Addressing the topic of fashion on May 22, 1941, Pius remarked to the girls of Catholic Action:

Some young ladies may remark that a certain form of dress is more convenient, or even more hygienic; but if it becomes a grave and proximate danger for the soul, it is certainly not hygienic for the spirit, and you must reject it. The salvation of their souls made heroines of the martyrs, like the Agneses and the Cecilias, amidst the sufferings and torturings of their virginal bodies: and will you, their sisters in the faith, in the love of Christ, in the esteem for virtue, not find at the bottom of your hearts the courage and the strength to sacrifice a little well-being --a physical advantage, if you like, to conserve safe and pure the life of your souls? And if, simply for one's own pleasure, one has not the right to endanger the physical health of others, is it not still less licit to compromise the health, or rather the very life of their souls? If, as some women say, a bold fashion does not leave them with any evil impressions, how can they know then that others do not draw therefrom incentives to evil? . . . Oh, how truly was it said that if some Christian women could only suspect the temptations and falls they cause in others with modes of dress and familiarity of behavior, which they unthinkingly consider of no importance, they would be shocked by the responsibility which is theirs.[62]

In this passage perhaps the most interesting aspect is the extent to which Pius feels that women can present temptations to evil for men, <u>even when women are not conscious of this</u>. This is the case, according to Pius, not only with certain modes of dress, but also in the case of familiar behavior. If familiar behavior is a temptation to men, distance, physical and emotional, seems to be necessary to eliminate the temptation. In a way this is to advocate the restriction of women's freedom because men are weak. This is, in fact, the entire thrust of Pius' views on the power of woman: such power needs to be controlled carefully, for men are easily seduced to sin.

Women and Work

There are three major points in the body of literature by Pius XII on women and work. The first is that proper work for women is caring for children and home. The second is that when women work outside the home, they deserve equal pay for equal work. The third is that there are a number of ways in which women working outside the home create problems, social and moral.

That the proper work for women was domestic work was primary in the thinking of Pius XII. This was the message of his July 26, 1955 address to women, Le vingtcinquieme[63]: the family is women's work. Motherhood and childcare is not only proper work for women; it is the way to salvation for her:

> When God in his goodness bestows on the bride the dignity of motherhood beside a cradle, the cries of the newly born will not disturb or destroy the happiness of the home. Rather, it will increase and transfigure it with divine light resplendent with the angels of heaven, whence descends a ray of life which surpasses nature and generates in the sons of man, sons of God. Herein lies the sanctity of the bridal bed: herein the dignity of Christian motherhood, and the salvation of the married woman. For the woman, proclaims the great Apostle Paul, shall be saved through motherhood if she continue in faith and love and sanctification with sobriety.

. . . . .

A cradle consecrates the mother; more
cradles sanctify her, and glorify her in the
eyes of her husband, her children, the Church,
and the nation. Those mothers who are filled
with regret when another child seeks the nour-
ishment of life at their breast, are foolishly
unhappy: they do not know of what stuff they
are made. Complaint at the blessing of God
which surrounds and increases the family
hearth is the enemy of domestic happiness.
The heroism of motherhood is the pride and
glory of the Christian wife. If she has not
the joy of having a little angel, the loneli-
ness and solitude in her home becomes a prayer
and invocation to heaven; her tears flow like
those of Anna, who at the door of the Temple
begged of God the gift of a son--Samuel.[64]

But not only are women to be saved through
motherhood, with the more children, the better;
Pius also instructed women in how to be good mothers,
even to such minutiae as the advantage of breast-
feeding infants:

Many of the moral characteristics which
you see in the youth or the man owe their origin to the manner and circumstances of his
first up-bringing in infancy: purely organic
habits contracted at that time may later prove
a serious obstacle to the spiritual life of
the soul. And so you will make it your special care in the treatment of your child to observe the prescriptions of a perfect hygiene,
so that when it comes to the use of reason its
bodily organs and faculties will be healthy
and robust and free from distorted tendencies.
This is the reason why, except where it is
quite impossible, it is most desirable that
the mother should feed the child at her own
breast. Who shall say what mysterious influ-

287

ences are exerted upon the growth of that little creature by the mother upon whom it depends entirely for its development![65]

Regardless of the fact that Pius felt that women's proper work was in the home, he recognized that many women were obliged to work for a living,[66] and insisted that such women deserved equal pay with men who performed the same work:

> We have no wish to deny the advantages to be derived from certain of these social measures, provided that they are administered in a proper manner. We have, in fact, Ourselves, insisted that, for the same work and the same service rendered, women have a right to equal pay with men.[67]

This stand on "equal pay for equal work" is indeed found in numerous places in the documents of Pius XII.[68] Pius maintained that this had always been the position of the Church. Pius XII explained that to do otherwise than pay equal wages for equal work was unjust, and contrary to the common good. His diagnosis of harm to society, however, was based not only on his visions of unjustly paid women, but also on a vision of resulting male unemployment:

> First of all, We need not remind you, with your wide experience of social affairs, how the Church has always supported the principle that to the working woman is owed, for the same amount of work and production, a salary equal to that of the working man; that it would be an injustice, and contrary to the common good, to profit without consideration from the work of the woman, only because it is available at lower price. This would harm not only the working woman, but also the man, who would thus be exposed to the danger of unemployment.[69]

Regardless of Pius' support for "equal pay for equal work" he did not advocate that men and women be given equal work so as to be able to command equal pay. Instead he called for extreme prudence in decision-making about women's work:

> With reference to work, the physical and moral makeup of woman calls for prudent discrimination as to its quality and its quantity. The idea of using women in construction work, in the mines, and for various types of heavy labor--which is praised and practiced in certain countries which claim to be progressive--is not a modern achievement at all; instead it is more like a sad return toward an age that Christian civilization laid to rest long ago.
>
> It is true that woman is a force to be reckoned with in the economy of a nation, but only on the condition that she continue to carry on the lofty functions which are rightfully hers. She is certainly not an industrial force (to use the common terminology) such as man is, for a greater expenditure of physical energy can be expected of the latter. That genteel respect which every man of refined upbringing shows women whenever he meets them ought to be put into practice by the civil laws and institutions of the nation as well.[70]

Pius was not clear as to how his phrase, "physical and moral makeup of woman," should be interpreted. The reference to woman's physical makeup being restrictive is understandable because it is so explicit in the tradition. But "moral makeup" is ambiguous--are some occupations more of a moral threat to women than to men?

Pius found that the fact that woman was pri-

289

marily designed for domestic work should be the determining factor in deciding where and in what she should be employed. In his lengthy address to Italian women on October 21, 1945 Pius noted that since the war many women without hope of husbands and families were entering civil and political life. He pointed out what kinds of work _were_ appropriate to women's nature and calling:

This is one motive calling the Catholic woman to enter on the new path now opening to her activity. But there is another: her dignity as a woman. It is for her to work with man for the welfare of the _civitas_ in which she enjoys a dignity equal with his, and here each sex has its part to play according to its nature, its distinctive qualities, its physical, intellectual, and moral capabilities. Both sexes have the right and the duty to work together for the good of society, for the good of the nation. But it is clear that while man is by temperament more suited to deal with external affairs and public business, generally speaking the woman has a deeper insight for understanding the delicate problems of domestic and family life, and a surer touch in solving them—which, of course, is not to deny that some women can show great ability in every sphere of public life.

It is not so much that each sex is called to a different task; the difference is rather in their manner of judging and arriving at concrete and practical applications. Take the case of civil rights, for example; at the present time they are equal for both sexes. But just think how much more intelligently and effectively these rights will be used if men and women pool their resources in using them. The sensibility and delicacy which are characteristic of the woman may perhaps bias her judgement in the direction of her impressions, and so tend to the prejudice of wide and clear vision, cool decision, or farsighted prudence; but on the other hand they are most valuable aids in discerning the needs, aspirations, and dangers proper to the sphere of domestic life, public assistance, and religion.[71]

This passage causes one to wonder that a task supposedly so important as the rearing of children is entrusted (almost entirely) to such creatures who are impressionable, lacking either clear vision or farsighted prudence. But more than this, the reference to the fact that while today civil rights are equal for the sexes, it would be better if women and men divided civil duties and rights between them--this reference induces suspicion as to the extent of the rights which will fall to women. The specific work roles to which Pius assigned women were certainly limited, and obviously modelled on the duties of housewives and mothers:

> Associated with the work of man in the sphere of civil institutions, she will apply herself especially to matters calling for tact, delicacy, the maternal instinct, rather than administrative rigidity. In such questions as those of a woman's dignity, a girl's honor and integrity, the protection and education of the child, who better than a woman can understand what is needed? And what a number of problems there are of this kind which require the attention of government and legislature! In the suppression of licentious behavior, for example, only a woman has the gift which can temper firmness with kindness without sacrifice of efficiency; in dealing with morally abandoned children, only a woman will know how to save them from humiliation

and have them trained to a decent life and to
the practice of the religious and civic virtues; only she can be truly successful in ad-
ministering orphanages, in welfare work for
released prisoners, and rescue work for fallen
girls, she alone can give true expression to
the lament of a mother's heart when she sees
a totalitarian state--call it by what name you
will--trying to rob her of the right to educate her children.[72]

Those occupations, then, which are appropriate to
women are those which require personal relationships between persons, personal communication and
love. This is the work that only she is fit for.
Here we have come to the point when the appropriate
question for Pius is: How human are men? If they
cannot successfully handle jobs that call for expressions of the heart, what kind of Christians are
they? What kind of human beings? Are the jobs un-
fit for women fit for any human being? Perhaps the
work that needs to be done first is not the herding
of women into jobs that will not deform them and
will require their human warmth. Perhaps the task
which should come first is to make everyone's work
more human by a rearrangement of tasks and a questioning of the traditional views on work. This is
one objection of feminism to Pius XII's formulations of woman's place, and to those of his successors.

Because Pius felt that there were some jobs
which were appropriate to women because of their
nature and calling (and some jobs that were not
appropriate for women), one of the problems with
the order of his day was that women were working in
areas which were not appropriate for them. This
could cause, and did cause, in Pius XII's opinion,
serious problems for the whole of society. The
chief culprit in this threat to society seemed to

be that women were becoming not only equal with
men on the job, but were approaching dominance--or
at least, we shall see, so Pius viewed the trend.
This equality approaching dominance was, Pius said,
responsible for promoting a perfidious kind of un-
christian autonomy which caused people to refuse to
sacrifice for the good of others. It was also, he
said, destroying the domestic hierarchy upon which
all society depended.[73] This domestic hierarchy
to which Pius referred was the Pauline concept of
the headship of the man, a headship which was endangered when woman became involved in a sphere of
activity in which there was no male exercising a
position of authority over her. Pius was very explicit that this sphere in which a woman could be
free of male control was dangerous for the family
because it might give her ideas of general autonomy:

> And do you, O brides, lift up your hearts.
> Do not be content merely to accept, and--one
> might almost say--to tolerate this authority
> of your husband, to whom God has subjected you
> according to the dispositions of nature and of
> grace; in your sincere submission you must
> love that authority and love it with the same
> respectful love you bear toward the authority
> of Our Lord Himself, from Whom all authority
> flows.[74]
> We well understand that just as the parity
> in studies, in school, in science, in sports,
> in competition, makes many a woman's heart
> swell with pride, so the mistrustful sensi-
> bility of modern young women may not yield
> without difficulty to subjection in the home.
> Many voices will suggest rather a proud auton-
> omy; they will repeat that you are in every
> respect the equal of your husband, and in many
> respects his superior. Do not react like Eve
> to these lying, tempting, deceitful voices.

Do not be led astray from the path which alone will lead you to true happiness in this life as well as in the life hereafter.[75]

Here we have again the message that to be subject is not to be inferior or unequal; women's place is to be subordinate to her husband because both nature and the Creator have so ordained things. Pius went on to maintain that true freedom and independence lie not in autonomy, but in adherence to a conscience formed by the Church's teaching of the divine law. Therefore he called on women to continue to make the constant sacrifices which are necessary within any marriage to preserve the union necessary to allow the woman to properly raise children:

The greatest independence, that which is yours by sacred right, is the independence of a solidly Christian heart in the fact of the importunities of evil. There where duty makes itself heard, summons, warns your mind and your heart, when you are faced with an appeal which is contrary to the unexceptionable precepts of the divine law, and to the unchangeable duties of Christians, of wives, and of mothers, there you must preserve and defend respectfully, calmly, but yet firmly and immoveably, all the sacred and inalienable independence of your conscience. There come at times in one's life days in which dawns the hour of heroism or of a victory, whose only witnesses are God's angels--and they, invisible witnesses.

In any case, when you are called upon to sacrifice a dream, a personal taste--be it as legitimate as you will--rejoice to think that these small sacrifices will recompense by winning over more and more as the days pass, the heart which gave itself to you. These sacri-

fices will ever increase and cement that intimate union of thoughts, sentiments, of will,
which alone will enable you easily and sweet-
ly to carry out the noble mission entrusted
to you on behalf of your children: a mission
whose chances of success any lack of this
unity would seriously undermine.

And since in the family, as in any association of two or more persons with the same end
in view, an indispensable element is the authority which constitutes an efficacious safeguard of their union, and directs and governs
all to this end, you must love this bond which
makes of two wills only one, even though along
the path of life one leads and the other follows. You must love that bond with all the
love you bear your home.[76]

In the above paragraphs we have a new twist in
the papal teaching on women's subjection to men.
Not only is this subjection to be borne, it is to
be embraced, and the reason that women are to embrace the rule of men is that this is the only way
they can successfully fulfill their primary task
of raising children.

It is interesting that in his consideration of
women Pius XII was very selective about his use of
the Genesis account. He often referred to the se-
condariness of Eve, to her important role in the
Fall, and her punishment for the Fall. But when
he considered woman's role he did not refer to the
purpose Genesis alleges for her creation--to be a
helpmeet and companion for man, to share in the
dominion over the earth. Instead, as we see in
this passage, he looked to biology, to her body
and its differences from the male body, and defined her purpose in terms of those differences.
Her purpose is to have children and to raise them,
and whatever relationship is necessary with man in

order to enable her to raise those children is
therefore the appropriate relationship between man
and woman. The unspoken implication of this passage is that if the wife failed to submit to her
husband and were abandoned, she and the children
would be in a hopeless position: their survival
depends upon the maintenance of the marriage on
whatever terms are necessary. This was not always
far from the actualities of women's lives. But
the curious aspect of all this is that Pius here
took the often real dependence of women and children for survival on the husband and made this normative for the marital relationship _in place of_ the
relationship indicated as primary in the scriptural
account. Throughout his other writings on marriage
there is a continuing contradiction between the
idea of woman's primary task as motherhood and her
primary relationship as partner to man.[77] The tendency is, as above, to view the partnership as a
pragmatic one required by the necessarily joint
task of raising children.

Besides the subtle ways always touched upon in
which working women undermine the proper order in
the home and family, Pius XII was very clear that
the day-to-day needs of the family were unfilled
when women were obliged to fill two roles:

> Is it not a truth at once old and yet ever
> new--a truth rooted even in the very physical
> conditions of the life of the woman, a truth
> remorselessly proclaimed not only by the ex-
> perience of the remotest ages, but also in
> our own times of insatiable industry, of
> claims to equality, or sporting competitions
> --the truth that it is the woman who must
> mould and nourish the family hearth, and that
> in this, her place can never be taken by her
> husband.
> This is the task assigned her for the

good of society by nature and by marriage.
Drag her, draw her out of and away from her
family with the attractions of one or another
of the too many causes which compete to win
and subdue her: and you will find the woman
neglecting her hearth. Without this flame,
the atmosphere of the home cools, the family
circle practically ceases to exist, and becomes an occasional refuge for an odd hour;
the center of daily life will be found elsewhere for her husband, for the wife herself,
for the children.

Whether we want it so or not, the married
man or woman, who is resolved to remain faithful to the duties of this state, cannot build
the beautiful edifice of happiness except upon the firm foundation of family life. But
where can you find a true family without a
fireside, without a real, visible point of
union, where this life is centered, concentrated, rooted, maintained and deepened . . .
where it may bud and come to flower? It is
useless to reply that the visible hearth exists from the moment when the two hands were
joined, the rings placed on the fingers, when
the newlyweds took up a common abode in their
apartment or house, be it large or small, rich
or poor. No; for the material fireside is not
enough to form the spiritual edifice of happiness. The matter must be raised up to a rarer
atmosphere; from the earthly fire must spring
the living and life-giving flame of the new
family.

This is not the work of a day, especially
if the fireside is not the one hallowed by the
preceding generations, but rather--as is more
often the case today, at least in the city--in
some rented home which can be changed at will.
Who will create then, little by little, day by
day, the true spiritual fireside, if not the

action par excellence of her who has become a 'housewife', of her to whom the heart of her husband trusts? Whether her husband be a laborer or farmer, professional or literary man, scientist or artist or clerk or official, it is inevitable that his work should carry him for the most part outside the home, or, if in the home, it will confine him for long hours in his study, out of the current of family life. For him, the family hearth will become the place where, at the end of his working day, he will restore his physical and moral powers in rest, peace, in intimate enjoyment.[78]

In essence, this is an assertion that the world is not a humane place, and that it is the job of women to provide a human refuge from the world for husband and children. The burden of providing quality of life falls on the woman. In a sense, then, when women do from necessity work in the world, their task is to work for the humanization of the world, but for Pius this task seemed so immense that to withdraw women's energies from the maintenance of domestic refuges in order to humanize the whole world seemed to endanger the only human areas in the world.

Women and the Church

That the Church is responsible for having restored (and in some senses established) the dignity of woman is a major theme of Pius XII. In his October 14, 1956 allocution to Italian women's groups he declared:

Even now you can find some people who tend to play down or even completely ignore the Church's meritorious role in restoring womankind to its original dignity. They

298

never tire of claiming that the Church is
actually bitterly opposed to the so-called
'emancipation of woman from a feudal regime.'
They use false fragmentary evidence and give
a superficial interpretation of customs and
laws which were inspired by necessary proprie-
ties of the day; and they do this in an attempt
to associate the Church with something that it
has firmly opposed from its very beginning--
that unjust status of personal inferiority to
which paganism often condemned women.

Do we have to recall the famous sentence
of St. Paul which is reflected in the internal
nature and external attitude of all Christian
civilization? '[There is] neither Jew nor
Greek; there is neither slave nor freedman;
there is neither male nor female. For you are
all one in Jesus Christ.' This does not mean
that Christian law does away with the limitations or proper subjection which arise from
the demands of nature, of human and Christian
propriety, or from the needs of life together,
which cannot last long without some authority,
even in its smallest unit, the family.[79]

Here Pius claimed that the Church is responsible
for defending the worth of women. We observed earlier that Pius defended the Church's treatment of
women over that of paganism in that the Church insisted upon the necessity of female subjection to
males.[80] Though the stance attributed to paganism
in the two passages seems contradictory, it is important to see that the Church's defense of the
dignity of woman,[81] especially expressed in opposition to divorce, concubinage, and adultery (which
worked to woman's disadvantage in paganism[82]) was
intimately linked to the view that women are to be
protected because their proper condition of subjection makes this a duty for all men, and particularly for organizations with power. The protection of

women from the evils which degraded them in paganism is necessary precisely because of their dependence. It was not inconsistent for Pius to have condemned the pagan treatment of woman both for having granted her a false equality and for having degraded her when she proved unable to protect herself in that independence.[83]

The best illustration of the way in which Pius wove together these themes of Church defense of women and Church insistence upon womanly subjection is an extended passage from an address which Pius gave on the role of the Christian wife, given to one of the frequent groups of Italian newlyweds he addressed:

> The divine Redeemer came thus to restore what paganism had overthrown. However much light they threw upon the family bond, neither Athens nor Rome, focal points of civilization, succeeded either through the profound speculation of philosophy, or with the wisdom of their laws, or with the severity of censure, in giving the woman her true place in the family.
> In the Roman world, notwithstanding the respect and dignity surrounding the mother of the family--Uxor dignitatis nomen est, non voluptatis--she was withal according to the ancient law, juridically subject to the totally unlimited power of her husband or the pater familias, who had supreme power in the home . . .
> But with the passing of the centuries, the laws of the ancients concerning the family fell into disuse; their iron discipline disappeared, and women became practically independent of the authority of the husband.
> . . . there arose in vivid contrast the ever-growing numbers of women especially of

300

high society, who fled disdainfully from the
duties of motherhood, to give themselves rather to occupations, and to play a part till
then reserved to men alone.

At the same time, as divorces multiplied,
the family began to disintegrate, and womanly
affections and behavior deviated from the
straight path of virtue . . . The woman has a
great influence upon individual and social behavior, because she has a great influence upon
her husband. Remember that Eve, deceived by
the serpent, gave of the forbidden fruit to
Adam, and he too ate of it.

To reestablish in the family that hierarchy indispensable for unity and happiness, and
at the same time to restore the original and
true grandeur of conjugal love, was one of the
greatest undertakings of Christendom. And
this from the moment that Christ affirmed before the Pharisees and the whole world: 'What
God has joined together let no man put asun-
der.'

. . . . .

But granted this dependence of the wife on
her husband as it is sanctioned in the very
first pages of revelation, the Apostle of the
Gentiles reminds us that Christ, full of mercy
for us and for womankind, has sweetened that
little bitterness which remained at the basis
of the old law. He has shown, in His divine
union with the Church 'espoused in His precious blood' how the authority of the head and
the subjection of the spouse can become, without being the least diminished, transformed by
the power of love, of a love which intimates
that wherewith He is united to His Church. He
has shown how firm command and respectful,
docile obedience can and should find forget-
fulness of self and a generous, reciprocal
giving in active and mutual love.[84]

301

The last aspect of the treatment of the Church
and women to be considered is not one that Pius explicitly broached, but is one which is suggested to
us within his documents on women. In fact, the
subject is suggested by the fact that Pius wrote
so much on the subject of women. Pius did not consider the topic of men, their nature, role, treatment by the Church, or place in the man-woman relationship. In the above passage, Pius spoke of
Christ's mercy "for us and for womankind." This is
the only instance in any of the papal documents I
have seen in which Pius speaks of himself as a
male. In every other instance of the use of the
first person plural without the capitalization indicating what Webster's calls the "royal we", the
reference is to the human race, or the Church, as
a whole. The implication here is that Pius found
it necessary to assert that the "us" on whom Christ
had mercy also included woman. In addresses to
mixed groups of Catholics all the twentieth-century
popes have spoken of the "sons" of the Church,
their mission and the love of the Church for them.
This is so common as to be unremarkable. This issue as to the place of women within the Church became increasingly more important as the following
popes were pressed to define the role of women in
the Church and the extent to which they are full
members.

John XXIII: On Woman

The major changes in the writings of John
XXIII on the subject of woman are by no means revolutionary. He tended to dwell less on the differences of role between men and women, though he did
not differ one iota from Pius XII on woman's nature
and primary responsibility. In a number of his addresses to women, however, he spoke of the public
duties of women in the same terms he applied to
men.[85] This was especially clear in addresses to

302

the women of Catholic Action in which he spoke of
the duties of all members of Catholic Action, without distinguishing special duties for the members
of the two sexes.

Another change in emphasis in the writings of
John XXIII was his increased acceptance of working
women as a part of the modern world that was here
to stay. In a major address to the Italian Center
for Women on December 7, 1960, _Ci e gradito_, John
spoke to the topic of the "Woman of Today":

> There has been and still is some discus-
> sion over how wise it is, from certain points
> of view, to employ women in certain specified
> types of labor and certain professions. But
> we have to face facts as they are and make it
> clear that there is an ever greater flow of
> women toward sources of employment, of labor,
> and an ever more widespread desire on their
> part for some kind of activity that can make
> them economically independent and free from
> want.[86]

On September 6, 1961 John addressed groups of women's organizations (_Convenuti a Roma_), making
much the same point: it is a fact that women work,
regardless of discussions of the desirability of
this. What should be done, he said, is to ascer-
tain what measures can be taken to mitigate the
burdens on such women.[87]

One very interesting shift in emphasis in the
writings of John is that from a total focus on
marriage and motherhood (still a strong theme but
not so exclusive as under Pius) toward virginity.
There are many examples of John's urging women to
consider virginity, often explicitly declaring it
superior to other modes.[88] One reason for this
shift may have been the falling off of vocations

which began to become serious under John. The emphasis is clear, regardless of the cause. Previous popes had also placed a high value on virginity, but in speaking to and about women they did not tend to make virginity so major a theme.

John XXIII, like his predecessors, saw the chief task of women as motherhood. Following the lead of Pius XII, John affirmed that women had other tasks, too, especially as representatives of and lobbyists for the family. But, as he declared in a May 3, 1960 address, C'est pour nous, the chief task of women is the education of the child in the home.[89] In Convenuti a Roma, on September 6, 1961, John told a group of women:

> We would also like to remind you that the end for which the Creator fashioned women's whole being is motherhood. This vocation to motherhood is so proper to her and so much a part of her nature that it is operative even when actual generation does not occur.[90]

In his address to the Italian Center for Women, Ci e gradito, John elaborated on the subject of the woman in the family:

> In this picture of the family there is an irreplaceable role that belongs to the woman. There is a voice in the home that everyone will listen to, if it knows how to make itself heard, if it has always made itself respected; it is the watchful and prudent voice of the woman and mother. . . . When the voice of the mother encourages, invites, entreats, it remains engraved deep in the heart of her own, and is never again forgotten. Oh, only God knows how much good is stirred up by this voice and what benefits it brings to the Church and to human activity![91]

In his consideration of the respective roles of the husband and wife within the family, John's description did not diverge from that of Pius XII. In the second section of his first encyclical, Ad petri cathedram, he wrote:

> Within the family, the father stands in God's place. He must lead and guide the rest by his authority and the example of his good life.
>
> The mother, on the other hand, should [command] her children firmly and graciously by the mildness of her manner and by her virtue in the domestic situation. [In relation to her spouse she should behave kindly and lovingly.]
>
> Together the parents should carefully [instruct and educate] their children, God's most precious gift, to an upright and religious life.[92]

John used the same explanation of the situation of men and women with regard to equality as had Pius XII: they are equal in dignity, but not in function. It was therefore not contradictory to insist on the equality of women and their subjection to men in marriage. (John preferred to speak of the authority of the husband rather than the subjection of the wife, but the relation is not different from that of Pius XII.) This difference posited between dignity and function was explained by John in Convenuti a Roma:

> It is true that living conditions tend to bring about almost complete equality of the sexes. Nevertheless, while their justly-proclaimed equality of rights must extend to all the claims of personal and human dignity, it does not in any way imply equality of functions. The Creator endowed woman with

natural attributes, tendencies and instincts,
which are strictly hers, or which she possesses to a different degree from man; this means
that woman was also assigned specific tasks.

To overlook this difference in the respective functions of men and women or the
fact that they necessarily complement each
other, would be tantamount to opposing nature: the result would be to debase woman
and to remove the true foundation of her
dignity.[93]

John XXIII was very descriptive as regards
the kind of work that was appropriate for women.
In an address on women's work, given to the Federation of Young Catholic Women April 23, 1960, he
remarked:

And if one seeks to make precise what
ought to characterize the work of woman, it
must be affirmed without hesitation that the
task of woman, being directed immediately or
remotely toward maternity, consists of everything that is a work of love, of giving, of
welcoming, everything that is disinterested
service of other people--all this finds a
natural place in the feminine calling. Thus
has Providence ordained, and it is a major
duty to watch carefully lest some work unsuitable for the feminine nature should
change the personality of young workers by
its deleterious influence. Such is the price
that must be paid to safeguard the complete
dignity of the person, and, at the same time,
to assure their felicitous development of
their human potentialities.[94]

In a similar vein, John wrote in _Pacem in terris_:
"Women must be accorded such conditions of work as
are consistent with their needs and responsibili-

ties as mothers."[95]

Perhaps the most controversial aspect of John's writings on women is his message to working women concerning how they are to respond to their two roles and the conflict between them:

> But even if the economic independence of women brings certain advantages, it also results in many, many problems with regard to their fundamental mission of forming new creatures! Hence we have new situations that are serious and urgent, and that call for preparation and for a spirit of adaptability and self-sacrifice. These arise in the area of family life: in the care and education of youngsters, in homes that are left without the presence of someone that they need so much; in the loss or disturbance of rest resulting from the assumption of new responsibilities; and above all, in keeping feast days holy, and, in general, in fulfilling those religious duties which are the only thing that can make the mother's work of training her children really fruitful.
>
> Everyone knows that outside work, as you might naturally expect, makes a person tired and may even dull the personality; sometimes it is humiliating and mortifying besides. When a man comes back to his home after being away for long hours and sometimes after having completely spent his energies, is he going to find in it a refuge and a source for restoring his energies and the reward that will make up for the dry, mechanical nature of the things that have surrounded him?
>
> Here again, there is a great task waiting for women: let them promise themselves that they will not let their contacts with the harsh realities of outside work dry up the

richness of their inner life, the resources
of their sensitivity, of their open and delicate spirit; that they will not forget those
spiritual values that are the only defense of
their nobility; last of all, that they will
not fail to go to the fonts of prayer and
sacramental life for the strength to maintain
themselves on a level with their matchless
mission.

They are called to an effort perhaps
greater than that of men, if you take into
consideration women's natural fraility in certain respects and the fact that more is being
asked of them. At all times and in all circumstances they are the ones who have to be
wise enough to find the resources to face
their duties as wives and mothers calmly and
with their eyes wide open; to make their
homes warm and peaceful after the tiring
labors of daily work, and not to shrink from
the responsibility in raising children.[96]

The above passage makes very clear that the
self-sacrifice which is, in John's opinion, indicated is to be exclusively the province of the
working wife. Women who work in the jobs he described as dry and mechanical, humiliating and
mortifying, are asked to promise not to let this
harshness dry up their inner richness, their sensitivity and spirit. They are to avoid this so
that they can create a refuge for husband and
children fleeing from this same harshness. They
are asked not to let the double burden of tasks
inside and outside the home make them any less useful to those husbands who carry half their burden.
John did not seem to think that the enormity of the
demands he placed on women who work demanded any
special justification other than the fact that the
other members of the family depend on the wife to
keep them human.

It is strange that in the Christian civilization that was so important for both Pius and John
we find that it is the subject member of society,
woman, to whom the Christian qualities are ascribed
and from whom they are demanded. One is brought to
the question as to what is the connection between
the role of the <u>man</u> and the demands of Christian
living, since spirituality, love, compassion, self-
sacrifice, and piety are all considered feminine
traits. The male role almost seems redundant, until one considers that the importance of hierarchy
for John was not less than in his predecessors'
views.

Hierarchy was the assumption upon which John's
emphasis on good social order rested, though this
hierarchy was not the traditionally understood
hierarchy, which was permanent and unchanging. In
<u>Mater</u> <u>et</u> <u>Magistra</u> and <u>Pacem</u> <u>in</u> <u>terris</u> John often
spoke of the well ordered society. He considered
that good order was the result of the delegation of
authority to the select few:

> Human society can be neither well ordered
> nor prosperous without the presence of those
> who, invested with legal authority, preserve
> its institutions and do all that is necessary
> to sponsor actively the interests of all its
> members. And they derive their authority from
> God, for, as St. Paul teaches, 'there is no
> power but from God.'[97]

John observed that, though those in authority have
the right to rule and to compel obedience

> It must not be concluded, however, because
> authority comes from God, that therefore men
> have no right to choose those who are to rule
> the state, to decide the form of government,
> and to determine both the way in which author-

ity is to be exercised and its limits. It is
thus clear that the doctrine which we have
set forth can be fully consonant with any
truly democratic regime.[98]

John's approval of democracy, and his recon-
cilement of a kind of hierarchy with democracy in
government obviously did not extend into the family. The reasons that it did not are both clear
and instructive for understanding his view of democracy.

The understanding of democracy referred to
here is, significantly representative democracy,
in which the people choose their rulers; they do
not share in the ruling of society themselves, as
in direct democracy. The need for hierarchy, for
a strong authority over society, had historically
been the basis for papal objections to democracy.
It is only since the evolution of civil democracy
has proved that hierarchy can exist within democracy that papal objections to democracy have
ceased. Calls for democracy in the family are very
different in that family democracy entails the
sharing of power, a concept at odds with the papal
insistence on a strong authority.

When, therefore, John quoted Leo's Immortale
Dei: "society cannot hold together unless someone
is in command to give effective direction and unity
of purpose,"[99] this was meant to be true of all
societies, including the family. Every family required a head, though all the members of the family
held certain rights within it.

This insistence on the need for hierarchy not
only determined that every family had a head and
those subject to the head, but the authority of the
head determined that adaptation and self-sacrifice,
adjustment and flexibility fell to the lot of the

310

subjects. If those subject could decide what they would not accept as their role, they would not be subject. For John, there was no way to <u>share</u> ultimate responsibility.

This hierarchical principle is important in understanding how John could issue both these very traditional descriptions of the nature and role of woman and the following passage from <u>Pacem in terris</u> on the emerging role of women in the world:

> There are three things that characterize our present age:
>
> .   .   .   .   .
>
> Secondly, the part that women are now playing in political life is everywhere evident. This is a development that is perhaps of swifter growth among Christian nations, but it is also happening extensively if more slowly among nations that are heirs to different traditions and imbued with a different culture. Women are gaining an increasing awareness of their natural dignity. Far from being content with a purely passive role or allowing themselves to be regarded as a kind of instrument, they are demanding both in domestic and in public life the rights and duties which belong to them as human persons.[100]

John's approval of this trend was not an approval of similar social and political roles for men and women. He sincerely desired the end of women's passivity, as had Pius XII. Both felt that women needed to carry their support and defense of the home into the public sphere. Women were to decide what needed to be done, and do it, but only in those areas in which they had special duties and abilities. This was clear in a speech John made to the <u>men</u> of Catholic Action on May 13,

311

1962, just one year before _Pacem in terris_: "If
you say the word 'man' [uomo] what you mean first
of all is the connective tissue of society, for it
is to him that the responsible and burdensome tasks
of civil society are entrusted. . . ."101 John's
welcome to women entering public life was not a
general welcome to equal partnership, but a more
limited acknowledgement that there was a public
aspect of the duties of mother and wife.

One clear sign that John desired women to take
up a specific aspect of social and political life
as their own, and not social and political duties
in general, was the interpretation that he gave to
the Gospel story of Mary and Martha. This story
is probably the most explicit passage in the New
Testament favoring a break with the traditional
women's role. But John, in addressing contemplative sisters on October 20, 1960, _Notre joie est
grande_, interpreted this story in such a way that
Jesus' remark that Mary had "chosen the better
part" meant that the contemplative life was superior to the life spent in society.102 This, of
course, was not an original interpretation; it was
standard fare in spiritualistic theology. John
interpreted joining the group of followers who
heard Jesus' teaching as taking on the life of con-
templatives, and ignored the more unusual fact that
Jesus approved of a woman joining the learned group
in which theology was taught, rather than serving
meals. Such an interpretation cannot but throw
some light on John's approval of women's action and
participation in the public sphere.

Paul VI: On Woman

The documents of the Vatican Council provide
the first clues as to the inclination of Paul's
stance on woman. The Pastoral Constitution, _Gaudi-
um et Spes_, referred to women, their nature and

role, in two places, paragraphs 52 and 60. Concerning the specific role in the family that nature intended for women, the first paragraph stated:

> The family is a kind of school of deeper humanity. But if it is to achieve the full flowering of its life and mission, it needs the kindly communion of minds and the joint deliberation of spouses, as well as the painstaking cooperation of parents in the education of their children. The active presence of the father is highly beneficial to their formation. The children, especially the younger among them, need the care of the mother at home. This domestic role of hers must be safely preserved, though the legitimate social progress of women should not be underrated on that account.[103]

The most remarkable aspect of this passage is that it mentions the necessity of the presence of the father to the children. In addition, the traditional view that young children require the presence of the mother in the home, presumably full time, is qualified by approval of social progress for women. A later paragraph affirmed that women deserve equal rights with men in the public sphere:

> The possibility now exists of liberating most men from the misery of ignorance. Hence it is a duty most befitting our times that men, especially Christians, should work strenuously on behalf of certain decisions which must be made in the economic and political fields, both nationally and internationally. By these decisions universal recognition and implementation should be given to the right of all men to a human and civic culture favorable to personal dignity and free from any

discrimination on the grounds of race, sex, nationality, religious, or social conditions.[104]

And later in the same document the subject of women is returned to:

> Women are now employed in almost every area of life. It is appropriate that they should be able to assume their full proper role in accordance with their own nature. Everyone should acknowledge and favor the proper and necessary participation of women in cultural life.[105]

Gaudium et Spes thus took the position that discrimination against women on the grounds of sex is contrary to human dignity and to the position of the Church. The participation of women in civic and political life, however, is to be in accord with their own distinctive nature and proper duties. Taking into account the tradition on to which this document is appended, we see that these qualifications on the entry of women into public life are an affirmation of the traditional understanding of the nature of woman and her primary task of motherhood. Nevertheless, in the sections of the document concerning the family and marriage there is much less differentiation of the duties of the parents by sex than usually occurred in past papal documents. This was a continuation of a trend begun under John.

In the documents of Paul VI, apart from the conciliar documents, we find a generally ambiguous position on women. In some ways Paul made more positive statements concerning the similarities of the duties and functions of men and women in the world than did his predecessors. And yet it is true that Paul used many of the traditional formu-

314

lae and views of his predecessors concerning the special nature of women and the appropriate tasks determined by that nature.

One inescapable point is that it was only under Paul's pontificate that the question of the role of woman in the Church assumed the major importance it holds today. Today the issue of women's ordination is at the forefront of the debate concerning the place of women in the Church, though other issues, including the inclusion of women in the administration of the Church, are probably as important to the future of the Church as a whole.

Paul made it clear that he agreed with his predecessors' assessment of the nature of woman:

> A woman finds in her family not just a greater share of cares and concerns but also her most natural and loving mission, her best recognized dignity, her surest guarantee of salvation and of reward. 'Her salvation,' says St. Paul, 'will be in motherhood, provided that she remains modest and holy in faith and charity.'[106]

In a like manner, Paul's Octogesima adveniens had this to say of the changing place of women in the modern world:

> Similarly, in many countries a charter for women which would put an end to actual discrimination and would establish relationships of equality in rights and respect for their dignity is the object of study and at times of lively demands. We do not have in mind that false equality which would deny the distinctions laid down by the Creator Himself, and which would be in contradiction with woman's proper role, which is of such capital

315

importance, at the heart of the family as well as within society. Developments in legislation should on the contrary be direct- ed to protecting her proper vocation and at the same time recognizing her independence as a person, and her equal rights to participate in cultural, economic, social, and political life.[107]

If Paul had given an example of "false equality", this passage would be much easier to understand and to reconcile with the other message he sends concerning women. Women had equal rights in the civic and political fields, and were, he said, not to be discriminated against at any level. But evidently women were not to understand this declar- ation of equal right as papal approval of women in all social and political roles, for some of these roles for women were examples of "false equality". Which such social and political roles he thought acceptable for women are not clear, and the ban he placed on discrimination was therefore ambiguous.

In Paul's speech to the Study Commission on Women, January 31, 1976, he again touched on the theme of false equality, but again failed to give examples of such "deviations":

Dear sons and daughters, We wish also to put you on guard against some deviations which can affect the contemporary movement for the ad- vancement of women. Equalization of rights must not be allowed to degenerate into an egalitarian and impersonal elimination of differences. The egalitarianism blindly sought by our materialistic society has but little care for the specific good of persons; contrary to appearances it is unconcerned with what is suitable or unsuitable to women. There is, thus, a danger of unduly masculiniz-

316

ing women or else simply depersonalizing
them. In either case, the deepest things
in women suffer. Egalitarianism can even
favor forms of a hedonism which is a real
threat not only to the spiritual and moral
integrity of women but even of their basic
human dignity.

The genuinely Christian advancement of
women will not be limited to a vindication
of their rights. The Christian spirit obliges
all of us, men and women alike, to keep ever
in mind our duties and responsibilities. The
chief need today is to bring about a closer
and more extensive collaboration between men
and women, both in society at large and in
the Church, so that all may 'contribute their
respective resources and energies to the
building of a world which is not leveled into
uniformity but is harmoniously organized and
unified.' When thus understood, the advancement of women can help greatly in deepening
the unity of mankind and establishing peace
in the world.[108]

A consideration of these documents together does
not lead to a view of the work of women in the
world that is acceptable to the women's movement.
Paul insisted on the complementarity of women:

to speak of rights does not resolve the problem, which is more profound; it is necessary
to aim at an effective complementarity, so
that men and women bring their proper riches
and dynamism to the building of the world,
not levelled and uniform, but harmonious and
unified, according to the design of the Creator, or to use the terms of the Holy Year,
renewed and reconciled.[109]

This complementarity was the result of viewing the

317

natures of men and women as so different that their functions could not be but complementary. The use of the terms "not levelled and uniform, but harmonious and unified" which have been consistently used in the tradition to signify hierarchy gave these statements more continuity with the past than is at first apparent in Paul's treatment of complementarity.

Because of this emphasis on complementarity, Paul's words on the equality of women and his ban on sex discrimination must be understood as in accord with the basic position of his predecessors. The statement "But We cannot fail also to call attention here to the fact that in the more developed countries a prudent realism must mark the ascension of women to positions of policy-making and decisions which influence all areas of social life"[110]--this statement must be interpreted in the light of his predecessors' reservations regarding the abilities of women to make objective, realistic judgements, unbiased by excessive emotionalism or vanity. It is true that Paul did not repeat these views of feminine nature. But he did not reject them, and accepted the general picture of female nature as including sensitivity, generosity, intuition, sensibility, and emotionality:

> We rejoice especially on the eve of the International Women's Year, proclaimed by the United Nations, at the ever wider participation of women in the life of the society, to which they bring a specific contribution of great value, thanks to the qualities God has given them. These qualities of intuition, creativity, sensibility, a sense of piety and compassion, a profound capacity for understanding and love, enable women to be in a very particular way the creators of reconciliation in families and in society.[111]

318

Yes, Christian women, civil society and the
ecclesial community expect much in the future
from your sensitivity and capacity for understanding, your gentleness and perseverance,
your generosity and humility. These virtues,
which harmonize so well with the psychological makeup of women and were so splendidly
developed in the Blessed Virgin, are also the
fruits of the Holy Spirit.[112]

Paul's most important document on women, and
the one most complete in its treatment of the
question of women in the modern world, was his
address to the Union of Italian Catholic Jurists
of December 8, 1974. This document was also an
example of Paul's ability to combine a traditional
view with the modern, contradictory demands of women without reconciling the differences. Note the
presence of both the traditional and the modern
egalitarian elements in the following passage:

Neither We nor any other observer of the
contemporary scene are unaware of the socio-
cultural transformation that has caused,
among other things, a remarkable change in
the position and roles of women. A rather
rapid transition has brought us from a primarily agricultural society to a society
characterized by industrialization and its
satellite phenomena: urbanization, population mobility and instability, and a revolution in domestic life and social relationships.
One effect of this shift has been to put
woman at the center of an as yet unresolved
crisis in institutions and culture. The
crisis has affected especially her relationships within the family, her educational mission, her very identity as woman and her entire specific way of sharing in the life of

319

society through work, friendships and the
help and comfort she gives to others. Even
her religious outlook and practice have been
affected. Today, then, we are faced with
developments of enormous importance: first
and foremost, the equal rights given to women,
along with their increasing emancipation from
the control of men; a new conception and interpretation of their roles as wives, mothers,
daughters and sisters; the ever increasing
availability to them of a vast and expanding
range of specialized professional occupations;
their growing tendency to prefer jobs outside
the home, with its effects on the marital relationship, and above all, on the education
of the children, who are prematurely freed
from the authority of the parents and especially of the mother.

The new situation is evidently not wholly
negative in its impact. In these new circumstances the woman of today and tomorrow will
perhaps be able more easily to develop her
full potential. Even the misguided experiments of the present time can be useful, if
the sound universal principles of conscience
take firmer root in society and lead to a new
balance in family and social life.

The real problem is to bring about a recognition, respect, and, where necessary, a recovery of these principles, which are also
irreplaceable values proper to the civilization of a highly developed people. Let us
call them briefly to mind. We are referring,
above all, to the functional differentiation
of woman from man within the nature they
share; furthermore, the uniqueness of her
nature, her psychology, and her vocation as a
human being and a Christian; her dignity,
which must not be degraded as it so often is
today in the spheres of morality, work, ad-

vertising and entertaining, and through promiscuity; finally, the primordial place of
woman in all those areas of human existence
where we confront more directly the problems
of life itself, suffering, and help to our
fellow men, and especially in the area of
motherhood.

If we were to reduce to a few essentials
these brief indications concerning the place
women should have in a renewed society, we
might say: Let us willingly vote for

1) the recognition of the civil rights of
women as full equals of men, wherever these
rights have not yet been acknowledged;

2) laws that will make it really possible
for women to fill the same professional, social and political roles as men, according to
the individual capacities of the person;

3) the acknowledgement, respect, and protection of the special prerogatives of women
in marriage, family, education, and society.

4) the maintenance and defense of the dignity of women as persons, unmarried women,
wives and widows; and the help they need, especially when the husband is absent, disabled,
or imprisoned, that is, when he cannot fulfill
his function in the family.[113]

Those aspects of this treatment of women which
were traditional are obvious. But there are some
very new aspects to the stance taken in this address. Number (2) above (that women be enabled to
fill the same professional, social, and political
roles as men) seems to be a flat contradiction of
the stance Paul took up to, and even after, this
address. I see no way to avoid the fact that there
is a contradiction between advocating both the same
roles for men and women, and advocating complementary and necessarily different roles for the sexes
based on their different natures and functions.

One possible explanation of how Paul came to take such contradictory stands on this issue is the possibility that while he supported increased rights and opportunities for women in public life, he feared that the papal approval of the extension of such rights and opportunities might encourage women already tending to, in Paul's view, desert their primary calling, to reject the traditional and necessary roles in favor of the new opportunities. This could also explain his exhortations of gradualism:

> November 17, 1973 We defined the task of the Study Commission on Women in Society and the Church. The task was concerned with documentation and with reflection on the ways of promoting the dignity and responsibility of women. These purposes are certainly present in your minds. The fulfillment of the task of promotion must be gradual and none of the stages in the process may be bypassed. Prudent discernment is called for, for the question with which you deal requires tact. Nothing is gained by talking of the equalization of rights, for the problem goes far deeper.[114]

This explanation does not, however, eliminate all the contradictions in the papal stance toward women. Especially if we look at what Paul said about women in the Church, and compare this to his statements concerning the equality of dignity, personhood, and rights that men and women share as human beings, we do not seem to have a consistent stance.

In his last years Paul began his consideration of women in the Church with the affirmations of Vatican II regarding women:

322

Vatican II solemnly reminded us of the right and duty of all the baptized--men and women alike--to share as responsible members of God's people in the mission of the Church. The Council then noted specifically: 'Further, in our times women have an increasingly larger role in the life of society; it is then quite important that they participate more intensively also in the various areas of the apostolate.'[115]

In this same document, however, Paul went on to assume that although women do not receive the same call to the apostolate as was given to the Twelve "and therefore to ordained ministry, they are nevertheless invited to follow Christ as disciples and co-workers." He remarked that the women who accompanied Jesus from the first of his ministry, who saw him die and be buried, and who were present the morning of the Resurrection, though not, like the Apostles, the foundation of the Church, were all the same a valuable contribution to the strengthening of the early Church. Paul viewed the Church's treatment of women as set for all time by the example of Christ, which he recognized as daring and innovative for his day. Paul considered that the task of the Church must be to develop the role of women within the limits set by Christ's example. Thus he mentioned the apostolic work of some women in the area of pastoral care of families. A very few women, he said, are called to take part in the work of authoritative reflection on the pastoral scene, at the level of parish, diocese, or deanery. Paul expressed support for these "experiments".[116]

The earliest address of Pope Paul's on women came during the Council itself. On September 8, 1964 Paul VI addressed a group of female religious, and in the course of his talk broached the subject

of women in the Church, specifically in the work
of the Vatican Council:

> We will let you in on a little secret in this
> regard: We have given orders that some de-
> vout ladies are to attend as auditors several
> of the solemn ceremonies and several of the
> General Congregations of the coming third
> session of the Second Vatican Council; what
> We have in mind are those congregations that
> will discuss matters of particular concern to
> the lives of women. Hence We will have pre-
> sent at an ecumenical council, perhaps for
> the first time, a representation of women--
> only a small one, obviously, but still sig-
> nificant and you might say, symbolic--from
> you sisters, first of all, and then from the
> great Catholic Women's organizations. Women
> will thus know just how much honor the Church
> pays to them in the dignity of their being
> and of their mission on the human and the
> Christian levels.[117]

Though fourteen years ago it was certainly incon-
ceivable that women hearing this address would
think that this gesture on Paul's part indicated
just how little the Church honors and respects
women, the case is different now. Today the continuing and total exclusion of women from all the
decision-making within the Church--even these few
women to be admitted to the Council were admitted
as non-voting auditors, of course--is difficult to
understand in the light of Paul's other statements
concerning women. It is especially difficult to
understand in the light of the strong papal emphasis (from both John and Paul) on the importance of
participation in the decision-making processes of
society for all human beings. This participation
was often described, from Pacem in terris on, as
a basic human right. Are basic human rights not

valid in the Church?

The suspicion that women are not really, despite Paul's protestations, considered full members of the Church can only be strengthened by examination of Paul's _motu proprio_, _Ministeria quaedam_, of August 15, 1972. In this letter Paul revised the norms concerning the ministries of lector and acolyte. Paul quoted Vatican Council statements which he believed called from him the decision to open up the offices of lector and acolyte to the laity:

> Mother Church earnestly desires that all
> the faithful should be led to that full con-
> scious, and active participation in liturgi-
> cal celebrations which is demanded by the
> very nature of the liturgy. Such participa-
> tion by the Christian people as 'a chosen
> race, a royal priesthood, a holy nation, a
> purchased people' (1 Pt 2,9) is their right
> and duty by reason of their baptism. In the
> restoration and promotion of the sacred lit-
> urgy, this full and active participation _by_
> _all the people_ is the aim to be considered
> before all else; for it is the primary and
> indispensable source from which the faithful
> are to derive the true Christian spirit; and
> therefore pastors of souls must zealously
> strive to achieve it, by means of the neces-
> sary instruction, in all their pastoral
> work.[118]

Since women have normally considered themselves
numbered among the "faithful," as members of the
"Christian people," and among the baptized, it is
difficult not to sense a contradiction between
this explanation of allowing the laity to perform
these offices, and number VII under the new norms:

In accordance with the venerable tradition of
the Church, installation in the ministries of
lector and acolyte is reserved to men.[119]

This statement of course causes the subject
of tradition and its use by the Church to arise.
In the case of women, this question of the use of
tradition became even more critical with the publication of the Declaration on the Question of the
Admission of Women to the Ministerial Priesthood,
approved by Paul on October 15, 1976.[120] In this
document there were three kinds of tradition cited
against permitting the ordination of women: the
tradition established by the fact that Jesus was a
male, the tradition established by the fact that
none of the twelve apostles was a woman, and the
tradition established within the Church of the last
two thousand years which has not ordained women.
These "traditional" reasons for not ordaining women
are not the only ones used by the document. The
document also refers to the fact that the priest is
to be understood as the sign of Christ, and that
signs are to bear a natural resemblance to that
which they signify. The fact that the Church has
usually held that women, too, are made in the image
and likeness of God was not accounted sufficient
natural resemblance.

The last reason given why women cannot be ordained is that of traditional sexual symbolism.
The fact that the Church understands herself as
the bride of Christ, the chosen people as the bride
of Yahweh, and the minister as the representative
of Christ (male) ministering to a female Church was
held to invalidate the ministry of women, presumably because it would initiate divine homosexual-
ity. The fact that this could be seriously put
forth as a reason for denying ministry to over half
the members of the Church says something about the
level of theology in the Church today. Symbols are

constructs of people, created to imply that something from one context is also relevant in another.
The sexual symbolism used by the Church was begun
by St. Paul, who clearly desired to use the traditional Jewish symbol (bride) which had clarified
the love and authority aspects of the relationship
between God and people by reference to the relationship between man and wife in a patriarchal
culture. To insist on this sexual symbolism at
the very time that the Church has begun to abandon
the traditional insistence upon the subjection of
women (and therefore the traditional authority relationship) within marriage is a desperate attempt
to retain the exclusion of, and therefore control
over, women.

Conclusion

It is difficult to tell exactly what the overall development of the last hundred years has been
within this area of papal teaching. The Church no
longer affirms the inequality of the sexes, but has
not changed her understanding of male and female
nature and function upon which the former judgment
of inequality was based. Aside from this shift, it
is difficult to reach conclusions because of the
many themes which constantly reappear to give the
appearance of a static tradition. But the major
difficulty is that anything we might be tempted to
call change is, for the most part, merely a failure
of a particular pope to articulate a point made by
his predecessors. Silence on a particular point
can be a signal of an important breakthrough. But
until the breakthrough itself occurs, it can be
misleading to regard the silence as anything other
than a pause between similar affirmations of a
traditional point.

Even the papal shift away from affirmations of
female inequality was intended to apply to the

civil order, and not within the Church itself. It
has prompted no internal changes in the Church.
In the absence of implementation of new understandings of woman and her place in the world, and until
the traditional view of woman is explicitly dis-
avowed in the papal teaching, we must assume that
any movement within the papal teaching is negligible. Until women have some voice in creating the
Church's view of their nature and role, some voice
in the decision-making as to the extent and form of
their participation in the Church, it is impossible
to say that any of the themes we have examined have
been permanently relegated to the pages of anti-
quity.

NOTES

[1]Mary Daly, The Church and the Second Sex
(New York: Harper and Row, 1975--written and copy-
righted 1968) and Beyond God the Father (Boston:
Beacon Press, 1973). Rosemary Radford Ruether,
Religion and Sexism (New York: Simon and Schuster,
1974) and New Woman New Earth (New York: Seabury
Press, 1975). This is not to ignore the facts that
Mary Daly between 1968 and 1973 moved from Catholic
to "PostChristian," and that Ruether has included
non-Catholic, and even non-Christian, material in
her works.

[2]The teaching challenged is more than the
social teaching, for it extends beyond applied
theology into fundamental theology, and sometimes
into dogmatic theology (i.e., God as Father, Jesus
as male, etc.).

[3]With the possible exception of the Declaration on the Question of the Admission of Women to
the Ministerial Priesthood, October 15, 1976, AAS
69:98.

[4]Clara Maria Henning, "Celibacy as a Feminist
Issue," Women and Orders, edited by Robert J. Heyer
(New York: Paulist Press, 1974), p. 87.

[5]Sister Albertus Magnus McGrath, O.P., Women
and the Church (Garden City, New York: Doubleday
Image, 1976), p. 129.

[6]Arlene Swidler, "Partnership Marriage: Model
of Future Priesthood," in Women and Catholic
Priesthood, edited by Anne Marie Gardiner, SSND

(New York: Paulist Press, 1976), pp. 130-131. Swidler's belief that the injunction to obey is not aimed at women is not, however, typical of feminists.

[7]Shulamith Firestone, The Dialectic of Sex (New York: Bantam, 1970), p. 8.

[8]Dorothy Dinnerstein, The Mermaid and the Minotaur (New York: Harper and Row, 1976).

[9]Sheila Rowbotham, Woman's Consciousness, Man's World (London and New York: Pelican, 1973), p. 34.

[10]Mitchell began writing as a Marxist-feminist but is less Marxist now.

[11]Juliet Mitchell, "The Longest Revolution," New Left Review, No. 40, 1966.

[12]Eli Zaretsky, Capitalism, the Family, and Personal Life (New York: Harper and Row, 1975).

[13]Charnie Guettel, Marxism and Feminism (Toronto: Women's Press, 1974).

[14]Linda Jenness, Feminism and Socialism (New Jersey: Pathfinder, 1972).

[15]Sheila Rowbotham, Woman's Consciousness, Man's World; Women, Resistance and Revolution (Vantage, 1974).

[16]Karl Marx, The German Ideology, Part 1, "Feuerbach," in Karl Marx-Frederich Engels: Collected Works, Vol. 5 (New York: International Publishers, 1976), p. 44.

[17]Hilda Scott, Can Socialism Liberate Women?

<u>Experiences</u> <u>from</u> <u>Eastern</u> <u>Europe</u> (Boston: Beacon
Press, 1974), pp. 209-220.

[18]Clara Maria Henning, "Celibacy as a Feminist
Issue," <u>Women</u> <u>and</u> <u>Orders</u>, p. 102; "Canon Law and
the Battle of the Sexes," <u>Religion</u> <u>and</u> <u>Sexism</u>, pp.
272-273.

[19]<u>Women</u> <u>and</u> <u>the</u> <u>Church</u>, p. 23; <u>The</u> <u>Church</u> <u>and</u>
<u>the</u> <u>Second</u> <u>Sex</u>, pp. 76-77.

[20]<u>New</u> <u>Woman</u> <u>New</u> <u>Earth</u>, pp. 19-20.

[21]<u>Arcanum</u>, <u>ASS</u> 12:389.

[22]Ibid., p. 396.

[23]<u>ASS</u> 18:167-168.   The bracketed phrases are
inserted in a translation otherwise from Michael J.
Byrnes in <u>Papal</u> <u>Teaching</u>:   <u>Matrimony</u> (Boston:
Daughters of St. Paul, 1963), pp. 168-169.   The
first phrase is <u>debitum</u> <u>conservatur</u> <u>mulieri</u> <u>decus</u>,
omitted in translation; the second is <u>sed</u> <u>sinceri</u>
<u>amoris</u> <u>legibus</u>, which Byrnes translated "in order
that they be bound to their wives with a bond of
sincere love."

[24]<u>Quod</u> <u>apostolici</u> <u>muneris</u>, <u>ASS</u> 11:373-374,
December 28, 1878.

[25]<u>Supra</u>, pp. 257-258.

[26]This was a presupposition of Leo's demand
for the just wage in <u>Rerum</u> <u>novarum</u>:   a man should
be able to support his wife and children and be
able to save some in addition. <u>ASS</u> 23:662.

[27]For example, <u>Arcanum</u>, <u>AAS</u> 12:390 and <u>ASS</u> 12:
396.

[28] AAS 12 (1920):314.

[29] AAS 10 (1918):57; translation: Papal Teachings: Woman in the Modern World (Boston: Daughters of St. Paul, 1959), p. 27.

[30] Not in the Acta. From Papal Teachings: Woman in the Modern World, p. 28, which gives as its source La Civilta Cattolica, a fortnightly review.

[31] Ibid., p. 29.

[32] Ibid., p. 32.

[33] AAS 14 (1922):678; translation: Papal Teachings: Matrimony, p. 215.

[34] AAS 14 (1922):690; translation: Papal Teachings: Matrimony, p. 216. The original of the phrase beginning "where the authority of" is: in qua parentum potestas paternitatem divinam exprimat unde oritur ac nominatur. The nominatur refers to the alternative meaning of parens as author, cause, or origin, and not to divinam paternitatem. (AAS 14 (1922):690.)

[35] A Lei, Vicario Nostro, AAS 20 (1928):136-137. The last sentence is: Se mano do donna si deve alzare. Ci auguriamo e preghiamo che sia sempre e solo in atto di benefica azione. Translation: Papal Teachings: Woman in the Modern World, p. 35.

[36] AAS 22 (1930):72.

[37] AAS 23 (1931):516; translation: Michael J. Byrnes, Papal Teachings: Matrimony, pp. 292-293.

[38] AAS 29 (1937):71. The brackets enclose a

phrase left untranslated from the original in the translation of Joseph Husslein, S.J. in Social Wellsprings: Pius XI (Milwaukee: Bruce Publishing Co., 1942), pp. 345-346. The translation is otherwise Husslein's. The original clause reads: feminam a viri tutela prorsus liberam praedicent.

[39]AAS 22 (1930):549-550; translation: Papal Teachings: Matrimony, pp. 233-234.

[40]AAS 22 (1930):567-568; translation: Papal Teachings: Matrimony, pp. 258-260.

[41]A similar shift occurred concerning equality between classes at about the same time.

[42]AAS 37 (1945):287; translation: Papal Teachings: Woman in the Modern World, pp. 131-132.

[43]Allocution to Italian Education Association, October 24, 1955, AAS 47 (1955):780.

[44]April 24, 1952 allocution to Catholic Women's Organizations, AAS 44 (1952):423; translation: Papal Teachings: Woman in the Modern World, pp. 202-203. (Same theme in AAS 37 (1945):294-295.)

[45]February 25, 1942 allocution to newlyweds, Atti e discorsi di Pio XII (Romae: Instituto Missionaria, Pia societa San Paolo), Vol. 4, p. 40.

[46]AAS 39 (1947):353; translation: Papal Teachings: Woman in the Modern World, p. 163.

[47]Atti e discorsi, Vol. 2, p. 339; translation: Papal Teachings: Woman in the Modern World, p. 51.

[48]Papal Teachings: Woman in the Modern World,

pp. 178-179. No original available.

[49]Ibid., p. 179.

[50]_AAS_ 37 (1945):285, October 21, 1945 address
to Italian women: translation: _Papal Teachings:
Woman in the Modern World_, p. 109.

[51]April 24, 1943, _AAS_ 35 (1943):134; translation: _Papal Teachings: Woman in the Modern World_,

[52]_Atti e discorsi_, Vol. 3, pp. 224-225; translation from _Papal Teachings: Woman in the Modern
World_, pp. 63-64.

[53]Allocution to the World Union of Catholic
Women's Organizations, September 29, 1957. _Osser-
vatore Romano_, October 9, 1957.

[54]_Atti e discorsi_, Vol. 3, pp. 225-226; translation: _Papal Teachings: Woman in the Modern
World_, p. 64.

[55]Ibid.   [56]Ibid., p. 227.

[57]Ibid., pp. 223-224; translation: _Papal
Teachings: Woman in the Modern World_, pp. 62-63.

[58]_AAS_ 44 (1952):718-719; translation: _Papal
Teachings: Woman in the Modern World_, p. 210.

[59]Allocution to the Children of Mary, October
25, 1942. Not in _Acta Apostolicae Sedis_ or _Atti e
discorsi_; translation: _Papal Teachings: Woman in
the Modern World_, p. 100.

[60]September 10, 1941 address to newlyweds,
Atti e discorsi, Vol. 3, p. 328; translation:
Papal Teachings: Woman in the Modern World, p. 66.

[61]*Dos son los motives*, to young women of Spain, April 9, 1956. *Osservatore Romano*, April 12, 1956; translation: *Papal Teachings: Woman in the Modern World*, p. 260.

[62]*Atti e discorsi*, Vol. 3, pp. 139-140; translation: *Papal Teachings: Woman in the World Today*, pp. 59-60.

[63]*Osservatore Romano*, July 28, 1955; translation: *Papal Teachings: Woman in the Modern World*, p. 237.

[64]*Atti e discorsi*, Vol. 4, pp. 41-42; translation: *Papal Teachings: Woman in the Modern World*, pp. 82-83.

[65]*Atti e discorsi*, Vol. 3, p. 261; translation: *Papal Teachings: Woman in the Modern World*, p. 73.

[66]*AAS* 37 (1945):291, Allocution to Italian women, October 21, 1945; translation from *Papal Teachings: Woman in the Modern World*, p. 136.

[67]*AAS* 37 (1945):288; translation from *Papal Teachings: Woman in the Modern World*, p. 133.

[68]In addition to the above, also *AAS* 39 (1947):480, and *AAS* 37 (1945):214 (below).

[69]*AAS* 37 (1945):214; translation: *Papal Teachings: Woman in the Modern World*, p. 126.

[70]Radio message to Federation of Italian women, October 14, 1956, *AAS* 48 (1956):785; translation: *Papal Teachings: Woman in the Modern World*, p. 278.

[71]*AAS* 37 (1945):291-292; translation: *Papal Teachings: Woman in the Modern World*, p. 137.

[72]*AAS* 37 (1945):293; translation: *Papal Teach-

ings: Woman in the Modern World, pp. 139-140.

[73]Atti e discorsi, Vol. 3, pp. 225-226.

[74]Ibid., p. 231; translation: Papal Teachings: Woman in the Modern World, p. 68.

[75]Address to newlyweds, September 10, 1941, Atti e discorsi, Vol. 3, p. 231; translation: Papal Teachings: Woman in the Modern World, p. 68.

[76]Ibid.

[77]See especially Atti e discorsi, Vol. 3, pp. 223-224 and Vol. 4, pp. 41-42, notes 57 and 64 above.

[78]Allocution to newlyweds, February 25, 1942, Atti e discorsi, Vol. 4, pp. 38-40; translation: Papal Teachings: Woman in the Modern World, pp. 80-81.

[79]Dilette figlie, The Pope Speaks, Vol. 3, no. 4, p. 367; no original available.

[80]Supra, pp. 279-281.

[81]See also AAS 44 (1952):424.

[82]Atti e discorsi, Vol. 4, pp. 111-112.

[83]Ibid.

[84]September 10, 1941. Atti e discorsi, Vol. 3, pp. 236-239. Translation: Papal Teachings: Woman in the Modern World, pp. 65-68.

[85]Allocution to Vatican diplomatic corps, December 25, 1959, Osservatore Romano, December 28-29, 1959 (The Pope Speaks, Vol. 6, p. 149); address to the Young Women of Catholic Action in Rome, January 10, 1960, AAS 52 (1960):83-90; and his address

to girls of Catholic Action on September 29, 1960,
The Pope Speaks, Vol. 6, p. 348 (no original available).

[86]Osservatore Romano, December 8, 1960; translation: The Pope Speaks, Vol. 7, p. 171.

[87]AAS 53 (1961):610.

[88]Di gran cuore, September 29, 1960, The Pope
Speaks, Vol. 6, p. 648; Nous sommes particuliérement, April 23, 1960, The Pope Speaks, Vol. 6, p.
331; Era ben naturale, January 29, 1960, The Pope
Speaks, Vol. 6, pp. 210-213. No originals available.

[89]AAS 53 (1961):319-320.

[90]AAS 53 (1961):611; translation: The Pope
Speaks, Vol. 7, p. 345.

[91]Osservatore Romano, December 8, 1960; translation: The Pope Speaks, Vol. 7, p. 151.

[92]AAS 51 (1959):509-510. The translation is
from The Pope Speaks, Vol. 5, p. 368 except for the
sections in brackets: impero was translated "form",
a phrase and entire sentence were omitted from the
translation, and instruo and educo were translated
as "rear". One effect of these mistranslations was
to further erode the exercise of initiative by women.

[93]AAS 53 (1961):611; translation: The Pope
Speaks, Vol. 7, p. 345.

[94]Nous sommes particuliérement, no original
available; translation: The Pope Speaks, Vol. 6,
p. 331.

[95]AAS 55 (1963):262.

[96]Ci e gradito, Osservatore Romano, December 8, 1960; translation: The Pope Speaks, Vol. 7, pp. 172-173.

[97]AAS 55 (1963):269; translation: The Pope Speaks, Vol. 9, p. 22.

[98]Ibid., p. 270.

[99]Ibid.

[100]AAS 55 (1963):267-268; translation: The Pope Speaks, Vol. 9, pp. 21-22.

[101]AAS 54 (1962):403.

[102]AAS 52 (1960):897.

[103]AAS 58 (1966):1074; translation: The Gospel of Peace and Justice: Catholic Social Teaching Since Pope John, edited by Joseph Gremillion (New York: Orbis Press, 1976), pp. 288-289.

[104]AAS 58 (1966):1073; translation: Gospel of Peace and Justice, p. 296.

[105]AAS 58 (1966):1081; translation: Gospel of Peace and Justice, p. 297.

[106]Salutiamo con compiacenza, February 12, 1966, AAS 58 (1966):224.

[107]Octogesima adveniens, AAS 63 (1971):410-411; translation: Gospel of Peace and Justice, pp. 491-492.

[108]Après plus, Osservatore Romano, January 31, 1976; translation: The Pope Speaks, Vol. 21,p. 165.

[109]*Soyez les bienvenues*, April 18, 1975, *Osservatore Romano*, April 19, 1975; translation: *The Pope Speaks*, Vol. 20, p. 37.

[110]*Apres plus*, *Osservatore Romano*, January 31, 1976; translation: *The Pope Speaks*, Vol. 21, p. 165.

[111]*A tutti*, December 8, 1974, *Osservatore Romano*, December 20, 1974; translation: *The Pope Speaks*, Vol. 19, p. 345.

[112]*Soyez les bienvenues*, April 18, 1975, *Osservatore Romano*, April 19, 1975; translation: *The Pope Speaks*, Vol. 20, p. 40.

[113]*Ricordi antichi*, December 7, 1974, *Osservatore Romano*, December 8, 1974; translation: *The Pope Speaks*, Vol. 19, pp. 314-316.

[114]*Soyez les bienvenues*, *Osservatore Romano*, April 19, 1975; translation: *The Pope Speaks*, Vol. 20, p. 37.

[115]*Ibid.*, translation, p. 38.

[116]*Ibid.*

[117]*E motivo*, September 8,1964, *Osservatore Romano*, September 9, 1964; translation: *The Pope Speaks*, Vol. 10, p. 17.

[118]*Ministeria quaedam*, August 15, 1972, *AAS* 64 (1972):530; translation: *The Pope Speaks*, Vol. 17, p. 256. (Emphasis mine.)

[119]*Ibid.*, p. 553; translation: *The Pope Speaks*, p. 261. [120]*ASS* 69:98.

CHAPTER VI

FINAL CONCLUSIONS

This survey of papal teaching brings us to two conclusions. The first is that the size of the gaps remaining between papal teaching and the minimum requirements of a liberation stance is very different depending on the particular issue at hand. The second is that the pace of the development in the papal teaching also differs a great deal depending upon the particular issue.

Within the issues of racism and Third World culture we find a continuing development of the papal teaching over the period studied. Though there remain significant differences between the Third World theologians and the official teaching on these issues, the differences have substantively narrowed under most of the last few popes.

The gap between Third World liberation theology and the papal teaching is perhaps smallest regarding private property; this issue is also one in which the papal teaching has made steady progress since Leo XIII. On the issues of Marxism and the use of violence the pontificates of John XXIII and Paul VI have touched off a minor revolution in papal teaching; the gaps between the two sides are still significant, but the logjam has been broken.

The issue on which papal teaching and Third World liberation theologians remain oceans apart is that of theological method. There are, in the Vatican refusal to break with the traditional theo-

341

logical method, elements of both continuity and
discontinuity. There is a sense in which the continuity with the past on this point is to be expected. In liberation theology, theology is the
second step, dependent upon prior commitment to
the liberation struggle. Until the Church resolves
sufficient of its other differences with liberation
theology, or gets unwillingly drawn into the political struggle by the partisans of liberation theology in the clergy, the Church will not begin to
take up the theological task from within engagement in the liberation struggle, and therefore will
continue its traditional view as to how theology is
done. The element of discontinuity in the papal
stance on theological method concerns the sense in
which the papal tradition of the last century was
critical of both the liberal ideology and the
reality of the modern world. Liberation theologians maintain that they are carrying on this tradition of radical critique of the world, and that if
the papacy is to maintain this former critical
stance it must engage the Church in praxis, thus
altering its understanding of theological method.

Though the papal teaching, especially from Leo
XIII to Pius XII, often confused the critique of
modernity and capitalist ideology with concern for
its own declining power and prestige, most of the
religious values upon which that critique was based
are still viewed as pertinent by the liberation
theologians. Respect for the dignity and freedom
of human life yet call the Church to a radical critique of the modern world and to a stance against
those forces and ideologies which restrict and deny
such values. This is not a time, say the liberation theologians, for the Church to make peace with
the modern world; it is a time which calls for
careful discrimination and critique, and for praxis
on the part of the Church. Continuity in the critical stance toward the world seems to require dis-

342

continuity in theological method.

The attitude of Paul VI toward liberation theology, seemingly reversed in the years after <u>Octogesima</u> <u>adveniens</u>, hardened into clearcut opposition. Powerful segments of the Church in the First World joined Latin American ecclesial opponents of the theology of liberation. Not only is liberation theology today menaced by this powerful coalition of ecclesial forces, but it is also persecuted by the civil and economic powers it threatens. Beyond the question of the survival of the Latin American theology of liberation there is a question as to whether papal sensitivity to the Third World and its theologies--never before so acute as under the first years of Paul's papacy--was dulled by Paul's unsuccessful attempt to overcome fear of civil repression and political involvement in pushing the Church to become the Church of the poor. John Paul II's intention to attend the Latin American episcopal meeting in Puebla in January, 1979 demonstrates his interest in these questions. It is difficult to predict before Puebla what attitude this new pope will adopt in these questions.

Though Paul's earlier statements favorable to liberation theology did not reflect the actual practice of the Church, <u>Octogesima</u> <u>adveniens</u> and <u>Populorum</u> <u>progressio</u> were not mere rhetoric, either. They were rather an attempt to push the Church's position in the liberation theology direction. It is always necessary to consider papal teachings in the light of current Church practice, rather than as pronouncements of accepted Church stands, for such teaching may either reflect Church practice or be an attempt to alter it in one direction or another. The power of the papacy and the weight of papal statements in general prevent papal teaching from being solely rhetoric.

The issue of women--their nature, role, and place in the Church--is one on which there has been virtually no papal movement, in which the present gap between the official Church and the goals of liberation movement is very wide, and on which hopes for progress seem most bleak. On the whole it seems clear that papal accommodation to Third World liberation theology--stalled or reversing though it may now be--has not been matched by similar accommodation to the women's liberation movement or its theology. The very fact that Third World liberation theology has been taken up by segments of the clergy and even of the hierarchy has meant that the issues of that movement are somewhat heard in the Vatican and debated in the Church. Women have no such access to positions of power within the Church from which to force a hearing of their issues. Episcopal meetings, such as the Synod of 1971 and the regional meetings of CELAM in Medellin and Puebla, offer a forum in which liberation theology can be heard and comprehended. Without minimizing the powerful episcopal, papal and civil forces locked in a conspiracy to destroy the theology of liberation in Latin America, one can maintain, I think, that such forums offer a hope that the Vatican and conservative hierarchy can yet be influenced on the remaining issues--a hope that has no such basis in the case of women.

The situation of women in papal teaching, however, cannot be explained merely by the absence of women in the hierarchy, or even in the clergy. New national and racial groups have gained access to the Church, and become influential within it, from exactly the same outsider position that women occupy. For example, the modern creation of a black hierarchy only began with Pius XII, and yet the Church made continual progress before and after this in recognizing the equality and rights of

black people. Today we must ask how it is that
the Church can maintain the contradictions between
its position on women and its position on human
beings in general. The papal teaching on the
rights of all human beings to equality, freedom,
decision-making and participation in all aspects
of life contrasts vividly with the exclusion of
women from decision-making in the Church and from
participation in the offices of the liturgy. These
rights of all human beings contrast as well with
the limited social roles deemed fit for women in
the papal teaching: those which can accommodate
the primary domestic vocation she is assigned, and
concerning which she is given little choice.

It is impossible to accurately probe the
motives of any individual pope as to the reasons
for the impasse on the woman question. But the
overall pattern is so clear that we are left little
option but to assume that in the woman question
there is something more deeply rooted than in these
other areas. For the crucial sticking points in
papal teaching for black and Latin American liberation theology has concerned the posture that the
Church takes toward events in the world; the question as to the place of these peoples within the
Church has not been at issue for at least decades,
and in some instances centuries. With regard to
women, the primary issue now is not the Church's
advocacy of women's rights in the world, but the
simple recognition of equal rights in the Church.
It can only be assumed that the recognition of such
rights presents a vital threat to the Church's understanding of herself, upon which her structure
and teaching rest.

Only the high level of threat that the women's
movement poses to the Church explains the stubborn
clinging to the tradition of exclusion originally
based upon such outdated concepts as the defilement

345

of the altar by menstrual blood, feminine sinfulness, and the belief in female inferiority. The
extent of the threat results from the fact that
women are a clear majority within the Church.
Their empowerment would endanger conceptions of
authority and patterns of hierarchy, as well as
challenge the vestigial aspects of the medieval
worldview still operative in the Church: soul/
body dualism, the harmony model of the world, and
the understanding of Christian love as sacrificial
and vertical. Many of these changes are indeed
implied in the Third World challenges to the Vatican. But the centrality of the traditional understanding of the male/female relationship to the
papal view of harmony and authority, body and soul,
love and hierarchy, assures that a revolution in
the male/female relationship could not but call
these into question also.

The challenge liberation theologies pose to
the papacy, and indeed to the present Church leadership, must be, then, perceived in terms of
major alterations not only in praxis, in the way
in which the Church responds to the world, but in
the structure, personnel and theology of the
Church itself.

BIBLIOGRAPHY

Andrews, John. <u>Paul</u> <u>the</u> <u>Sixth</u>: <u>A</u> <u>Critical</u> <u>Apprai</u>-<u>sal</u>. Milwaukee: Bruce Publishing Co., 1973.

Aquinas, Thomas. <u>Summa</u> <u>Theologiae</u>. Blackfriars Dominicans, editors. New York: McGraw-Hill Book Co., 1964.

Aretin, Karl Otmar von. <u>The</u> <u>Papacy</u> <u>and</u> <u>the</u> <u>Modern</u> <u>World</u>. New York: McGraw-Hill Book Co., 1970.

Assman, Hugo. <u>Theology</u> <u>for</u> <u>a</u> <u>Nomad</u> <u>Church</u>. New York: Orbis Press, 1975.

Benedict XV. <u>Maximum</u> <u>illud</u>. <u>Acta</u> <u>Apostolicae</u> <u>Sedis</u> 11. 1919.

Bigo, Pierre. <u>La</u> <u>doctrine</u> <u>sociale</u> <u>de</u> <u>l'Eglise</u>. Paris: Presses de Universitaires de France, 1965.

Bigo, Pierre. <u>The</u> <u>Church</u> <u>and</u> <u>Third</u> <u>World</u> <u>Revolu</u>-<u>tion</u>. New York: Orbis Press, 1977.

Boesak, Allen. <u>Farewell</u> <u>to</u> <u>Innocence</u>: <u>A</u> <u>Socio</u>-<u>ethical</u> <u>Study</u> <u>of</u> <u>Black</u> <u>Theology</u> <u>and</u> <u>Power</u>. New York: Orbis Press, 1977.

Brown, William Eric. <u>The</u> <u>Catholic</u> <u>Church</u> <u>in</u> <u>South</u> <u>Africa</u>. London: Burns and Oates, 1960.

Calves, J. Y. and Perrin, Jacques. <u>The</u> <u>Church</u> <u>and</u> <u>Social</u> <u>Justice</u>. London: Burns and Oates, 1961.

Calves, J. Y. <u>Politics</u> <u>and</u> <u>Society</u> <u>in</u> <u>the</u> <u>Third</u> <u>World</u>. New York: Orbis Press, 1973.

Camp, Richard L. The Papal Ideology of Social Reform. Leiden: E. J. Brill, 1969.

Catholic Archdiocese of Capetown. The Catholic Church in Southern Africa. Capetown: Diocese of Capetown, 1951.

Commission Theologique Internationale. Declaration Sur Le Promotion Humaine et Le Salut Chretien. La Documentation Catholique. No. 1726.

Cotter, A. C. The Encyclical Humani Generis. Weston, Mass.: Weston College Press, 1952.

Daly, Mary. Beyond God the Father. Boston: Beacon Press, 1972.

Daly, Mary. The Church and the Second Sex. New York: Harper and Row, 1975.

Dinnerstein, Dorothy. The Mermaid and the Minotaur. New York: Harper and Row, 1976.

Dussel, Enrique. Ethics and the Theology of Liberation. New York: Orbis Press, 1978.

Dussel, Enrique. History and the Theology of Liberation. New York: Orbis Press, 1976.

Eagleson, John, editor. Christians for Socialism. New York: Orbis Press, 1975.

Eckhardt, Karl C. The Papacy and World Affairs. Chicago: University of Chicago Press, 1937.

Elwood, Douglas J. What Asian Christians Are Thinking. Quezon City, Philippines: New Day Publishers, 1976.

Encyclopedia Americana. New York: Americana Corp.

1953.

Falconi, Carlo. *The Popes in the Twentieth Century*. Boston: Little, Brown and Co., 1967.

Firestone, Shulameth. *The Dialectic of Sex*. New York: Bantam, 1970.

Gilson, Etienne. *The Social Teachings of Leo XIII*. Garden City, New York: Doubleday, 1954.

Gremillion, Joseph, editor. *The Gospel of Peace and Justice*. New York: Orbis Press, 1976.

Guerry, Emile. *Social Teaching and the Church*. London: St. Paul Publishers, 1961.

Guettel, Charnie. *Marxism and Feminism*. Toronto: Women's Press, 1974.

Gutierrez, Gustavo and Shaull, Richard. *Liberation and Change*. Atlanta: John Knox Press, 1977.

Gutierrez, Gustavo. *A Theology of Liberation*. New York: Orbis Press, 1973.

Hales, E.E.Y. *Pope John and His Revolution*. Garden City, New York: Doubleday, 1966.

Harte, Thomas. *Papal Social Principles*. Gloucester, Mass.: Peter Smith Co., 1960.

Hatch, Alden. *Pope Paul VI*. New York: Random House, 1966.

Hebblethwaite, Peter. "CELAM Draft Drops Latin Input." *National Catholic Reporter*. Vol. 14, no. 28. April 21, 1978.

Hebblethwaite, Peter. "Liberation Theology Under
    Attack." National Catholic Reporter. Vol.
    14, no. 22. March 24, 1978.

Henning, Clara Maria. "Celibacy as a Feminist
    Issue." Women and Orders, edited by Robert
    Heyer. New York: Paulist Press, 1974.

Henning, Clara Maria. "Canon Law and the Battle
    of the Sexes." Religion and Sexism, edited
    by Rosemary Radford Ruether. New York:
    Simon and Schuster, 1974.

Hoare, F. R. The Papacy and the Modern State.
    London: Burns and Oates, 1940.

Howell, Leon. "Chavez for the Defense." Christi-
    anity and Crisis. Vol. 37, no. 17. Novem-
    ber 14, 1977.

Hughes, Philip. The Pope's New Order: A Systema-
    tic Study of the Social Encyclicals and Ad-
    dresses from Leo XIII to Pius XII. London:
    Burns and Oates, 1942.

Husslein, Joseph, editor. Social Wellsprings:
    Leo XIII. Milwaukee: Bruce Publishing Co.,
    1940.

Husslein, Joseph, editor. Social Wellsprings:
    Pius XI. Milwaukee: Bruce Publishing Co.,
    1942.

Jenness, Linda. Feminism and Socialism. New Jer-
    sey: Pathfinder, 1972.

John XXIII. Accueillant avec. Acta Apostolicae
    Sedis 52. 1960.

John XXIII. Ad petri cathedram. Acta Apostolicae

Sedis 51. 1959.

John XXIII. _C'est pour nous_. _Acta Apostolicae_
Sedis 53. 1961.

John XXIII. _Ci e gradito_. _Osservatore Romano_.
December 8, 1960.

John XXIII. _Convenuti a Roma_. _Acta Apostolicae_
Sedis 53. 1961.

John XXIII. _Di gran cuore_. _The Pope Speaks_.
Vol. 6.

John XXIII. _The Encyclicals and Other Messages of_
Pope John XXIII. Washington, D.C.: The Pope
Speaks Press, 1964.

John XXIII. _Hac trepida hora_. _Acta Apostolicae_
Sedis 50. 1958.

John XXIII. _In questa luminosa_. _Acta Apostolicae_
Sedis 51. 1959.

John XXIII. _Mater et Magistra_. _Acta Apostolicae_
Sedis 53. 1961.

John XXIII. _Notre joie est grande_. _Acta Aposto-_
licae Sedis 52. 1960.

John XXIII. _Nous sommes particulierement_. _The_
Pope Speaks. Vol. 6.

John XXIII. _Pacem in terris_. _Acta Apostolicae_
Sedis 55. 1963.

John XXIII. _Princeps pastorum_. _Acta Apostolicae_
Sedis 51. 1959.

John XXIII. _Ringrazia di vero_. _Acta Apostolicae_

<u>Sedis</u> 50. 1958.

Kappen, Sebastian. <u>Jesus</u> <u>and</u> <u>Freedom</u>. New York: Orbis, 1977.

Latourette, Kenneth. <u>A History of Christianity</u>. New York: Harper and Row, 1975. Vol. 2.

Latourette, Kenneth. <u>The Twentieth Century in Europe</u>. Vol. 4 of <u>Christianity in a Revolutionary Age</u>. New York: Harper and Row, 1961.

Leo XIII. <u>Ad extremas orientis oras</u>. <u>Acta Sanctae Sedis</u> 25.

Leo XIII. <u>Arcanum</u>. <u>Acta Sanctae Sedis</u> 12.

Leo XIII. <u>Diuturnum</u>. <u>Acta Sanctae Sedis</u> 14.

Leo XIII. <u>Graves de communi</u>. <u>Acta Sanctae Sedis</u> 33.

Leo XIII. <u>Immortale Dei</u>. <u>Acta Sanctae Sedis</u> 18.

Leo XIII. <u>In plurimis</u>. <u>Acta Sanctae Sedis</u> 20.

Leo XIII. <u>Inscrutabile</u>. <u>Acta Sanctae Sedis</u> 10.

Leo XIII. <u>Libertas humana</u>. <u>Acta Sanctae Sedis</u> 20.

Leo XIII. <u>Quod Apostolici muneris</u>. <u>Acta Sanctae Sedis</u> 11.

Leo XIII. <u>Rerum novarum</u>. <u>Acta Sanctae Sedis</u> 23.

Leo XIII. <u>Sapientiae Christianae</u>. <u>Acta Sanctae Sedis</u> 22.

Lewis, Carlos A. <u>Catholic Negro Bishops</u>. Bay St. Louis: Divine Word Publications, 1958.

Lopez-Trujillo, Alfonso. _Liberation_ or _Revolu-tion_? Huntington, Ind.: Our Sunday Visitor Press, 1977.

MacEoin, Gary. "Will the Latin American People Be Heard at CELAM III?" _Latin_ _America_ _Press_, Vol. 10, no. 1. March 9, 1978.

MacEoin, Gary. "CELAM III Will Test the Reality of Medellin." _Latin_ _America_ _Press_, Vol. 10, no. 1. January 5, 1978.

Marx, Karl. _The_ _German_ _Ideology_. Part I. "Feuerbach," in _Karl_ _Marx-Frederich_ _Engels:_ _Collected_ _Works_, Vol. 5. New York: International Publishers, 1976.

McGrath, Sister Albertus Magnus. _Women_ _and_ _the_ _Church_. Garden City, New York: Doubleday Image, 1976.

Memorandum _From_ _Theologians_ _in_ _the_ _Federal_ _Repub-lic_ _of_ _Germany_ _Concerning_ _the_ _Campaign_ _Against_ _the_ _Theology_ _of_ _Liberation_. Mimeographed.

Michel, Virgil. _Christian_ _Social_ _Reconstruction_. Milwaukee: Bruce Publishing Co., 1958.

Miranda, Jose Porfirio. _Marx_ _and_ _the_ _Bible_. New York: Orbis, 1971.

Miranda, Jose Porfirio. _Being_ _and_ _the_ _Messiah_. New York: Orbis, 1977.

Mitchell, Juliet. "The Longest Revolution." _New_ _Left_ _Review_, No. 40, 1966.

Moore, Basil, editor. _The_ _Challenge_ _of_ _Black_ _The-ology_ _in_ _South_ _Africa_. Atlanta: John Knox

353

Press, 1973.

Nell-Bruening, Oswald von. Reorganization of
Social Economy. Milwaukee: Bruce Publishing
Co., 1939.

New Catholic Encyclopedia. New York: McGraw-Hill
Book Co., 1967.

O'Brien, David and Shannon, Thomas. Renewing the
Earth: Catholic Documents on Peace, Justice
and Liberation. New York: Doubleday Image,
1977.

Outka, Gene. Agape: An Ethical Analysis. New
Haven: Yale University Press, 1972.

Papal Teachings: Matrimony. Boston: Daughters
of St. Paul, 1963.

Papal Teachings: Woman in the Modern World. Boston: Daughters of St. Paul, 1959.

Paul VI et al. De Justitia in Mundo. Acta Apostolicae Sedis 63. 1971.

Paul VI et al. Gaudium et Spes. Acta Apostolicae
Sedis 58. 1966.

Paul VI. Après plus. Osservatore Romano. January 31, 1976.

Paul VI. A tutti. Osservatore Romano. December
20, 1974.

Paul VI. E motivo. Osservatore Romano. September 9, 1964.

Paul VI. Libentissimo sane animo. Osservatore
Romano. October 2, 1966.

Paul VI. Ministeria Quaedam. Acta Apostolicae Sedis 64. 1972.

Paul VI. Nous nous appris. Osservatore Romano. June 8, 1966.

Paul VI. Nous voudrions d'abord. Osservatore Romano. June 26, 1966.

Paul VI. Octogesima adveniens. Acta Apostolicae Sedis 63. 1971.

Paul VI. Populorum progressio. Acta Apostolicae Sedis 59. 1967.

Paul VI. Ricordi antichi. Osservatore Romano. December 8, 1974.

Paul VI. Salutiamo con compiacenza. Acta Apostolicae Sedis 58. 1966.

Paul VI. Soyez les bienvenues. Osservatore Romano. April 19, 1975.

Paul VI. Voi avete participato. Acta Apostolicae Sedis 55. 1963.

Pius IX. Qui pluribus. Acta Pii PP IX. Romae: Typis Rev. Camarae Apostolicae, 1865.

Pius IX. Syllabus of Errors. Acta Pii PP IX. Romae: Typis Rev. Camarae Apostolicae, 1865.

Pius XI. A Lei, Vicario Nostro. Acta Apostolicae Sedis 20. 1928.

Pius XI. Casti connubi. Acta Apostolicae Sedis 22. 1930.

Pius XI. Divini illius Magistri. Acta Apostoli-

355

cae Sedis 22. 1930.

Pius XI. Divini Redemptoris. Acta Apostolicae
Sedis 29. 1937.

Pius XI. Firmissimam constantiam. Acta Apostolicae Sedis 29. 1937.

Pius XI. Lux veritatis. Acta Apostolicae Sedis
23. 1931.

Pius XI. Mit brennender sorge. Acta Apostolicae
Sedis 29. 1937.

Pius XI. Non abiamo bisogno. Acta Apostolicae
Sedis 23. 1931.

Pius XI. Officiorum omnium. Acta Apostolicae
Sedis 14. 1922.

Pius XI. Quadragesimo anno. Acta Apostolicae
Sedis 23. 1931.

Pius XI. Rerum ecclesiae. Acta Apostolicae
Sedis 18. 1926.

Pius XI. Sixteen Encyclicals of His Holiness,
Pope Pius XI. Washington, D.C.: National
Catholic Welfare Conference, 1937.

Pius XI. Ubi arcano. Acta Apostolicae Sedis 14.
1922.

Pius XII. Ad ecclesiam Christi. Acta Apostolicae Sedis 47. 1955.

Pius XII. Amadissimo hijos. Acta Apostolicae
Sedis 43. 1951.

Pius XII. Atti e discorsi di Pio XII. Romae:

356

Instituto Missionaria, Pia Societa San Paolo, 1939-1945, 6 Vols.

Pius XII. <u>C'est</u> <u>un</u> <u>geste</u>. <u>Acta Apostolicae Sedis</u> 38. 1946.

Pius XII. <u>Chers</u> <u>fils</u>. <u>Acta Apostolicae Sedis</u> 42. 1950.

Pius XII. <u>Chers</u> <u>fils</u> <u>et</u> <u>cheres</u> <u>filles</u>. <u>Acta Apostolicae Sedis</u> 46. 1954.

Pius XII. <u>Con</u> <u>sempre</u> <u>nuova</u>. <u>Acta Apostolicae Sedis</u> 35. 1943.

Pius XII. <u>Datis</u> <u>nuperrine</u>. <u>Acta Apostolicae Sedis</u> 48. 1956.

Pius XII. <u>Dequelle</u> <u>consolation</u>. <u>Acta Apostolicae Sedis</u> 43. 1951.

Pius XII. <u>Der</u> <u>Katholische</u> <u>Deutsche</u>. <u>Acta Apostolicae Sedis</u> 44. 1952.

Pius XII. <u>Dilette</u> <u>Figlie</u>. <u>The Pope Speaks</u>. Vol. 3, no. 4.

Pius XII. <u>Dos</u> <u>son</u> <u>los</u> <u>motives</u>. <u>Osservatore Romano</u>. April 12, 1956.

Pius XII. <u>Dum</u> <u>maerenti</u> <u>animo</u>. <u>The Pope Speaks</u>, Vol. 3, no. 1.

Pius XII. <u>E'ancora</u> <u>vivo</u>. <u>Acta Apostolicae Sedis</u> 47. 1955.

Pius XII. <u>Ecce</u> <u>ego</u> <u>de</u> <u>clinabo</u>. <u>Acta Apostolicae Sedis</u> 47. 1955.

Pius XII. <u>Evangelii</u> <u>praecones</u>. <u>Acta Apostolicae</u>

<u>Sedis</u> 43. 1951.

Pius XII. <u>Fidei donum</u>. <u>Acta Apostolicae Sedis</u> 49.
1957.

Pius XII. <u>Fulgens corona</u>. <u>Acta Apostolicae Sedis</u>
45. 1953.

Pius XII. <u>Humani generis</u>. <u>Acta Apostolicae Sedis</u>
42. 1950.

Pius XII. <u>In questo giorno</u>. <u>Acta Apostolicae
Sedis</u> 32. 1940.

Pius XII. <u>In the liturgical office</u>. <u>Acta Apostolicae Sedis</u> 43. 1951.

Pius XII. <u>La nostra casa</u>. <u>Acta Apostolicae Sedis</u>
48. 1956.

Pius XII. <u>La solennita</u>. <u>Acta Apostolicae Sedis</u>
33. 1941.

Pius XII. <u>Le vingt-cinquieme</u>. <u>Acta Apostolicae
Sedis</u> 47. 1955.

Pius XII. <u>Leva Jerusalem</u>. <u>Acta Apostolicae Sedis</u>
50. 1958.

Pius XII. <u>Luctuoissimi eventus</u>. <u>Acta Apostolicae
Sedis</u> 48. 1956.

Pius XII. <u>Meminisse juvat</u>. <u>Acta Apostolicae Sedis</u>
50. 1958.

Pius XII. <u>The memorable message</u>. <u>Acta Apostolicae
Sedis</u> 32. 1940.

Pius XII. <u>Nel vedere el cielo</u>. <u>Acta Apostolicae
Sedis</u> 40. 1948.

Pius XII. <u>Nous</u> <u>nous</u> <u>addressons</u>. <u>Acta</u> <u>Apostolicae</u> <u>Sedis</u> 42. 1950.

Pius XII. <u>Nous</u> <u>nous</u> <u>souhaitons</u>. <u>Acta</u> <u>Apostolicae</u> <u>Sedis</u> 47. 1955.

Pius XII. <u>Oggi</u> <u>al</u> <u>compiers</u>. <u>Acta</u> <u>Apostolicae</u> <u>Sedis</u> 36. 1944.

Pius XII. <u>Que</u> <u>hermoso</u> <u>espectaculo</u>. <u>Acta</u> <u>Apostolicae</u> <u>Sedis</u> 43. 1951.

Pius XII. <u>Quoniam</u> <u>Paschaliam</u>. <u>Acta</u> <u>Apostolicae</u> <u>Sedis</u> 31. 1939.

Pius XII. <u>Poco</u> <u>piu</u> <u>di</u> <u>dieci</u> <u>anni</u>. <u>Osservatore</u> <u>Romano</u>. May 28, 1955.

Pius XII. <u>The</u> <u>Pope</u> <u>Speaks</u>: <u>The</u> <u>Words</u> <u>of</u> <u>Pius</u> <u>XII</u>. New York: Harcourt, Brace and Co., 1940.

Pius XII. <u>Se</u> <u>a</u> <u>tempere</u>. <u>Acta</u> <u>Apostolicae</u> <u>Sedis</u> 32. 1940.

Pius XII. <u>Sertum</u> <u>laetitiae</u>. <u>Acta</u> <u>Apostolicae</u> <u>Sedis</u> 31. 1939.

Pius XII. <u>Summi</u> <u>Pontificatus</u>. <u>Acta</u> <u>Apostolicae</u> <u>Sedis</u> 31. 1939.

Pinchon, Charles. <u>The</u> <u>Vatican</u> <u>and</u> <u>Its</u> <u>Role</u> <u>in</u> <u>World</u> <u>Affairs</u>. New York: E. P. Dutton and Co., 1950.

Poulet, Charles. <u>History</u> <u>of</u> <u>the</u> <u>Catholic</u> <u>Church</u>. St. Louis: S. Herder and Co., 1940. Vol. 2.

Poynter, J. W. <u>The</u> <u>Popes</u> <u>and</u> <u>Social</u> <u>Problems</u>. London: Watts and Co., 1949.

Riding, Alan. "Catholic Bishops in Latin America
    Wage Bitter Struggle Over Church's Leftist
    Trend." The New York Times, April 6, 1978.

Rowbotham, Sheila. Woman's Consciousness, Man's
    World. London: Pelican, 1973.

Rowbotham, Sheila. Women, Resistance and Revolu-
    tion. New York: Vantage, 1974.

Ruether, Rosemary. Liberation Theology. New York:
    Paulist Press, 1972.

Ruether, Rosemary. New Woman New Earth. New York:
    Seabury Press, 1975.

Ruether, Rosemary. Religion and Sexism. New York:
    Simon and Schuster, 1974.

Ryan, James N., ed. The Encyclicals of Pius XI.
    St. Louis, Mo.: Herder and Herder, 1927.

Sacred Congregation for the Doctrine of the Faith.
    Declaration on the Question of the Admission
    of Women to the Ministerial Priesthood. Acta
    Apostolicae Sedis 69. 1977.

Scott, Hilda. Can Socialism Liberate Women? Ex-
    periences from Eastern Europe. Boston:
    Beacon Press, 1974.

Segundo, Juan Luis. The Liberation of Theology.
    New York: Orbis Press, 1976.

Seven Great Encyclicals. New York: Paulist
    Press, 1963.

Swidler, Arlene. "Partnership Marriage: Model of
    Future Priesthood." Women and Catholic
    Priesthood, edited by Anne Marie Gardiner,

360

SSND. New York: Paulist Press, 1976.

"Taking on the Vatican." _Time_. May 8, 1978.

Torres, Sergio and Eagleson, John. _Theology in the Americas_. New York: Orbis, 1976.

Torres, Sergio and Fabella, Virginia, editors. _The Emergent Gospel_: _Theology from the Underside of History_. New York: Orbis Press, 1977.

Watt, Lewis. _Catholic Social Principles_. London: Burns and Oates, 1929.

Zaretsky, Eli. _Capitalism, The Family, and Personal Life_. New York: Harper and Row, 1976.

INDEX

A Lei, Vicario Nostro, 332 n35

A l'occasion, 242 n 68; 243 n70

A tutti, 339 n111

Acerba animi, 186,187

Accueillant avec, 164 n119

Action through the Word, 75

Ad ecclesiam Christi, 134

Ad extremas Orientis oras, 131

Ad petri cathedram, 6; 40; 50 n43,46; 51 n58; 52
    n61; 56n99; 57 n116; 217-219; 220; 222; 245
    n103; 305

Aeterni patris, 156 n14

Allende, S., 85

Allo strazio, 215

Anticlericalism, 87

Aquinas, Thomas, see Thomas Aquinas

Applied theology, 66

Après plus, 338 n108; 339 n110

Arcanum, 56 n67; 257; 259; 331 n21,22; 331 n27

Aretin, Karl Otmar von, 48 n24; 49 n25,26,27,29;
    50 n45; 102 n49; 103 n59; 105 n65; 244 n89

Assman, Hugo, 65; 75; 99 n1,2,6,8,10; 100 n13,15;
    101 n36; 106 n75; 138; 162 n96; 164 n125;
    237 n13,15

Benedict XV, 130; 131; 135; 137; 140; 145; 260-
    263

Bigo, Pierre, 46 n6; 113; 117; 156 n13; 157 n26

Boesak, A., 155 n2

Boff, Leonardo, 99 n9; 237 n13

Bonum sane, 260-261

Byrnes, M. J., 331 n23

Calves, J. Y., 2; 31; 38; 47 n7,11,12,13; 48 n25;
     53 n72; 55 n92; 56 n108; 57 n115; 113; 117;
     118; 157 n12,25,26,27; 158 n43; 243 n79,82
Camp, R. L., 7; 48 n23; 158 n43,47; 159 n60
Capetown, Diocese of, 163 n109; 112; 115
Caritate Christi, 186
Casti Connubi, 51 n56; 52 n60; 53 n67,73; 101 n30;
     182; 266; 267-271
Catholic Action, 89; 94; 187
CELAM, 81; 82; 167; 235 n2,5,6; 236 n11
C'est bien volontiers, 140
C'est pour nous, 304
C'est un geste, 122
Chers fils, 105 n67
Chers fils et cheres filles, 242 n65
Christendom mentality, 86
Christians for Socialism, 172; 237 n13; 238 n16
Church of the poor, 67; 84
Ci e gradito, 303; 304-305; 338 n96
Colonization, 145
     Spanish and Portugese, 131;141
Comanagement, 121; 123
Comblin, J., 138
Communism, 27; 39; 42; 122; 174; 233
Communist Manifesto, 175
Con sempere nuoua, 157 n31; 158 n40
Cone, J., 105 n71
Contextualization, 139
Convenuti a Roma, 303; 304; 305-306
Co-optation of liberation theology, 97
Corporatism, 7

Daly, Mary, 329 n1; 331 n19
Datis Nuperrine, 215
Declaration On The Question of The Ordination of
     Women To The Ministerial Priesthood, 326;
     327; 329 n3
Declaration Sur Le Promotion Humaine et Le Salut
     Chretien, 107 n83,84; 235 n1, 236 n8, 247 n
     127

<u>De</u> <u>Justitia</u> <u>In</u> <u>Mundo</u>, 40; 45; 46 n1; 48 n17,19;
    56 n100; 57 n118; 160 n68
Democracy, 87; 88
<u>Dequelle</u> <u>consolation</u>, 105 n67
<u>Der</u> <u>Katholische</u> <u>Deutsche</u>, 282-283
Detroit Conference on the Ordination of Women, 251
Development, 109; 110; 127-129; 130; 148-154
<u>Di</u> <u>gran</u> <u>cuore</u>, 337 n88
Diez-Alegria, Jose Maria, 237 n15
<u>Dilectissimo</u> <u>nobis</u>, 186
<u>Dilette</u> <u>figlie</u>, 336 n79
Dinnerstein, Dorothy, 253; 330 n8
<u>Divini</u> <u>illius</u> <u>magistri</u>, 53 n67; 48 n21; 74; 101 n30,
    31; 265-266
<u>Divini</u> <u>Redemptoris</u>, 39; 47 n16,22; 49 n31; 52 n59,
    61; 53 n67; 55 n96; 74; 87; 95; 101 n30,32,
    35; 104 n64; 105 n67,69; 106 n77; 157 n30,33;
    181; 183; 186; 187; 189-190; 191-192; 194;
    198; 239 n32; 240 n36,37,42-50; 266-267
Dogmatic theology, 66-67
<u>Dos</u> <u>son</u> <u>los</u> <u>motives</u>, 335 n61
<u>Dum</u> <u>maerenti</u> <u>animo</u>, 206
Dussel, E., 138; 155 n2; 162 n90,97; 164 n125;
    237 n14; 238 n16,17

<u>E</u> <u>motivo</u>, 339 n117
<u>E'ancora</u> <u>vivo</u>, 209; 243 n76,77
<u>Ecce</u> <u>ego</u> <u>declinabo</u>, 242 n65
Egalitarianism, 27; 39; 42; 44; 143; 144
<u>Ehrwurdige</u> <u>Bruder</u>, 83
Ellwood, D. J. 162 n98
Engels, F., 254
England, 141
    clergy in, 130
Enlightenment, 63
Epistemological privilege, 111
<u>Era</u> <u>ben</u> <u>naturale</u>, 337 n88
<u>Evangelii</u> <u>praecones</u>, 47 n15; 82; 102 n41; 105 n69;
    130; 134; 135; 138; 145; 155 n10; 158 n40;
    160 n80; 161 n86,87,88; 162 n95; 164 n116,117

Fabella, V., 104 n63; 106 n71; 162 n98
Falconi, C., 103 n59; 104 n60; 105 n65,67; 244 n89
Fidei donum, 102 n40; 130; 145; 160 n69
Firestone, Shulamith, 252; 253; 330 n7
Firmissimam constantiam, 187-189; 240 n40
France, 141
French workers, 80
Fulgens corona, 242 n65
Fundamental theology, 66

Gaudium et Spes, 18; 34; 40; 41; 48 n17; 50 n48;
     54 n80; 56 n101; 124; 126; 127; 139; 159 n62,
     63; 224; 246 n114-117; 312-314
Gera, Lucio, 236 n12
Gilson, E., 156 n20
Goretti, Maria, 275
Graves de communi, 53 n67
Gregory VII and Norwegian clergy, 130
Gremillion, J., 105 n68
Guettel, Charnie, 253; 330 n13
Gutierrez, Gustavo, 58; 59; 67-68; 86; 99 n1,3,4,
     7,8,10; 100 n11,12,13,14,17,18; 104 n63; 105
     n71; 155 n1,2; 164 n125; 237 n13,15

Hac trepida hora, 244 n97
Hales, E.E.Y., 56 n2,10
Harte, T., 106 n74
Henning, Clara Maria, 329 n4; 331 n18
Historical change, 6
     Paul VI and, 18-21
     Pius XI and, 6-10
     Pius XII and, 11-16
     John XXIII and, 16-17
Historical project, 59; 61; 64; 95
Humani generis, 12-15
Hungarian revolt, 84; 214-216; 238 n25
Husslein, J., 48 n18

Idealism, 75
Immortale Dei, 53 n67; 258; 310

In _questo giorno_, 33 n67; 103 n59
In _plurimis_, 51 n58; 140; 178-79; 239 n26
In _the liturgical office_, 143
India, 131
Iniquiis afflictisque, 187; 240 n39
Inesaurabili mistero, 216
Inscrutabili, 175; 238 n20
Integral development, 127
International Commission on Theology, 91; 97; 168;
    247 n127
Iguniz, Javier, 236 n13

Jenness, L., 253; 330 n14
John XXIII
    as conservative, 16
    on Church and culture, 135-136
    on colonialism, 146-147
    on development, 129; 148-151
    on the distinction between movement and
        ideology, 220-221
    on hierarchy, 309-312
    on historical change, 16-17
    on mission of the Church, 78
    on native clergy, 138
    on natural equality, 40; 44
    on partnerships, 43
    on the poor, 69; 71
    on private property, 113; 118; 119; 123-124;
        125
    on racism, 139
    on rights of human beings, 43
    on spiritual and temporal planes, 84; 85
    on women, 302-312
    on worker-priests, 80
    optimism regarding modern world, 16: 35; 44;
        123; 124; 149; 231
Johnson, P., 245 n106
Jus gentium, 114; 116
Just wage, 119
Just war, 117; 214-217; 232; 238 n24

367

Justice, 1
    general, 2
    particular, 2
    commutative, 2; 21; 29-37
    distributive, 2; 22
    social, 2; 21-45

Kappan, S., 162 n98
Kingdom of God, 60
Korea, 145

La nostra casa, 242 n69
La solennita, 31; 47 n14; 53 n67; 85; 86; 93; 103
    n58; 113; 157 n30; 158 n37,40,42,47
Lacrimabili statu, 140
Le vingtcinquieme, 286; 287
Lenin, V., 180; 183
Leo XIII, 1; 43; 79
    and freedom, 23
    and poverty, 111; 112; 113
    objections to Marxism, 175-176
    on just wage, 43
    on native clergy, 131; 137
    on natural equality, 119
    on private property, 112; 113; 115-118; 119;
        121; 128
    on slavery, 140; 178-179
    on Thomas, 115; 156 n114
    on women, 257-260
Les paroles si élevées, 205
Leva Jerusalem, 244 n77
Lewis, C. A., 160 n71,72; 161 n81,93
Liberation theology
    African, 139
    Asian, 139
Libentissimo sane animo, 71; 91
Libertas humana, 53 n67
Litteras a vobis, 139
Living wage, 34
Lopez-Trujillo, Bishop Alfonso, 236 n6

Luctuoissimi eventus, 214
Lux veritatis, 266

Marx, K., 183; 254; 330 n16
    early writings of, 181
Marxism, 33; 167-248
    and liberation theology, 170-173
    class struggle in, 181; 189-193; 200-201; 211-
        213; 233
    early papal teaching on, 174-180
    in Spain and Mexico, 180; 185; 189; 239 n25
    on marriage and family, 182; 183
    Pius XI on, 180-205
    Pius XII on, 205-217
Marxist analysis, 170; 171
Marxist atheism, 175; 181-186; 189-190; 206; 219;
    224-226
Marxist feminists, 254; 255
Marxist ideology, 170; 172-174
Marxist materialism, 75; 172; 181; 205-207; 219
Marxist organizations, 94
Mater et Magistra, 27; 28; 32; 43; 47 n14; 48 n17;
    50 n44,46; 51 n58; 52 n60; 54 n79; 57 n109,
    116; 69; 78; 84; 85; 86; 89; 90; 92; 102 n42,
    43,44; 106 n76; 113; 146; 148; 149; 150; 155
    n5; 157 n30,31; 159 n51,52,53,54,55,56,58,61;
    160 n70; 161 n89,90; 164 n120,123,126-128;
    169; 219; 245 n104; 309
Maximum illud, 130; 131; 135; 161 n85
McGrath, Sister A. M., O.P., 251; 329 n5; 331 n19
Medellín Conference, 68; 167
Meminisse juvat, 51 n58
Memorandum from Theologians in the Federal Repub-
    lic of Germany Concerning the Campaign Against
    the Theology of Liberation, 236 n6
Mexican Revolution, 188; 189
Middle Ages, 7, 9
Ministeria quaedam, 325; 339 n118,119
Miranda, J. P., 169-170; 236 n10; 237 n13,15
Miserentissimus Redemptor, 186

Mit brennender sorge, 53 n67
Mitchell, J., 253; 330 n10,11
Moore, B., 162 n98

Natalis trecentesimi, 261
Native clergy, 129-139
Nationalization, 122; 123
Natural law, 114-118
Nel vedere il cielo, 242 n68
Nell-Breuning, Oswald von, S.J., 169; 170
Neminem fugit, 266
Neocolonialism, 36
Non abiamo bisogno, 53 n67
Notre joie est grande, 312
Nous nous addressons, 121; 158 n43,44
Nous nous appris, 100 n24
Nous nous souhaitons, 46 n6; 156 n14
Nous sommes particulièrement, 337 n88,94
Nous voudrions d'abord, 101 n24

O'Brien, D., 105 n68
Octogesima adveniens, 18; 19; 20; 32; 35; 42; 45;
      46 n1,2; 50 n49; 51 n50; 54 n79,85,86; 79;
      80; 92; 93; 94; 95; 102 n46; 153; 154; 155
      n5; 165 n138; 167; 168; 173; 227; 232-233;
      246 n120-124; 315-316; 338 n107; 343
Officiorum omniun, 46 n6; 156 n14
Oggi al compiers, 157 n31
Outka, G., 42; 56 n104

Pacem in terris, 28; 29; 43; 46 n1,2; 47 n15; 50
      n47; 51 n57,58; 52 n60; 53 n70; 57 n114; 90;
      146-147; 150-151; 159 n50,57,58,59; 163 n
      104; 164 n121; 220-224; 245 n105; 245 n107-
      109; 246 n112,113; 306; 307; 309; 311; 312;
      324
Papal documents, ranking of, 106 n74
Papal reformism, 23
Paterna sane solicitudo, 187
Patrick, St., 130

370

Paul VI
    on change, 96; 97
    on Church and culture, 136; 137
    on collaboration with Marxism, 226-231
    on colonialism, 147
    on commemoration of _Rerum novarum_, 93; 94
    on complementarity of the sexes, 317; 318
    on development, 129; 151-154
    on human sciences, 95-96
    on Marxism, 224-233
    on mission of the Church, 79; 80; 91-93
    on native clergy, 138
    on natural equality, 40-42; 44-45; 95
    on the poor, 69; 71
    on private property, 118; 120; 124-128
    on racism, 139
    on utopia, 95
    on violence, 232
    travels of, 231
Perrin, J., 2; 31; 38; 47 n8,11-13; 48 n25; 53 n
    72; 55 n92; 113; 117-118; 156 n12,25,26,27;
    158 n43; 243 n79,82
Pius IX, 174-175
Pius XI
    and social justice, 2-3
    attitude toward Germany, 178
    on authority of the Church, 72-73
    on Catholic Action, 89
    on colonialism, 145
    on condemnation of Marxism, 198; 203-205
    on duty of the Christian state, 87
    on Marxism, 180-205
    on native clergy, 132-135; 138
    on natural equality, 39; 44; 119; 132-133
    on necessity of the Church, 74-75
    on private property, 112-113; 117-118; 120-
        121
    on racism, 132-133; 139
    on subsidiarity, 52 n64
    on wage labor and partnership, 43

Pius XI (continued)
    on women, 264-272
Pius XII
    on evangelical idealism, 76-77
    and historical change, 11-16
    and South Africa, 142-143
    and worker-priests, 80
    Christmas message 1939, 102 n38
    letter to Roosevelt, 1940, 104 n59
    on Catholic Action, 89
    on Church and culture, 135-136, 144
    on Church demand for freedom, 83
    on colonialism, 145; 146
    on condemnation of Marxism, 217
    on corporative units, 159 n64
    on development, 129
    on Marxism, 205-217
    on native clergy, 133-135; 138
    on natural equality, 40; 44; 119; 133; 134
    on partnership, 43
    on the poor, 69
    on private property, 113; 118-119; 120-123;
      125
    on racism, 133-134; 139
    on slavery, 140-141
    on spiritual and temporal planes, 84-85
    on totalitarianism, 207-208
    on women, 272-302
        on the nature of woman, 273-277
        on the relation between men and women,
          277-283
        moral considerations on women, 283-286
        on women in the Church, 298-302
    partiality to Germany, 85
    teaching documents of, 102 n37
    to visiting groups, 255

Quadragesimo anno, 1; 9; 31; 32; 46 n1; 47 n15,16;

Quadragesimo anno (continued)
    48 n17,21,22,23; 49 n30-36; 49 n37; 51 n56;
    52 n59-62,65; 53 n66,71; 54 n77; 55 n93,94;
    56 n106,107; 71; 72; 86; 95; 105 n69; 106 n
    77; 112; 118; 155 n5; 156 n23,24; 157 n30,
    31; 158 n38,39; 169; 186; 198; 199; 203; 239
    n29; 241 n51-59; 242 n61-64; 244 n96
Quae mari sinico, 137
Que hermoso espectaculo, 158 n46
Qui pluribus, 238 n18
Quod apostolici muneris, 156 n21; 157 n29; 175-
    176; 331 n24
Quoniam Paschaliam, 46 n1,2; 47 n13; 51 n56

Racism, 139-145; 132-136
Rerum novarum, 1; 10; 24; 31; 32; 40; 48 n17,22;
    51 n56; 52 n60,62,63; 54 n77-79; 55 n93; 56
    n105; 57 n113; 71; 72; 74; 79; 84; 85; 93;
    111; 112; 119; 155 n6; 156 n21,22; 157 n29,
    31-34; 157 n35; 158 n36; 179; 239 n27; 331
    n26
Ricordi antichi, 339 n113
Ringrazia di vero, 50 n56; 100 n33
Rowbotham, S., 253; 330 n9,15
Ruether, R. R., 329 n1; 331 n20

Sacred Congregation for the Propagation of the
    Faith, 131
Salutiamo con compiacenza, 338 n106
Sapientia Christianae, 53 n67
Scannone, Juan Carlos, 236 n12
Scott, H., 254-255; 330 n17
Se a tempore, 105 n67
Segundo, J. L., 57 n115; 65; 68; 83; 85; 100 n16,
    18; 99 n1,5,6,10; 103 n55; 139; 162 n99; 163
    n100; 237 n13,15
Sertum laetitiae, 38; 53 n67; 69; 157 n33; 158 n
    40; 243 n80,81; 244 n94
Shannon, T., 105 n68
Sie Haben, 161 n88

Silva, Cardinal, 172; 237 n13
Slavery, 140-141
Social option, 65
Social sciences, 65-66
Socialism, 39; 87; 88; 117; 174
South Africa, 141-145
South American Indians, 140
Soyez les bienvenues, 339 n109; 112; 114-116
Stalinism, 180-181
Subsidiarity, principle of, 24-29; 126
Summi Pontificatus, 6; 11-12; 39; 40; 46 n1,2;
        48 n17; 53 n67; 102 n38,39; 133-134; 161
        n88
Swidler, A., 251; 329 n6
Syllabus of Errors, 238 n19
Synod of Bishops 1971, 68; 128

Thomas Aquinas, 55 n89,90; 46 n5,6; 47 n7,8,9,10;
        51 n54,55; 109; 113-116; 122; 202; 223
        on justice, 1; 2; 37; 38; 156 n14,15,16,17,
        18; 157 n28
Torres, S., 104 n63; 106 n71; 162 n98

Ubi arcano, 4; 48 n20; 51 n57; 74; 101 n30; 182;
        239 n34,35; 264
Utopia, 61; 95

Vatican II, 6; 16; 18; 34; 63; 124; 126; 127;
        226; 323; 324
Villegas, B., 237 n13
Violence, 90
Voi avette participato, 246 n118

We are deeply touched, 242 n65
Women and work, 286; 298
Women's liberation movement, 249
Worker-priests, 80-81

Zaretsky, E., 253; 330 n12